PC LEARNING LABS TEACHES WORD PRO 96 FOR WINDOWS 3.1

PC LEARNING LABS TEACHES WORD PRO 96 FOR WINDOWS 3.1

By Sue Reber for

Logical Operations®

Ziff-Davis Press
Emeryville, California

Writer	Sue Reber
Curriculum Development	Logical Operations
Editor	Jan Jue
Technical Reviewer	Leigh Yafa
Project Coordinator	Ami Knox
Proofreader	Jeff Barrash
Production Coordinator, Logical Operations	Marie Boyers
Cover Illustration	Regan Honda
Cover Design	Regan Honda
Book Design	Laura Lamar/MAX, San Francisco
Word Processing	Howard Blechman
Page Layout	Russ Stolins
Indexer	Valerie Haynes Perry

Ziff-Davis Press, ZD Press, PC Learning Labs, and PC Learning Labs Teaches are licensed to Macmillan Computer Publishing USA by Ziff-Davis Publishing Company, New York, New York.

Ziff-Davis Press imprint books are produced on a Macintosh computer system with the following applications: FrameMaker®, Microsoft® Word, QuarkXPress®, Adobe Illustrator®, Adobe Photoshop®, Adobe Streamline™, MacLink®*Plus*, Aldus® FreeHand™, Collage Plus™.

If you have comments or questions or would like to receive a free catalog, call or write:
Macmillan Computer Publishing USA
Ziff-Davis Press Line of Books
5903 Christie Avenue
Emeryville, CA 94608
1-800-688-0448

ISBN 1-56276-224-9

Manufactured in the United States of America
10 9 8 7 6 5 4 3 2 1

CONTENTS AT A GLANCE

Introduction xvii

Chapter 1: Word Pro Basics 1

Chapter 2: Navigating in Word Pro 32

Chapter 3: Editing Text 62

Chapter 4: Text Formatting 92

Chapter 5: Text Enhancements 112

Chapter 6: Page Layouts 154

Chapter 7: Proofing Your Documents 176

Chapter 8: Advanced Editing and Formatting Techniques 190

Chapter 9: Paragraph Styles and Style Sheets 206

Chapter 10: Working with Tables 234

Chapter 11: Form Letters, Labels, and Envelopes 268

Appendix A: Installation 296

Appendix B: Keyboard Shortcut Reference 302

Appendix C: Exchanging Documents with Other Programs 308

Appendix D: Team Computing 316

Index 327

TABLE OF CONTENTS

Introduction xvii

Chapter 1: Word Pro Basics 1

Creating Your Work Directory 2

Introduction to Windows 4

Starting Windows 6

The Program Manager Window 6

Introduction to Word Pro 9

Starting Word Pro 9

The Word Pro Application and Document Windows 10

Issuing Commands through the Menu Bar 14

Practice Your Skills 15

The Basics of Entering Text 15

The Typing Area 16

Word Wrap and the Enter Key 16

Using Tabs to Align Text 17

Deleting Text with the Backspace Key 18

Practice Your Skills 19

Displaying Nonprinting Symbols 20

Saving Your Document 21

The File, Save As Command 21

The File, Save Command 22

Naming a Document 23

Printing a Document 25
Closing a Document 26
Creating a New Document 27
Exiting Word Pro 28
Summary 29
A Note on How to Proceed 30

Chapter 2: Navigating in Word Pro 32

Using File, Open to Open a Document 34
Understanding the Document Path 37
  Changing the Default Document Path 37
Scrolling through a Document 38
Moving through a Document 41
  Using the Keyboard to Move through a Document 42
  Using Edit, Go To to Move to a Page 43
  Using the Status Bar to Move to a Page 44
  Practice Your Skills 45
Using Edit, Find & Replace Text to Search for Text 45
  Practice Your Skills 50
Controlling Document Magnification 50
  Practice Your Skills 51
Obtaining On-Line Help 51
  Using the Help Table of Contents 52
  Obtaining Context-Sensitive Help 54
Saving a Modified Document 56

Practice Your Skills 56

Summary 59

If You're Stopping Here 61

Chapter 3: Editing Text 62

Basic Editing Techniques 64

Using a SmartIcon to Open a Document 64

Deleting Text with the Delete Key 66

Deleting Blocks of Text 67

Replacing Text 70

Practice Your Skills 70

More Techniques for Selecting Text 71

Practice Your Skills 75

Using Edit, Find & Replace to Replace Found Text 76

Moving and Copying Text 78

Understanding the Windows Clipboard 79

Moving Text 79

Copying Text 80

Using Edit, Undo to Undo Your Most Recent Operation 82

Practice Your Skills 83

Summary 86

If You're Stopping Here 90

Chapter 4: Text Formatting 92

Understanding Text Formatting 94

Applying Text Attributes 94

Using the Text Infobox to Apply and Remove Text Attributes 95
Using the Status Bar Buttons to Apply and Remove Text Attributes 97
Practice Your Skills 99
Changing Fonts 100
Using the Text Infobox to Change Fonts 100
Practice Your Skills 101
Using the Status Bar to Change Fonts 102
Practice Your Skills 104
Using Fast Format to Copy Text Formatting 104
Practice Your Skills 106
Summary 106
If You're Stopping Here 110

Chapter 5: Text Enhancements 112
Displaying the Ruler 114
Selecting Paragraphs for Text Enhancements 116
Working with Tabs 117
Tab Types 117
Using Short Cut Menus 118
Setting Custom Tabs in the Ruler 118
Setting Various Types of Tabs 123
Practice Your Skills 124
Moving Custom Tabs 125
Clearing Individual Tabs 125
Setting Indents and Line Breaks 126
The Ruler's Indent Markers 127

Setting Indents with the Ruler 128
Setting Indents Using the Text Infobox 130
Practice Your Skills 132
Setting Hanging Indents 133
Practice Your Skills 134
Using Shift+Enter to Create a New Line 135
Changing Paragraph Alignment 138
Practice Your Skills 142
Changing Line Spacing 142
Practice Your Skills 145
Summary 151
If You're Stopping Here 152

Chapter 6: Page Layouts 154
Creating Headers and Footers 156
Creating a Header 157
Creating a Footer 158
Adding a Date 158
Adding Page Numbers 161
Editing Headers and Footers 164
Setting Margins 164
Changing Document Margins through the Page Layout Infobox 165
Practice Your Skills 166
Paginating a Document 166
Viewing Page Layouts in Full Page View 168
Inserting Manual Page Breaks 169

Removing a Manual Page Break 171
Practice Your Skills 171
Controlling the Printing of Your Documents 171
Summary 172
If You're Stopping Here 175

Chapter 7: Proofing Your Documents 176
Checking Spelling 178
Using Spell Check 178
Using SmartCorrect 182
Finding and Placing Synonyms with Thesaurus 184
Checking Grammar, Style, and Mechanics 186
Using Grammar Check 186
Readability Statistics 187
Summary 188
If You're Stopping Here 189

Chapter 8: Advanced Editing and Formatting Techniques 190
Copying and Moving Text with Drag & Drop 192
Copying Text between Documents 195
Adding Bullets 198
Practice Your Skills 200
Using Format Check 200
Summary 203
If You're Stopping Here 204

Chapter 9: Paragraph Styles and Style Sheets 206
Understanding Paragraph Styles 208
Assigning Styles 209
Assigning Styles with the Style Status Button 210
Practice Your Skills 211
Redefining Styles 212
Redefining a Style's Spacing 215
Practice Your Skills 216
Overriding Styles 217
Creating Styles 219
Creating a New Style Based on Selected Text 219
Using the Style Hierarchy Definition Dialog Box to Inherit Properties 221
Practice Your Skills 226
Copying Styles 226
Understanding SmartMasters 228
Using SmartMasters 229
Using a SmartMaster to Create a Calendar 230
Summary 231
If You're Stopping Here 233

Chapter 10: Working with Tables 234
Creating Tables 236
Displaying Row and Column Headings 239
Moving a SmartIcons Bar 240
Moving in a Table 243
Practice Your Skills 244

Selecting Table Components 244
Entering Text in a Table 248
Practice Your Skills 248
Modifying Tables 249
Inserting Rows and Columns 249
Practice Your Skills 250
Deleting Rows, Columns, and Entire Tables 252
Changing Column Width 253
Practice Your Skills 254
Enhancing Tables 254
Aligning a Table 255
Adding and Changing Borders 255
Converting Tabbed Text to a Table 258
Practice Your Skills 259
Practice Your Skills 260
Summary 264
If You're Stopping Here 267

Chapter 11: Form Letters, Labels, and Envelopes 268

The Components of a Merge Operation 270
The Merge Data File 270
The Merge Document 272
The Merged Documents 273
Creating Form Letters 273
Creating a Merge Data File 274

Editing an Existing Merge Data File 278
Editing a Merge Document 282
Merging the Form Letters 285
Merging Records That Contain Blank Fields 286
Practice Your Skills 288
Creating Mailing Labels 288
Sorting Records in a Merge Data File 288
Creating an Envelope 290
Summary 291

Appendix A: Installation 296
Preparing Your Computer for Word Pro Installation 298
Installing Word Pro 96 on Your Computer 299

Appendix B: Keyboard Shortcut Reference 302
Movement 304
Text Selection 304
Menu Commands 305

Appendix C: Exchanging Documents with Other Programs 308
Opening Non–Word Pro 96 Files 310
Saving Word Pro 96 Documents in Other File Formats 311
Importing and Exporting for Unsupported Programs 313
Loss of Formatting When Importing and Exporting 313

Appendix D: Team Computing 316
TeamReview 318
TeamMail 321
TeamConsolidate 322

Index 327

INTRODUCTION

Welcome to *PC Learning Labs Teaches Word Pro 96 for Windows 3.1*, a hands-on instruction book designed to help you attain a high level of Word Pro fluency in as short a time as possible. And congratulations on choosing Word Pro 4.0, a powerful and feature-rich program that helps you create professional-looking documents with a minimum of work.

We at PC Learning Labs believe this book to be a unique and welcome addition to the ranks of "how-to" computer publications. Our instructional approach stems directly from over a decade of successful teaching in a hands-on classroom environment. Throughout the book, we have consistently mixed theory with practice; a topic is explained and then immediately drilled in a hands-on activity. These activities employ sample Word Pro documents provided on the Data Disk bound into the back of the book.

When you finish working your way through this book, you will have a solid foundation of skills in these Word Pro functions:

- *Documents* Creating, editing, printing, storing, and retrieving text
- *Navigation* Getting around in large documents
- *Editing* Deleting, replacing, selecting, moving, and copying text
- *Formatting* Controlling a document's appearance
- *Proofing* Checking documents for spelling, grammar, and word choices
- *Styles and SmartMasters* Quickly and uniformly creating and formatting complex documents

- *Tables* Organizing text and numbers into rows and columns
- *Merging* Generating form letters, mailing labels, and envelopes

Note: Throughout this Introduction, we have italicized terms with which you may not be familiar. Don't worry; we'll explain them in the chapters of the book. In the interim, please bear with us.

WHO THIS BOOK IS FOR

This book was written with the beginner in mind. Though experience with word processing and personal computers will certainly be helpful to you, little or none is required. You should know how to turn on your computer, monitor, and printer; how to use your keyboard; and how to move your mouse. Everything beyond that will be explained in the text.

HOW TO USE THIS BOOK

This book is designed to be used as a learning guide, a review tool, and a quick reference.

AS A LEARNING GUIDE

Each chapter covers one broad topic or a set of related topics. Chapters are arranged in order of increasing Word Pro proficiency; skills you acquire in one chapter are used and developed in subsequent chapters. For this reason, you should work through the chapters in strict sequence.

Each chapter is organized into explanatory topics and hands-on, step-by-step activities. Topics provide the theoretical overview you need to master Word Pro; activities enable you to apply this understanding immediately to specific examples.

AS A REVIEW TOOL

Any method of instruction is only as effective as the time and effort you are willing to invest in it. For this reason, we encourage you to review the more challenging topics and activities presented in this book.

AS A QUICK REFERENCE

General procedures (such as opening a document or selecting text) are presented as a series of bulleted steps; you can find these bullets (•) easily as you page through the book.

At the end of every chapter, you'll find a quick reference that lists the actions required to perform the techniques introduced in that chapter.

WHAT THIS BOOK CONTAINS

The contents of this book are divided into the following 11 chapters:

Chapter 1	Word Pro Basics
Chapter 2	Navigating in Word Pro
Chapter 3	Editing Text
Chapter 4	Text Formatting
Chapter 5	Text Enhancements
Chapter 6	Page Layouts
Chapter 7	Proofing Your Documents
Chapter 8	Advanced Editing and Formatting Techniques
Chapter 9	Paragraph Styles and Style Sheets
Chapter 10	Working with Tables
Chapter 11	Form Letters, Labels, and Envelopes

In addition, there are four appendices:

Appendix A	Installation
Appendix B	Keyboard Shortcut Reference
Appendix C	Exchanging Documents with Other Programs
Appendix D	Team Computing

The following features of this book are designed to facilitate your learning:

- Carefully sequenced topics that build on the knowledge you've acquired from previous topics
- Frequent hands-on activities, designed to sharpen your Word Pro skills
- Numerous illustrations showing how your screen should look at key points during the activities
- The Data Disk, which contains all the document files you'll need to complete the activities
- A quick reference at the end of each chapter, listing in easy-to-read table form the actions required to perform the techniques introduced in the chapter

THE EQUIPMENT YOU NEED

To run Word Pro 4.0 and complete this book, you need several pieces of computer equipment: a computer, monitor, keyboard, and a pointing device such as a mouse. A printer is strongly recommended, but optional.

A COMPUTER AND MONITOR

To install and run Word Pro, you need an IBM or IBM-compatible personal computer that has an 80386 or higher processor (80486 and so on) that is capable of running Microsoft Windows version 3.1 or higher. To completely install and use Word Pro and this book's Data Disk document files, your computer's *hard-disk drive* (or *hard drive*) must have at least 45 megabytes of free storage space. To run Word Pro, your computer must have at least eight megabytes of random access memory (although more is strongly recommended). Finally, you need an EGA or higher (VGA, SVGA, and so on) graphics card and computer monitor to display Windows and Word Pro at their intended screen resolution.

Before starting Chapter 1, you must have DOS 3.1 (or higher) and Windows 3.1 (or higher) installed on your computer; if they are not, see your DOS and Windows documentation for instructions. Word Pro 4.0 must also be installed, preferably *freshly* installed. See Appendix A for help on installing or reinstalling Word Pro.

A KEYBOARD

IBM-compatible computers come with various styles of keyboards; these keyboards function identically, but have different layouts. Figures I.1, I.2, and I.3 show the three most popular desktop-computer keyboard styles and their key arrangements. If you are using a portable computer, your keyboard may not exactly match any of these three keyboard styles, but should contain all of the keys necessary to run Word Pro.

Word Pro uses the three main areas of the keyboard:

- The *function keys* (F1, F2, and so on) enable you to use many of Word Pro's features. On the PC-, XT-, and AT-style keyboards, there are ten function keys at the left end of the keyboard; on the PS/2-style Enhanced Keyboard, there are 12 function keys at the top of the keyboard.
- The *typing keys* are located in the main body of all the keyboards. These keys include letters, numbers, and punctuation marks, as well as the Shift, Ctrl, and Alt keys.

Figure I.1 **IBM PC–style keyboard**

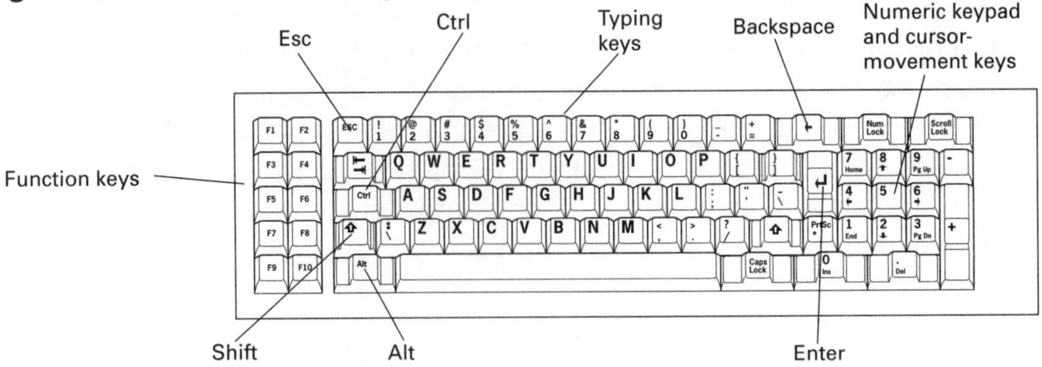

Figure I.2 **XT/AT–style keyboard**

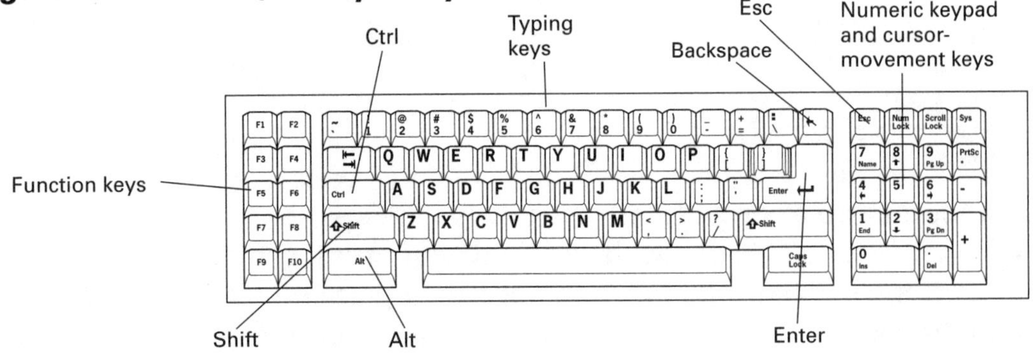

Figure I.3 **The 101-key Enhanced Keyboard**

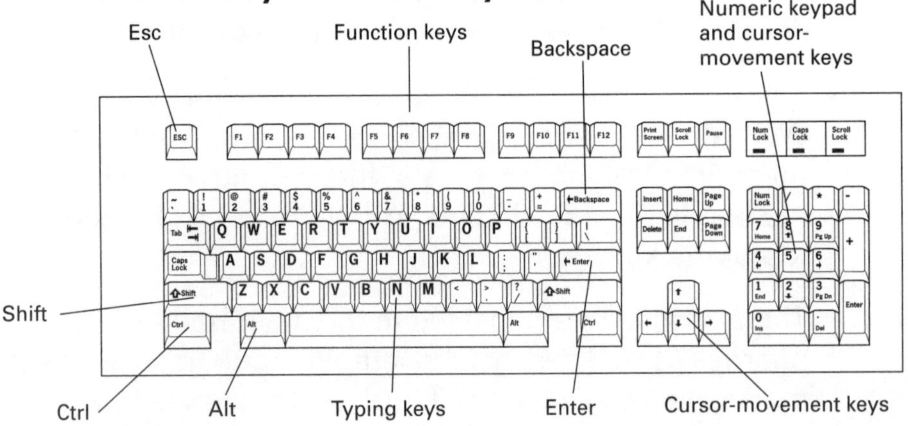

- The *numeric keypad* contains a group of number keys (the same ones found across the top row of the typing keys) for convenient numeric data entry. The numeric keypad also contains the *movement keys*: the Up, Down, Left, and Right Arrow keys; Home; End; PgUp (Page Up); and PgDn (Page Down).

  Pressing the Num Lock key toggles Num Lock on and off. For you to enter numeric data using the numeric keypad, Num Lock must be on. For you to use the movement keys on the keypad, Num Lock must be off. To enter numeric data when Num Lock is off, use the number keys on the top row of the typing area. The Enhanced Keyboard has an additional movement keypad to the left of the numeric keypad. This enables you to use the numeric keypad for numeric data entry (with Num Lock on) and still be able to use movement keys.

A MOUSE, TRACKBALL, OR OTHER POINTING DEVICE

You will need a mouse, trackball, or other pointing device to work through the activities in this book. Any Windows-compatible PC mouse, trackball, or other pointing device will do.

Throughout this book, we direct you to use a mouse, not a trackball or other pointing device. If you have a pointing device other than a mouse, you can use it to perform all the tasks that call for mouse techniques: pointing, clicking, dragging, and so on.

A PRINTER

Although you aren't absolutely required to have a printer to work through the activities, we strongly recommend it. A PostScript-type laser printer is ideal because that is the type of printer we used when preparing the activities and illustrations in this book. However, a non-PostScript laser or dot-matrix printer is acceptable.

To use your printer, you must first select it in Windows. If you have already printed successfully from Windows or any Windows accessory (for example, Windows Write or Windows Paintbrush), then your printer most likely will print from Word Pro. If you have never printed from Windows or a Windows accessory, refer to your Windows documentation.

Even if you have no printer, select a PostScript printer in Windows, anyway. Then you'll be able to follow most of the steps in activities that involve printing. Either way, you'll learn in Chapter 1 how to view on your computer screen how a document will look when printed.

CONVENTIONS USED IN THIS BOOK

Certain conventions used in this book are designed to help you learn Word Pro 4.0 easily and efficiently. Each chapter begins with a short introduction and ends with a summary that includes a quick-reference guide to the techniques introduced in the chapter. Main chapter topics (large, capitalized headings) and subtopics (headings preceded by a cube) explain Word Pro features.

Hands-on activities enable you to practice using Word Pro's features. In these activities, the menu choices, keystrokes, and anything we ask you to type are all presented in **boldface**. Here's an example from Chapter 2:

> **11.** Click on **OK** to open the document.

Throughout the book, we've also used a **boldface** word to call your attention to important notes and tips, and we've used *italic* for new terms, for words we direct you to look at on screen, and for emphasis.

Activities in this book follow a cause-and-effect approach. Most steps tell you what to do (cause) and then what will happen (effect). In the preceding Step 11 example,

Cause:	Click on **OK**.
Effect:	The document opens.

A plus sign (+) is used with the Shift, Ctrl, and Alt keys to denote a multiple-key keystroke. For example, Ctrl+F10 means "Press and hold down the Ctrl key; then press the function key F10; and then release both."

To help you distinguish between steps presented for your general knowledge and steps you should carry out at your computer as you read, we have adopted the following system:

- A bulleted step, like this, is provided for your information and reference only.

1. A numbered step, like this, indicates one in a series of steps that you should carry out in sequence on your computer.

ABOUT THE ILLUSTRATIONS IN THIS BOOK

This book contains numerous illustrations, or *figures*. Most picture how your computer screen should look as you work through the activities.

When creating these figures, we ran Word Pro 4.0 under Windows 3.1 using a VGA monitor and a PostScript laser printer. If you run Word Pro under a different version of Windows, or use a different type of monitor, or select a non-PostScript laser printer, your screen may not *exactly* match the figures in this book. For the most part, however, Word Pro will still run as described in the text.

Also, Word Pro often displays the current date on the screen. Most likely, your current date will not match the date we have used throughout this book. When you are comparing your screen to figures that display dates in the book, your screen should display your current date.

BEFORE YOU START

The activities in each of the following chapters are designed to proceed sequentially. In many cases, you cannot perform an activity until you have performed one or more of the earlier activities. For this reason, we recommend that you allot enough time to work through an entire chapter in each session.

You are now ready to begin. Good learning...and *bon voyage!*

CHAPTER 1: WORD PRO BASICS

Creating Your Work Directory

Introduction to Windows

Introduction to Word Pro

The Basics of Entering Text

Saving Your Document

Printing a Document

Closing a Document

Creating a New Document

Exiting Word Pro

Summary

A Note on How to Proceed

Welcome to Word Pro 4.0 and the exciting world of word processing! In this first chapter, we'll lead you through one complete Word Pro work session; you'll start the Word Pro program, create and edit a document, save and print the document, create a new document, and, finally, exit Word Pro. This, in a nutshell, is the procedure you'll use in your daily word processing work with Word Pro.

When you're done working through this chapter, you will know how to

- Start Word Pro
- Enter text
- Delete text
- Save and name a document
- Print and close a document
- Create a new document
- Exit Word Pro

Note: Before you can continue with this chapter, you must have Word Pro 4.0 and Windows (version 3.1 or higher) already installed on your computer. For directions on installing Word Pro 4.0, see Appendix A; for directions on installing Windows, see your Windows documentation.

CREATING YOUR WORK DIRECTORY

When you use this book, you'll work with several Word Pro document files that you'll copy from this book's Data Disk to your hard drive. To keep these files together on your hard drive, you need to create a *work directory*. (A hard drive functions like a big filing cabinet, holding an assortment of files; a directory functions like a hanging-file folder within that cabinet, storing a group of related files.)

Follow these steps to create your work directory and copy the files on the Data Disk into that directory:

1. Turn on your computer; after a moment, your *operating environment* loads automatically. If you are in Windows, please skip to step 2. If you are in DOS, please skip to step 4. If you are in a non-Windows, non-DOS operating environment (DOS Shell or GeoWorks, for example), exit to DOS, and then skip to step 4. (For help with exiting to DOS, consult your operating environment's documentation.)
2. Within Windows, locate the Program Manager, an on-screen window with the words *Program Manager* in its overhead title bar. If Program Manager is running as an *icon* (a small picture with the words *Program Manager* beneath it) instead

of as a *window* (a framed, large area on screen), use the mouse to *point*—that is, use the mouse to move the very tip of the on-screen *mouse pointer*—to the icon. Then *double-click*—that is, press the *left* mouse button twice in rapid succession—to open the icon into a window.

3. Move the mouse pointer to the word *File* in the upper-left corner of the Program Manager window. Click on **File** to open the File menu, and then click on **Exit Windows....** A *dialog box* entitled *Exit Windows* appears in the middle of the screen. Click the mouse pointer once on the **OK** button within this dialog box to exit from Windows to DOS.

4. The DOS prompt will appear on a line by itself

   ```
   C:\>
   ```

   (Your DOS prompt may look somewhat different.)

5. Type **dir** and then press **Enter**. The contents of the current directory are displayed, followed by a final line reporting the number of free bytes on your hard disk. If you have 600,000 or more bytes free, skip to step 6. If you have fewer than 600,000 bytes free, you may not be able to create your work directory and perform all the hands-on activities in this book. Before you proceed, you'll need to delete enough files from your hard disk to bring the free-byte total up to 600,000. If you need help doing this, please refer to your DOS documentation. **Caution:** *Be sure to back up all important files before deleting them!*

6. Remove the Data Disk from the back of this book and insert it, label up, into the appropriately sized disk drive.

7. Type **a:** if the Data Disk is in drive A, or type **b:** if the Data Disk is in drive B. Then press **Enter** to change the current drive to the Data Disk drive.

8. Type **install c: wordpro\wprowork** (be sure to leave a space between **install** and **c:** and another space between **c:** and **wordpro**). Then press **Enter** to begin the installation. (If you wish to create your work directory on a hard drive that is not designated as drive C, substitute that hard drive's letter for the **c** in this install command. For example, to install on a drive D hard drive, you would type *install d: wprowork.*)

9. If all is well, the message

```
Installation begun.
```

appears, followed by a message about copying files. When the procedure is complete, the message

```
Installation successful!
```

appears, followed by a line reporting the name of your work directory—for example,

```
c:\wordpro\wprowork
```

If you get an error message indicating that the hard drive you specified does not exist, or that the directory name you specified already exists, repeat step 8, substituting a new hard drive letter or work directory name as appropriate. For example, you might type *install d: wprowork* or *install c: wordwork*.

Note: Your work-directory name can be up to eight letters long. Do not use spaces, periods, or punctuation marks, and do not use the name *wordpro,* as that name is normally used by the Word Pro program itself.

Caution: If you use another work directory name, be aware that the activities in this book will all refer to your work directory as C:\WORDPRO\WPROWORK. You'll need to remember to substitute your chosen name for the name C:\WPROWORK as you work through the book.

INTRODUCTION TO WINDOWS

Because Word Pro is a *Windows application*—a program designed to run in the Microsoft Windows environment—you must start Windows before you can start Word Pro. (You can use the terms *application* and *program* interchangeably.)

Before you start learning about Word Pro itself, let's take a few moments to learn more about Windows. If you are already familiar with Windows, you may want to skip ahead to "Introduction to Word Pro," later in this chapter.

Windows is a program that provides a *graphical user interface*. This is a fancy way of saying that Windows gives your computer a new face—a graphical one—that makes Windows and

Windows applications more intuitive and fun to use than many DOS programs.

Windows and Windows applications operate around a set of interactive *windows*—on-screen boxes of varying sizes through which information is passed between the user (you) and the computer. Instead of having to type complex commands at your keyboard, you can give your computer the same instructions simply by using a mouse (or the keyboard, if you prefer) to manipulate the windows and elements within those windows. This enables you to spend less time telling your computer *how* you would like to work, and more time actually working.

In addition to providing a graphical user interface, Windows provides other functions that are important to effective and efficient computer use:

- It enables you to run more than one application at a time on the same computer. (This is sometimes referred to as *multitasking*.) For example, you might play a game of Solitaire while you print a letter from Word Pro.
- It manages your computer's memory and disk storage, thus enhancing your computer's performance and extending its capabilities.
- It provides a standard way to communicate with applications. Many Windows applications have the same commands for common tasks such as saving a file and printing. This means you do not have to learn a different set of commands for each application you use.
- It supports common window elements that help standardize the way your screen appears. As you'll soon see, Windows and Windows applications look similar.

These last two functions are the most important when learning Word Pro and other Windows applications. Because Windows helps to standardize how applications operate, you can transfer many of the procedures that you use in one Windows application to another. For example, if you already use Excel or 1-2-3 for Windows, you already have a jump start on learning Word Pro! In addition, because Windows applications look similar, you can concentrate more on your work and less on the screen's appearance.

STARTING WINDOWS

To start Windows, you must copy the Windows program from your hard disk into the computer's memory or *RAM* (random-access memory). Windows will remain in memory as long as you continue running it or any Windows application. When you exit Windows, it will remove itself from memory, freeing space for non-Windows programs to use. (Note that computer memory is a temporary data-storage space. When you exit Windows, the program clears itself from computer memory but remains installed on the hard drive, ready to copy again into computer memory when needed.)

Follow these steps to start Windows:

1. Type **win** and then press **Enter** to start Windows.
2. Examine the screen. An hourglass may appear momentarily, indicating that the computer has not yet finished with the task of starting Windows. Once Windows is running, the hourglass disappears and you will see the *Program Manager window*. You can recognize this window by its *title bar*, located along the top of the window; it reads *Program Manager*. If you don't see a window entitled Program Manager, continue with step 3; otherwise, skip the rest of this activity.
3. Look for a small picture, or *icon*, with *Program Manager* beneath it. Use your mouse to move the tip of the on-screen *mouse pointer*, which appears as a left-pointing arrow, over the icon. Then, *double-click*—that is, press and release the left mouse button twice in rapid succession—to open the icon into a window. If you do not double-click quickly enough, a *menu* may appear above the icon. If this happens, *click*—press and release the left mouse button just once—on the word **Restore**. (From here on, when we say "click" or "double-click," we mean that you should use the *left* mouse button. If we want you to click or double-click with the right mouse button, we'll tell you that.)

THE PROGRAM MANAGER WINDOW

The Program Manager window serves as a command center, enabling you to start an application from within the window by double-clicking on the application's *program icon*. Because Windows is a *customizable* program, its screen appearance and overall setup upon start-up can vary significantly from computer to computer. For this reason, we at PC Learning Labs cannot know exactly how your screen now appears. If your screen differs somewhat from Figure 1.1, don't worry. As long as the Program Manager window is open, you most likely will be able to start Word Pro.

Figure 1.1 **The Program Manager window**

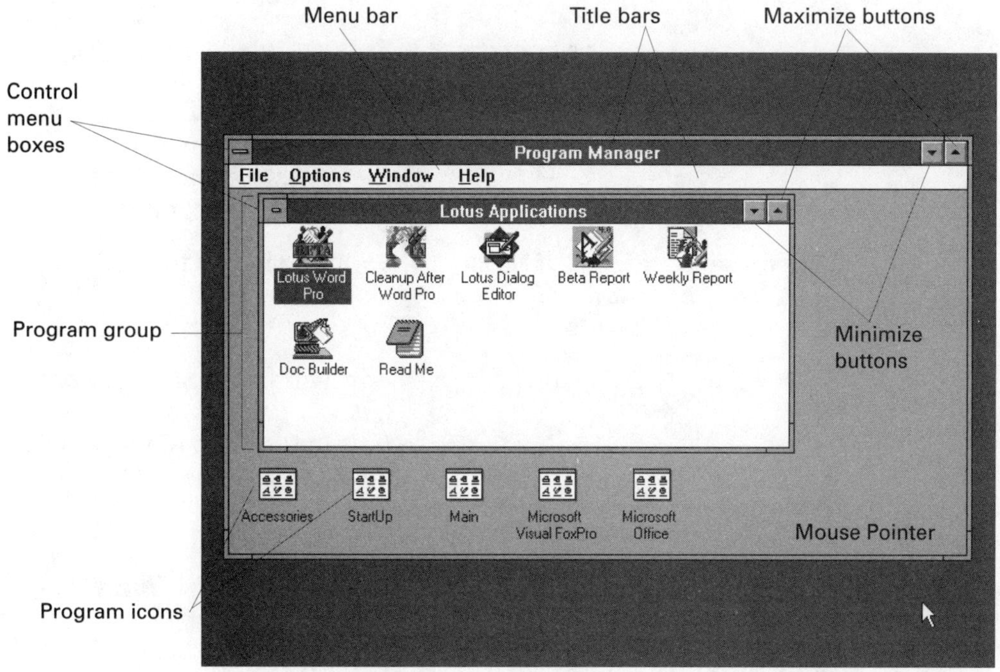

Figure 1.1 labels many of the elements of the Program Manager window. Table 1.1 defines the elements that are common to many windows, and Table 1.2 defines the elements that are specific to the Program Manager window. Your screen may contain some or all of these elements and may display elements not shown in Figure 1.1. Again, don't worry if your screen does not match the figure exactly. We're just familiarizing you with many of the window elements that you'll see when working in the Windows environment.

Table 1.1 Common Window Elements

Element	Location	Definition
Control menu box	Upper-left corner of window	Controls size and position of window; enables you to close window
Title bar	Across top of window	Displays name of window; at times, may display additional information
Maximize/ Restore button	Upper-right corner of window	Expands window to largest possible size; when window is maximized, button changes to Restore button, which you can use to restore window to its previous (unmaximized) size
Minimize button	To left of Maximize or Restore button	Shrinks window to icon
Menu bar	Below title bar	Lists window's *menu options* (*File, Options, Window*, and *Help* in Program Manager window)

Table 1.2 Window Elements Specific to the Program Manager

Element	Location	Definition
Program group	Inside Program Manager window	Window that holds set of related program icons
Program icon	Inside a program group window	Enables you to start program
Program group icon	Usually at bottom of Program Manager window	Opens into program group window when double-clicked

INTRODUCTION TO WORD PRO

Now that you've learned a little about Windows, you are ready to get started in Word Pro.

A word processor such as Word Pro is an application that enables you to create, edit, print, and save documents for future retrieval and revision. You enter text into the computer using a keyboard. As you type, your computer displays your words on a screen, or *monitor*, and stores them in memory or on a disk instead of on paper.

One of the chief advantages of a word processor over a conventional typewriter is that a word processor enables you to make changes to a document without retyping the entire document. For example, you can create a letter in a word processor and then, after you are finished, go back and change margins, add sentences, delete words, move paragraphs, correct spelling errors, and so on. You can do all of this without retyping the original text.

STARTING WORD PRO

To start Word Pro from the Program Manager window, you must locate the *Lotus Word Pro* program icon, and then double-click on it. The following steps will help you search for this icon. (We cannot know how your version of Windows is set up, so some of these instructions may not apply to you.)

1. In the Program Manager window, look for an icon entitled *Lotus Word Pro* (refer to Figure 1.1 for the appearance of this icon). If you see this icon on your screen, skip ahead to step 4. If you cannot see the icon, continue with step 2.
2. Windows stores program icons in program groups. Within the Program Manager window, program groups can appear as program group icons (*Accessories*, *StartUp*, and *Main* in Figure 1.1) or as windows (*Lotus Applications* in Figure 1.1). By default, Windows stores the Lotus Word Pro program icon in a program group called *Lotus Applications* (because Word Pro is a product of the Lotus Development Corporation). If you see a program group icon with this title, double-click on the icon to open it into a window. If the window contains the Lotus Word Pro program icon, skip to step 4.

3. If you do not have a Lotus Applications program group icon, or if the Lotus Applications program group does not contain the Lotus Word Pro program icon, you will have to search for the icon in the other program groups. Start by opening program groups that are likely to hold the Lotus Word Pro program icon, such as *Applications* or *Windows Applications*, and then continue on to less-likely groups. Once you've found the icon, skip to step 4. If you cannot find the icon, there is a good chance that Word Pro is not properly installed on your computer. In this case, refer to Appendix A for information on installing Word Pro, and then return to step 1 of this activity.
4. Double-click on the **Lotus Word Pro program icon** to load Word Pro into memory. A dialog box entitled *Welcome To Lotus Word Pro* is displayed. Observe the Welcome To Lotus Word Pro dialog box. It has two tabs: Create A New Document From A SmartMaster and Open An Existing Document. Depending upon which tab you display, you can either create a new document or open an existing one. (**Note:** You'll learn about SmartMasters in Chapter 9.)
5. Click on **OK** to create a new Word Pro document.

Note: Word Pro, like Windows, is a user-customizable program. If you have already used Word Pro after installing it on your computer, or if Word Pro was installed on your computer previously, some of Word Pro's basic settings, called *defaults*, may have been changed. In addition, many of Word Pro's features (the SmartIconbar, for example) are context-sensitive and change depending upon where you are in the program and what you are doing. Therefore, Word Pro may behave in a manner that we at PC Learning Labs cannot anticipate.

THE WORD PRO APPLICATION AND DOCUMENT WINDOWS

When you start Word Pro, two windows appear on the screen, one within the other. The larger of these, called the *application window*, usually fills the entire screen; you use it to communicate with Word Pro. The smaller window, called the *document window*, usually fits seamlessly within the application window; you use it to create and edit your Word Pro documents.

Note that the two Word Pro windows contain many of the elements that you've already seen in the Program Manager window: a title bar (it currently displays *Lotus Word Pro - [Untitled #1]*); Control menu boxes (the one on top is for the application window, and the one below is for the document window); a Minimize button; and a menu bar.

Figure 1.2 illustrates many elements of the Word Pro windows that you have not already seen; Table 1.3 defines these elements.

Figure 1.2 **Word Pro windows and window elements**

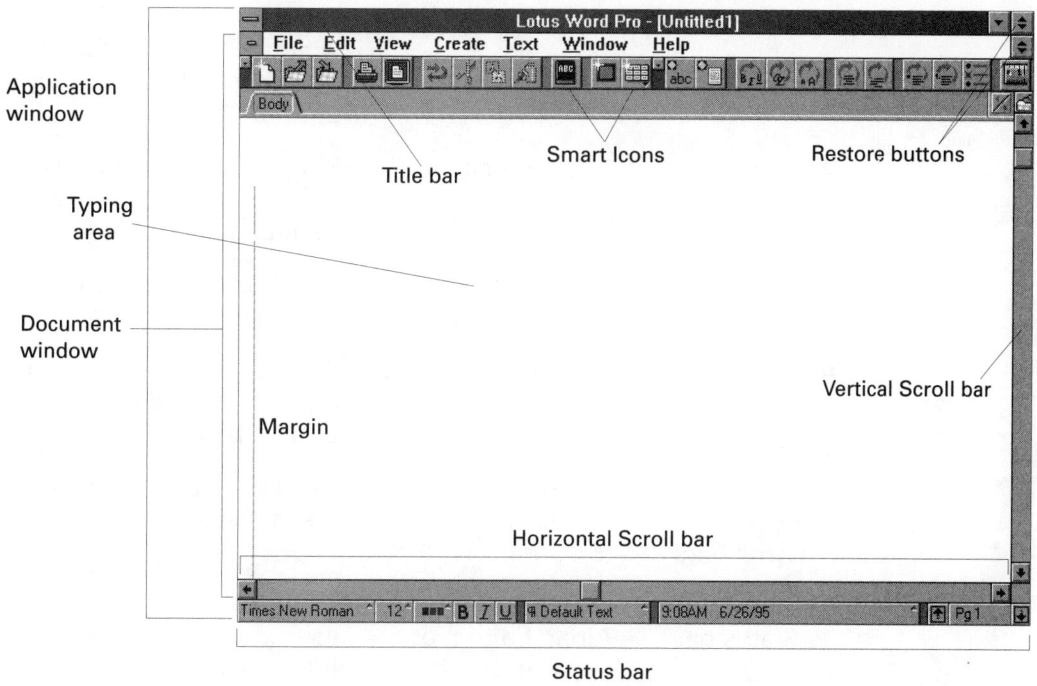

Let's take a closer look at some of these screen elements. (We will discuss the remaining elements in detail over the next few chapters.)

1. Click on the application window's **Control menu box** (the upper of the two Control menu boxes) to open the application's Control menu; *do not* double-click, as this will cause you to exit Word Pro. Notice the Control menu items: *Restore, Move, Size, Minimize,* and so on. Click on the **Control menu box** again to close the menu.

Table 1.3 **Word Pro Window Elements**

Term	Location	Definition
Application window	Usually fills entire screen	Larger of the start-up windows; provides interface between you and Word Pro
Document window	Within application window	Smaller of two start-up windows; holds active document
Restore buttons	Upper-right corner of screen	Control size of application window (upper button) and document window (lower button)
SmartIcons	Below menu bar	Provide quick access to some of Word Pro's most frequently used commands
Typing area	Inside document window	Provides area for you to type text
Margins	Around typing area	Represent space between typing area and edge of printed page
Vertical and horizontal scroll bars	Along right side (vertical) and bottom (horizontal) of document window	Used to display various areas of document
Status bar	Along bottom of application window	Its buttons display variety of information and enable you to perform various tasks; you'll learn more about these buttons throughout this book

2. Click on the document window's **Control menu box** (the lower of the two Control menu boxes). Observe that the Control menu items for the document window are similar to

those for the application window. Click on the **Control menu box** again to close the menu.

3. Click on the application window's **Restore button** (the upper of the two Restore buttons). The application window shrinks (is *restored*) to a smaller size. Notice that the Restore button has now changed to a Maximize button; it displays a single up-pointing triangle rather than both up- and down-pointing triangles (see Figure 1.3).

Figure 1.3 **Word Pro's application and document windows, unmaximized**

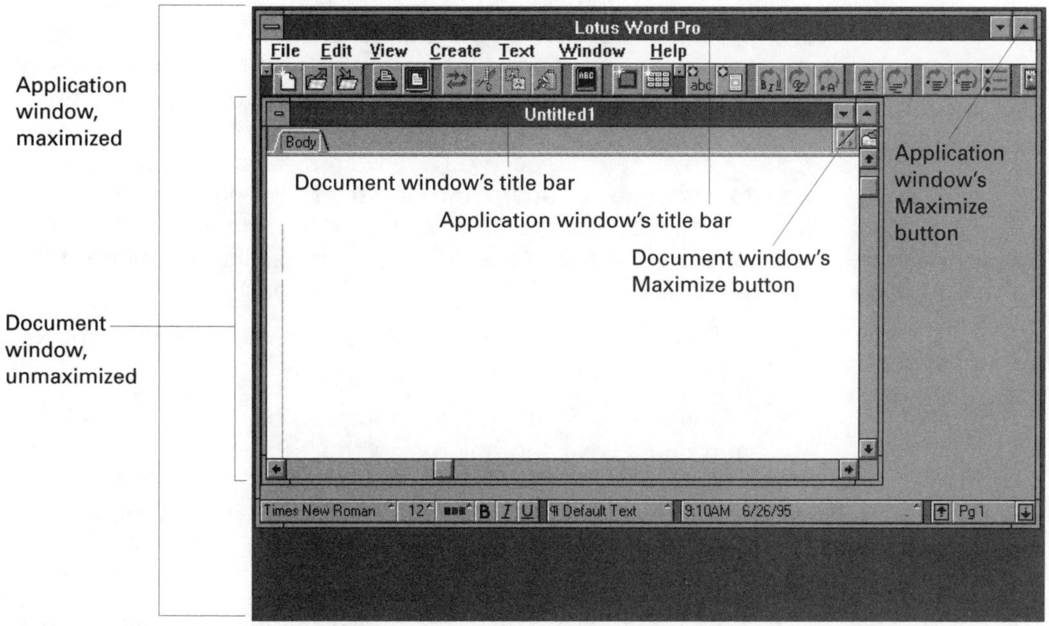

4. Click on the application window's **Maximize button** to maximize the application window. The window once again fills the screen, and the Maximize button changes back to a Restore button.

5. Repeat steps 3 and 4, substituting the document window's Maximize and Restore buttons for the application window's Maximize and Restore buttons. Observe that when you click

on the document window's Restore button, the button moves to the upper-right corner of the restored document window and becomes a Maximize button; this is the button you click on to maximize the document window (see Figure 1.3). Notice, also, that when you restore the document window, it gets its own title bar; when you maximize the document window, it shares the application window's title bar. (Leave both the application and document windows maximized for the remainder of this book.)

ISSUING COMMANDS THROUGH THE MENU BAR

To perform your daily word processing tasks (such as saving a document, setting new margins, and so on), you must issue the appropriate Word Pro commands. Because of Word Pro's flexibility, you can issue commands through a variety of mouse and keyboard methods. However, the menu bar is the only method that enables you to issue *every* available Word Pro command. For this reason, anytime we teach you a new command, we'll show you how to issue the command through the menu bar. After you've learned the menu bar technique, we'll often show you alternate methods. (In addition, Appendix B provides a list of keyboard shortcuts for techniques covered in this book.)

Let's practice using the menu bar to explore Word Pro's menus and to learn more about how they operate:

1. Move the tip of the mouse pointer to the **File** menu option, and then press and hold down the **left mouse button**. (Do not release this button until you're told to in step 3.) The File menu opens, displaying a set of file-related menu items: *New Document, Open, Close, Save, Save As...*, and so on.
2. Without releasing the button, *drag* the mouse pointer down to highlight **Save As...**. (You'll learn more about dragging in Chapter 3.) When you *highlight* an item in Word Pro, the item is displayed in *reverse video*; the words change from dark on light to light on dark.
3. Release the mouse button to open the Save As dialog box.
4. Click on the dialog box's **Cancel** button to close the dialog box. Whenever you inadvertently open a dialog box, you can

click on Cancel to close the dialog box without affecting any settings.

5. Click on **Edit**. The Edit menu opens, displaying Word Pro's editing commands. Note that, to open a menu, you can either press and hold the mouse button (as you did in steps 1 through 4), or press and release (click) the mouse button.

6. Observe that Word Pro has dimmed several Edit commands (*Undo, Cut, Copy, Paste*, and so on). Word Pro dims menu items to show that they are unavailable in the current context. For example, the Undo menu item is dimmed because you have not yet performed any actions that the Undo menu item can undo. (You'll learn about Undo in Chapter 3.)

7. Observe that an ellipsis (...) follows several Edit menu items (*Go To..., Find & Replace Text..., Check Spelling...*, and so on). Word Pro adds an ellipsis to menu items that, when clicked on, open dialog boxes. To keep this book easy to read, from this point on we will no longer use the ellipsis when referring to such menu items. For example, we will ask you to "Click on *Go To*," even though *Go To...* is how the item actually appears on your screen.

8. Click on **View** to open the View menu. Notice that the Edit menu closes automatically when you open the View menu.

PRACTICE YOUR SKILLS

1. Use the menu bar to examine the rest of Word Pro's menus, being careful not to select any menu items.

2. Close any open menu.

THE BASICS OF ENTERING TEXT

Word Pro is a WYSIWYG (what you see is what you get) word processor; the screen closely approximates how your document will look when you print it. Many computer users prefer WYSIWYG word processors because they eliminate the arcane codes and unpredictable page layouts that characterize non-WYSIWYG word processors. Word Pro's WYSIWYG feature encourages you to work in a "visually intuitive" style, in which you treat the word processor as a computerized extension of a typewriter.

In the next several sections, we'll discuss the basics of entering text into an Word Pro document.

THE TYPING AREA

When you start Word Pro and click on OK, a new document window opens, providing you with a blank typing area. Word Pro provides default settings for the margins, page size, line spacing, and several other document characteristics. Because of these default settings, you can begin to type immediately, without having to first specify any of these settings yourself.

As you type, you insert characters in front of a blinking vertical bar called the *insertion point*. To move the insertion point, simply click the mouse pointer at the desired place in the text.

Let's examine Word Pro's typing area:

1. Observe the insertion point (see Figure 1.4). Its location determines where you will insert the next character you type. Note that the insertion point of a new, blank document appears in the upper-left corner (at the beginning) of the typing area.
2. Watch the mouse pointer as you move it around your screen. Whenever it is within the document window, the pointer changes to an *I-beam*. When you move it outside the document window, it turns back into a left-pointing arrow.

WORD WRAP AND THE ENTER KEY

The Enter key on your computer's keyboard works similarly to the Return key on a typewriter. There is an important difference, however: When using a typewriter, you need to press the Return key whenever you want to end a line. When you run out of room on a line in word processing, the last word in the line automatically drops to the beginning of the next line. This feature is called *word wrap*.

You do need to use the Enter key to

- End a short line (one that does not extend to the right margin)
- End a paragraph
- Create a blank line

Figure 1.4 **The typing area with the insertion point and I-beam**

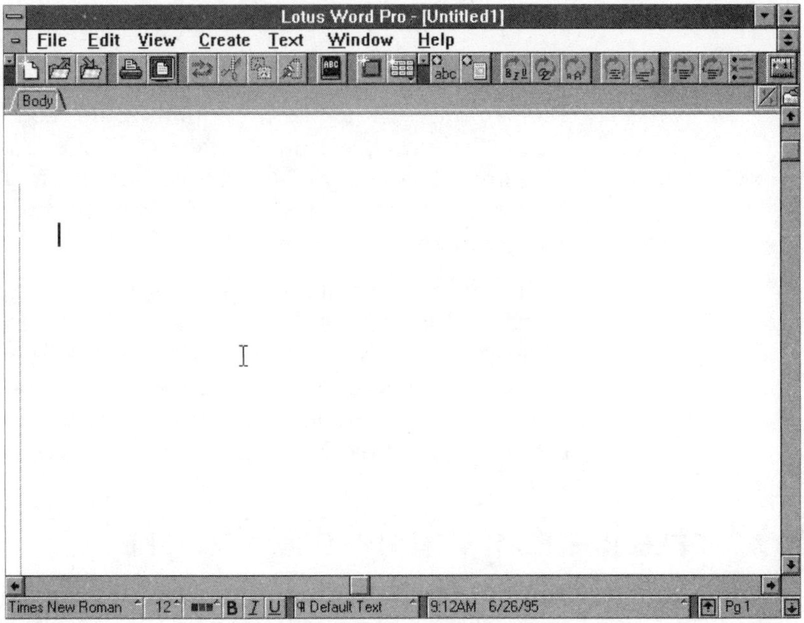

Insertion point

I-beam

Let's type some text in the new document window and practice using the Enter key. (We will demonstrate word wrap later in this chapter under "Deleting Text with the Backspace Key.")

1. Type **Interoffice Memo** to enter these characters at the insertion point, and then press **Enter** to end the line. Notice that the insertion point moves down and to the beginning of the next line.
2. Press **Enter** again to create a blank line.
3. Type **To:**.

USING TABS TO ALIGN TEXT

In word processing, *tabs* enable you to align text vertically. These two lines are properly aligned:

```
Line 1 ....
Line 2 ....
```

These two are not:

```
Line 1 ....
 Line 2 ....
```

Tabs are fixed horizontal positions within a line, and pressing the Tab key moves the insertion point to the next tab position to the right. By default, Word Pro's tabs are set at 1/2" increments, so pressing Tab once moves the insertion point 1/2" to the right; pressing Tab again moves it another 1/2", for a total of 1" (1/2" + 1/2"); and so on.

We created the properly aligned example shown just above by pressing Tab once at the beginning of each line. We created the improperly aligned example by using the Spacebar to insert blank spaces at the beginning of each line. When working in a WYSIWYG word processor, try not to align text using the Spacebar; it probably won't work.

DELETING TEXT WITH THE BACKSPACE KEY

You can use the Backspace key to delete text one character at a time. When you press Backspace, you delete the single character immediately to the left of the insertion point.

Let's experiment with Word Pro's Tab and Backspace features:

1. Press **Tab** to insert a *tab character* at the beginning of the line. This moves the insertion point to the first tab, 1/2" to the right. (Note that the tab character you have just inserted is invisible. You'll learn how to display it in the next activity.)
2. Press **Tab** again to insert a second tab character. This moves the insertion point to the second tab, 1" from the left margin.
3. Press **Backspace** to remove the second tab character.
4. Type **All Employees**.
5. Press **Enter** twice to end the *To:* line of the memo and add a blank line.
6. Type **From:**, press **Tab**, type **Deb Harding**, and press **Enter** twice to create the From line for our memo.
7. Type **Re:**, press **Tab**, type **Car Rentals**, and press **Enter** twice.

8. Type **We recently renewed our corporate agreement with Capital Rentals. They continue to be our primary car rental service.** Then press the **Spacebar** to insert a space before the next sentence.
9. Examine the screen. Notice that the word *primary* has automatically wrapped to the next line, even though you did not press Enter. This is an example of word wrap. (If you have not set up Windows and Word Pro to use a PostScript printer, your text may wrap at a different word.)

PRACTICE YOUR SKILLS

Complete your memo as shown in Figure 1.5. Use **Backspace** to correct any typing mistakes you make.

Figure 1.5 **The completed memo**

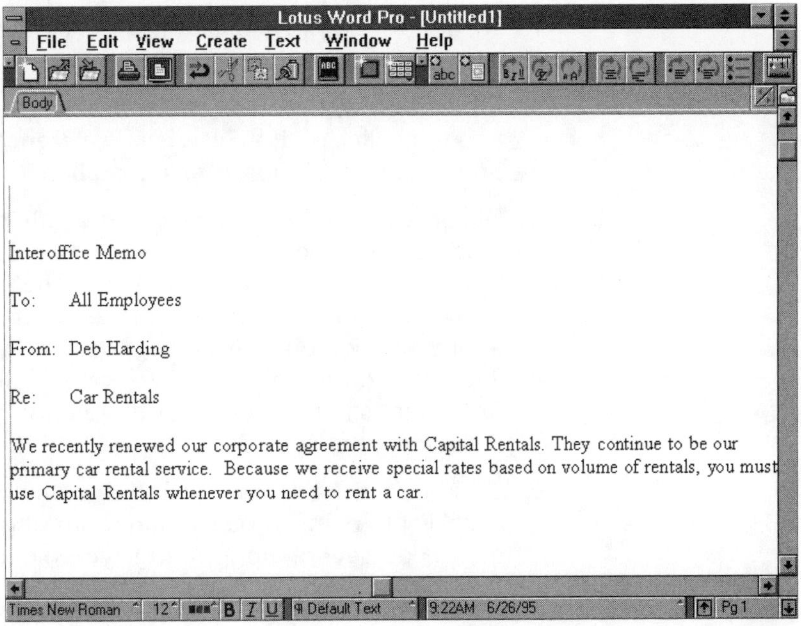

DISPLAYING NONPRINTING SYMBOLS

You can have Word Pro display special symbols on the screen that show the places in the text where you press the Enter and Tab keys. These *nonprinting symbols* (so called because they do not appear on paper when you print the document) are often useful to see. This is particularly true when you are working with heavily formatted documents and need to keep track of your tabs, blank lines, and so on.

To control the display of Word Pro's nonprinting symbols, you can use the View, Set View Preferences command.

Let's display some of the nonprinting symbols contained in your document so that you can see on-screen where you have pressed the Enter and Tab keys:

1. Examine the first four lines of text in your document. The lines are short, not reaching the right margin, but there are no symbols marking the ends of these lines.
2. Examine the *To:* line of the memo. There is a tab between *To:* and *All Employees,* but it is difficult to tell because you can't see any symbol for the tab character you inserted there.
3. Choose **View, Set View Preferences** (open the **View** menu, and then click on the **Set View Preferences** menu item) to open the View Preferences dialog box.
4. Observe the dialog box (see Figure 1.6). It consists of four tabs—Show, Zoom, Outline, and Clean Screen—that control the way you view your documents. The check boxes on the Show tab control what is displayed in your document and application windows (rulers, grids, graphics, and so on). (**Note:** We do not discuss the Zoom, Outline, and Clean Screen tabs in this book. For more information about these tabs, see your Word Pro documentation.)
5. Click on the **check mark** next to the Show Marks drop-down checklist to display the list of nonprinting symbols. Word Pro offers you several nonprinting symbols to display.
6. Select **Tabs**. Word Pro places a check mark to the left of *Tabs,* indicating that tab characters will display.
7. Select **Returns** and click on the **check mark** again to close the Show Marks drop-down checklist.

Figure 1.6 The Show tab in the View Preferences dialog box

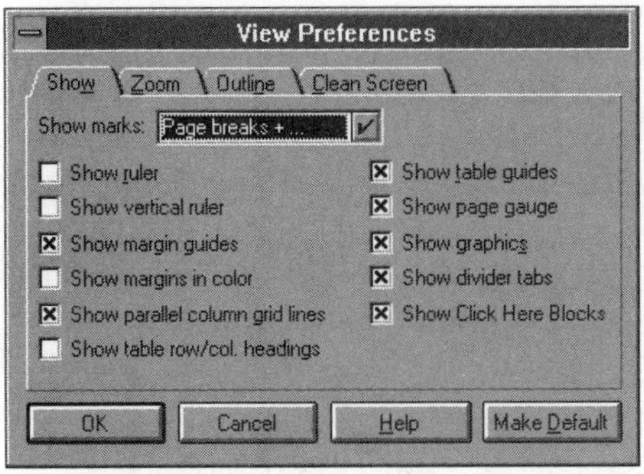

8. Click on **OK** to close the View Preferences dialog box.
9. Observe your screen. Word Pro now displays a *return symbol* (¶) at each point where you pressed Enter in the document. Where you pressed the Tab key, Word Pro now displays a *tab symbol* (·····>) to represent the tab character you inserted. Remember—these nonprinting symbols only appear on the screen; they will not appear on your printed document. (**Note**: if there is not enough space between the text, Word Pro may not display a tab symbol. Don't worry, it's there.

SAVING YOUR DOCUMENT

Before you save it, a document exists only in computer memory, a temporary storage area. For permanent storage, you must save the document as a file on a hard or floppy disk. Word Pro provides two commands you can use to save documents: *File, Save As* and *File, Save*.

THE FILE, SAVE AS COMMAND

You use the File, Save As command to save a document for the first time, to save a document with a new name, or to save a document in a different location (on another disk or in another directory, for example).

To save a document using File, Save As:

- Choose *File, Save As* to open the Save As dialog box.
- In the File Name *text box*, type a name for your document.

- If the appropriate disk drive is not already selected, use the Drives drop-down list box to select the drive onto which you want to save your document.
- If the appropriate disk-drive directory is not already selected, use the Directories list box to choose the *directory* or *subdirectory* into which you want to save your document. (Computer disks are arranged much like filing cabinets, with directories acting as hanging file folders that each hold a group of files. Subdirectories are a type of directory that act as file folders within file folders; they let you subdivide your files within a directory.)
- If desired, type a document description in the Description text box.
- Click on OK.

Note: When you save a document, Word Pro adds the .LWP *file name extension* to identify the file as a Word Pro document file. Your hard disk and floppy disks can hold many other types of files, such as .EXE program files, .WK3 spreadsheet files, .DBF database files, and so on. Do not add file name extensions yourself; let Word Pro do it for you automatically.

THE FILE, SAVE COMMAND

After you save a document once, you can use the File, Save command (instead of File, Save As) to save the document again with its current name and in its current location. File, Save updates a saved document by replacing the last-saved version of the document with the new version of the document on your screen.

For example, let's say you use File, Save As to save a business report to your reports directory as JAN-REPT, and then you go back and revise the report by adding an extra closing paragraph. If you then choose File, Save, the new report version (with the extra paragraph) will replace the last-saved version (no extra paragraph) on the disk.

Once you've used File, Save As to name and save a document, you should generally use File, Save for all subsequent updates of that document. However, if you later want to rename it or save it in a different location (while retaining a copy of the original file in the current location), you should use File, Save As.

Note: It's very important to save your active documents frequently. That way, if something happens to your computer's memory (for example, a power failure, which erases the contents of RAM), you will have a recent copy of your document safe on a disk. This precaution will keep retyping tasks to a minimum.

General rules for saving are as follows:

- Save at least once every 15 minutes.
- Save before printing.
- Save before using Word Pro's spelling checker (which you'll learn about in Chapter 7).

NAMING A DOCUMENT

When you save a document for the first time, you must name it. Follow these guidelines for naming documents:

- A file name can contain from one to eight letters, numbers, or the following special characters: ! @ # $ % ( ) - { } ' ~ (not counting the .LWP file name extension, which Word Pro supplies automatically).
- A file name cannot contain spaces.
- A file name should be descriptive, so that you can remember the file's contents (for example, JAN-REPT rather than X117-A).

Let's save and name your document in the directory you created in the "Creating Your Work Directory" section of this chapter. (If you named your work directory something other than C:\WPRO-WORK, the following steps may not work exactly as described. You will need to substitute your own work directory's name for C:\WPRO-WORK.)

1. Choose **File, Save As** to open the Save As dialog box.
2. Observe the File Name text box. It currently contains the highlighted, or *selected*, file name extension, .LWP.
3. Type **mymemo** to replace the selected text. (Letter case is not important when you are typing file names.)
4. Observe the Directory line to the right of the File Name text box. By default, Word Pro sets it to *c:\wordpro\docs*, meaning

that if you clicked on OK now, you would save your document on the C drive, in the DOCS subdirectory of the WORDPRO directory. (If your Directory line displays something other than c:\wordpro\docs, don't worry; we'll get you set up properly in a moment.) Returning to our filing-cabinet analogy, C is the filing cabinet, WORDPRO is a hanging file folder within that cabinet, and DOCS is a file folder within the WORDPRO hanging file folder.

5. Observe the Drives drop-down list box. It is set to the drive specified in the Directory line. (If you specified a different drive for your work directory, click on the drop-down list box's **drop-down list arrow** to open the list, and then select the appropriate drive letter. If the drive letter you want is not visible, use the **Up Arrow** and/or **Down Arrow** keys on your keyboard to select the appropriate drive, and then click again on the box's **drop-down list arrow** to close the drop-down list.)
6. In the Directories list box, double-click on **wordpro** to display the entire list of directories under *wordpro*.
7. Scroll to the end of the list of available directories by clicking repeatedly on the **down scroll** arrow in the lower-right corner of the Directories list box (as shown in Figure 1.7). Your WPROWORK directory should appear at the bottom of the list. Double-click on **wprowork** to select it. This is the work directory you created earlier in this chapter; here you will store and retrieve all of the documents you work with in this book.
8. Observe the Directory line. It confirms that you've selected the WPROWORK directory.
9. Position the mouse pointer inside the Description text box (the pointer changes to an I-beam), and click once to place the insertion point. Then type **This is my first document.** (Document descriptions are optional when saving a document. In Chapter 2, however, you'll learn how they can be useful when retrieving saved documents.) Your dialog box should now resemble Figure 1.7.
10. Click on **OK** to save your document. Word Pro closes the Save As dialog box.

Figure 1.7 **Saving a document for the first time**

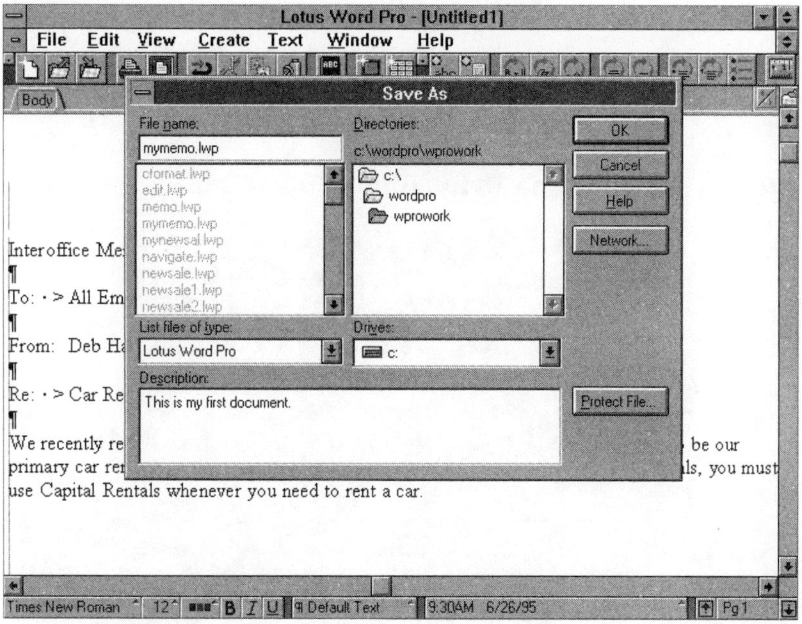

11. Observe the title bar. It now displays your document's name, *MYMEMO.LWP*, rather than *Untitled*. (Notice that Word Pro has added the .LWP file name extension automatically.)

PRINTING A DOCUMENT

By default, Word Pro prints one copy of the entire active document. You can also choose to print multiple copies, the current page only, a specific range of pages, just the even-numbered pages (2, 4, 6, and so on), or just the odd-numbered pages (1, 3, 5, and so on).

To print the active document:

- Choose *File, Print*.
- Select the desired options from the Print dialog box.
- Click on *OK*.

Let's print MYMEMO.LWP:

1. Choose **File, Print** to open the Print dialog box (see Figure 1.8). (Because Word Pro uses your Windows default printer, your dialog box may not match Figure 1.8 exactly.)

Figure 1.8 **The Print dialog box**

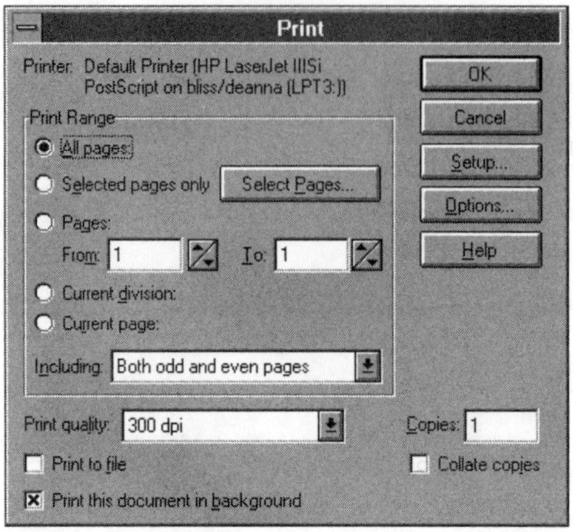

2. Click on **OK**. (Or, if you do not have a printer, click on Cancel to close the dialog box without printing.) Compare your printout with Figure 1.9. Depending on the printer you are using, your printout may vary slightly from the one pictured.

3. If your document failed to print, make sure your printer is on-line, and then try again. If it still won't print, refer to your printer and Windows documentation for information on setting up your printer properly.

CLOSING A DOCUMENT

When you're finished working with a document—that is, after you've completed, saved, and (if desired) printed it—you should close the document window. To do this, choose File, Close (or double-click on the document window Control menu box).

Figure 1.9 **The printed memo**

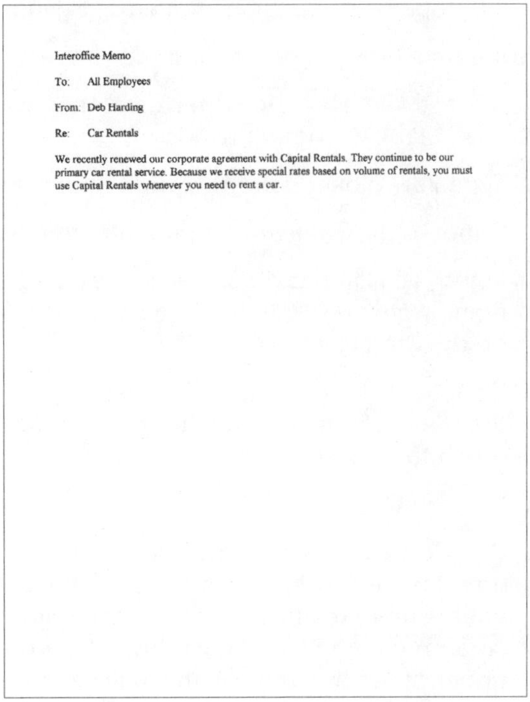

Interoffice Memo

To: All Employees

From: Deb Harding

Re: Car Rentals

We recently renewed our corporate agreement with Capital Rentals. They continue to be our primary car rental service. Because we receive special rates based on volume of rentals, you must use Capital Rentals whenever you need to rent a car.

Let's close MYMEMO.LWP:

1. Choose **File, Close** to close the document window and remove the document from computer memory. (Remember, because you used File, Save earlier, a copy of the document is still stored safely in your work directory.)
2. Observe the screen. Word Pro remains loaded, but no document window is open. The title bar displays only *Lotus Word Pro,* the scroll bars have disappeared, and the status bar is completely blank.

CREATING A NEW DOCUMENT

Once you've closed the active document, you're ready—if you choose—to create a new document. To do this,

- Choose *File, New Document.*

- Click on *OK*.

Word Pro opens a new, blank document window.

Let's create a new document and then save it:

1. Choose **File, New Document** and then click on **OK** to open a new, blank document window.
2. Type **Joe, please send the phone number for Capital Rentals.**
3. Choose **File, Save As** to open the Save As dialog box.
4. In the File Name text box, type **mysecond** to name the document. Note that Word Pro once again displays c:\wordpro\docs on the Directory line.
5. Double-click on **wordpro** in the Directories list box, then double-click on **wprowork** (you might still need to scroll down to find it).
6. Click on **OK**.
7. Double-click on your new document window **Control menu box** (the lower of the two boxes in the upper-left corner of your screen) to close the document window. *Do not* double-click on the application window's Control menu box (the upper of the two boxes); this will cause you to exit Word Pro. You can choose File, Close or you can double-click on the Control menu box to close a document window.

EXITING WORD PRO

Your final step in every Word Pro session is to exit Word Pro. *Never turn off your computer before doing so,* as this could harm your computer and/or result in the loss of data. To exit Word Pro and return to Windows, you can either choose File, Exit Word Pro, or double-click on the application window's Control menu box. As a safeguard, if you have not saved the latest version of an active document, Word Pro will prompt you to do so before exiting.

Let's exit Word Pro:

1. Choose **File, Exit Word Pro**. The Word Pro application window closes, revealing the Windows Program Manager once again.

SUMMARY

In this chapter, you learned the basics of the document creation-revision-saving-printing cycle, a procedure you'll use frequently in your daily word processing work. You now know how to start Windows and Word Pro; how to enter and delete text; how to save, name, print, and close a document; how to create a new document; and how to exit Word Pro. Congratulations! You're well on your way to mastering Word Pro.

Here's a quick reference guide to the Word Pro features introduced in this chapter:

Desired Result	**How to Do It**
Start Windows	From DOS, type **win**; then press **Enter**
Start Word Pro	In Program Manager window, double-click on **Lotus Word Pro program icon**
Maximize window	Click on window's **Maximize button**
Close window	Double-click on window's **Control menu box**
Restore window	Click on window's **Restore button**
Minimize window	Click on window's **Minimize button**
Choose menu commands	Click on menu option to open that drop-down menu; click on menu item. Or press and hold mouse button on menu option; drag down to menu item; release mouse button
End paragraph or short line	Press **Enter**
Create blank line	Press **Enter**
Insert tab character	Press **Tab**
Delete one character to left of insertion point	Press **Backspace**

Display nonprinting symbols for tabs and returns	Choose **View, Set View Preferences**; click on Show Marks **check mark**; select **Tabs**; select **Returns**; click on **check mark**; click on **OK**
Save new document, or save existing document with new name or in new location	Choose **File, Save As**; type document name in File Name text box; select appropriate drive and directory (if necessary) in Drives drop-down list box and Directories list box; click on **OK**
Save previously saved document with same name and location	Choose **File, Save**
Print active document	Choose **File, Print**; click on **OK**
Close active document window	Choose **File, Close**; or double-click on document window's **Control menu box**
Create new document	Choose **File, New Document**; click on **OK**
Exit Word Pro	Choose **File, Exit Word Pro**; or double-click on application window's **Control menu box**

In the next chapter, we'll show you how to navigate through multiple-page Word Pro documents. You'll learn how to open a document, change the default document path, scroll and move through a document, search for text, control document magnification, and obtain on-line Help.

A NOTE ON HOW TO PROCEED

If you wish to stop here, feel free to do so. If you wish to press onward, please proceed directly to the next chapter. Remember to allot enough time to work through an entire chapter at one sitting.

CHAPTER 2: NAVIGATING IN WORD PRO

- Using File, Open to Open a Document
- Understanding the Document Path
- Scrolling through a Document
- Moving through a Document
- Using Edit, Find & Replace to Search for Text
- Controlling Document Magnification
- Obtaining On-Line Help
- Saving a Modified Document

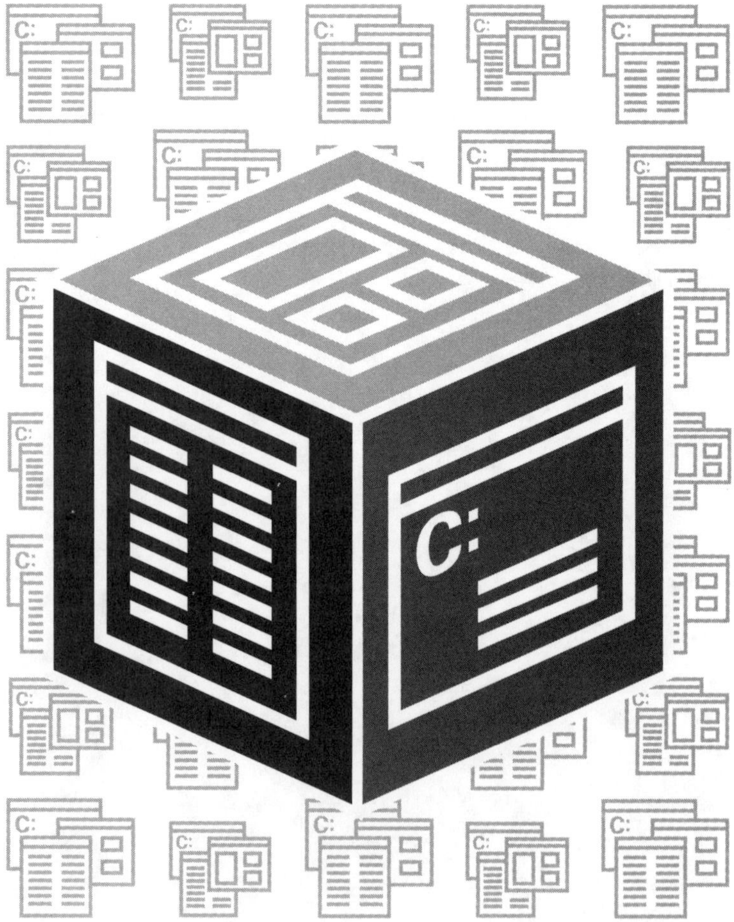

In Chapter 1, you learned how to start Windows and Word Pro, how to enter text, and how to create, save, print, and close documents. Because the one-page documents you created in Chapter 1 were short enough to fit all at once on your screen, you didn't need to *navigate* in Word Pro; in this chapter, however, you'll learn how to use the mouse and the keyboard to navigate through multiple-page documents that don't conveniently fit on one screen. It's essential for you to master these navigational techniques as early as possible in your Word Pro career. The more comfortable you feel navigating through a document, the more you'll be able to concentrate on the contents of the document.

When you're done working through this chapter, you will know how to

- Open a document
- Set a default document path
- Use the mouse to scroll through a document
- Use the keyboard, menus, and status bar to move through a document
- Use the Edit, Find & Replace Text command to search for text
- Use the View menu to control document magnification
- Use Word Pro's Help window to obtain on-line Help

USING FILE, OPEN TO OPEN A DOCUMENT

In Chapter 1 you learned how to create and save new documents. Here you'll learn how to open (*retrieve*) a saved document. This way, you'll be able to revise previously saved documents, and then save and print them again.

Follow these steps when you want to open a document:

- Choose *File, Open.*
- If necessary, use the Drives drop-down list box and the Directories list box to select the appropriate disk drive and directory.
- In the Files list box, click on the desired document name and then click on *OK*, or simply double-click on the desired document name.

When you open a document, Word Pro places a copy of the saved document in a document window on your screen. Because this is a *copy* of the saved document, and not the saved document itself, you can revise it to your heart's content without changing the original document stored on your disk.

Caution: If you save your revised document with the same name and in the same location as the original, you *do* change the original saved document. Whenever you want to preserve the original document, be sure to save the revised version with a new name and/or location.

Word Pro also provides a convenient shortcut for opening a file: It keeps track of up to the last five documents (the last four, by default) you opened, and places their names (preceded by a number) as menu items at the bottom of the File menu. To open one of these documents, you can open the File menu and click on the desired document name.

Let's begin by opening a document, NAVIGATE.LWP, that is stored in your work directory:

1. Start Word Pro. (For step-by-step instructions, refer back to "Starting Word Pro" in Chapter 1.)
2. Click on **Cancel** to close the Welcome to Lotus Word Pro window.
3. Choose **File, Open** to open the Open dialog box (see Figure 2.1).

Figure 2.1 **The Open dialog box**

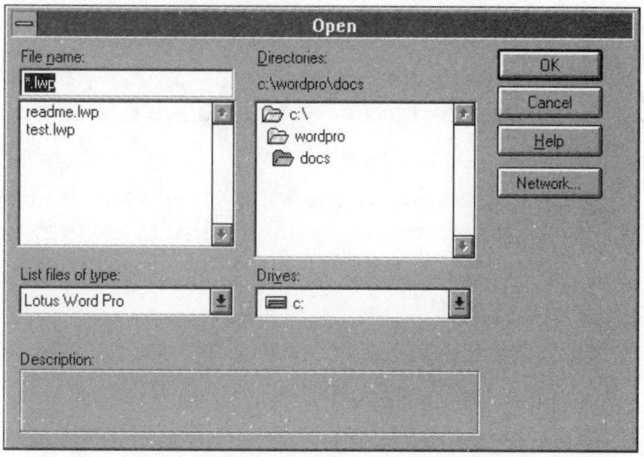

4. Observe the Directories line (located to the right of the File Name text box). The active directory is c:\wordpro\docs.
5. If necessary, use the Drives drop-down list box to select the drive containing your work directory.
6. In the Directories list box, double-click on **wordpro**. Then double-click on **wprowork** (or whatever name you gave your work directory).

7. Observe the File Name list box. It now lists in alphabetical order every Word Pro document stored in your work directory. Because there are too many documents to display at one time, *navigate.lwp* is not visible.

8. Observe the vertical scroll bar on the right edge of the File Name list box. It enables you to scroll down through the list of document names. Click on the scroll bar's **down scroll arrow** until *mymemo.lwp, mysecond.lwp,* and *navigate.lwp* are visible. Notice that your work directory contains documents you created, such as *mymemo.lwp,* as well as documents we supplied on this book's Data Disk, such as *navigate.lwp.*

9. Click on **mymemo.lwp**, and then observe the Description text box (located near the bottom of the dialog box). It displays the document description you typed when saving this document. Document descriptions can help you determine the contents of documents *before* you open them.

10. Click on **navigate.lwp**, and then observe the Description line. This document, too, contains a document description: *Document for Chapter 2.*

11. Observe the File Name text box. By clicking on *navigate.lwp,* you automatically inserted the document's name in this text box.

12. Click on **OK** to open the document. A copy of the document appears in the active document window (see Figure 2.2). Notice that the title bar now reads *Lotus Word Pro - [navigate.lwp].*

13. Close NAVIGATE.LWP (choose **File, Close** or double-click on the document window's **Control menu box**).

Now let's try the shortcut method for opening this document:

1. Open the **File** menu, and then observe the bottom of the menu. It now lists the NAVIGATE.LWP document.

2. Click on **1 C:\WORDPRO\WPROWORK\NAVIGATE.LWP** to re-open the document.

Figure 2.2 **The newly opened document NAVIGATE.LWP**

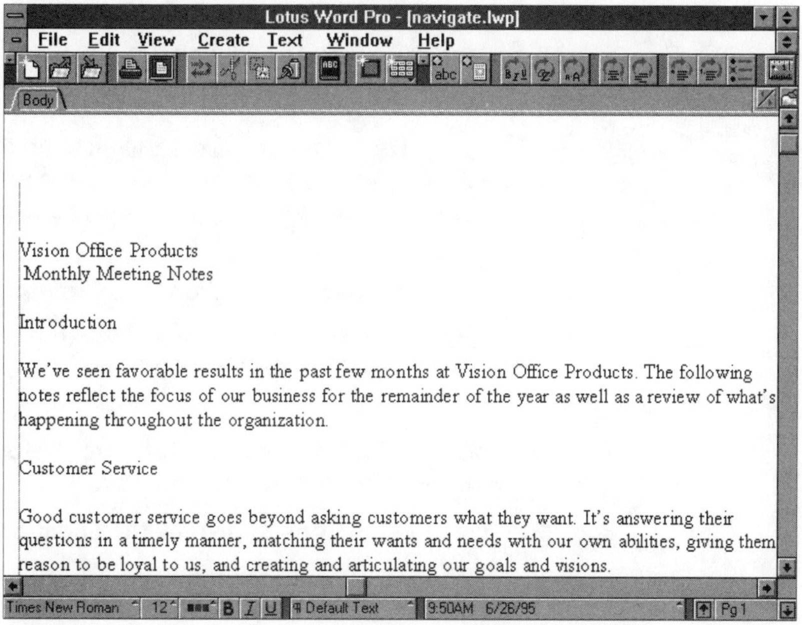

UNDERSTANDING THE DOCUMENT PATH

Word Pro by default wants to open and save documents to the c:\wordpro\docs disk drive and directory. Word Pro calls this combination of drive and directory the *document path*. The document path determines the appropriate avenue for saving and opening documents, and fortunately you can change it. In fact, until you change it, Word Pro automatically resets the document path to the original directory (usually, C:\WORDPRO\DOCS). Having to change the document path every time you want to open or save a document can be time-consuming. Luckily, Word Pro offers a solution: the Word Pro Preferences dialog box.

CHANGING THE DEFAULT DOCUMENT PATH

By using the Locations tab in the Word Pro Preferences dialog box, you can define a new default document path. That way, Word Pro will automatically set itself to that directory for opening and saving files.

To set a new default document path:

- Choose *File, User Setup, Word Pro Preferences.*
- Click on *Locations* to display the Locations tab.
- In the Documents text box, type the desired document path.
- Uncheck *Use Working Directory* if it is checked. (**Note**: if you check Use Working Directory, Word Pro will remember the directory you were working in when you last opened or saved a document.)
- Click on *OK* to close the Word Pro Preferences dialog box.

Let's set the document path to your working directory so that you will no longer have to designate it in the Save As or Open dialog boxes:

1. Choose **File, User Setup, Word Pro Preferences** to open the Word Pro Preferences dialog box.
2. Click on **Locations** to display the Locations tab.
3. Observe the Locations tab. It enables you to set default paths for documents and other Word Pro-related files.
4. In the Documents text box, type **c:\wordpro\wprowork** (or whatever disk drive and directory name are appropriate).
5. Uncheck **Use Working Directory**, if necessary. If this option is selected, Word Pro will ignore the document path you typed in the Documents text box (see Figure 2.3).
6. Click on **OK** to close the Word Pro Preferences dialog box.

SCROLLING THROUGH A DOCUMENT

At normal (100 percent) magnification, a Word Pro document window can only display about half of a standard business-size (8 1/2" × 11") page at a time. To view the remainder of a page (or other pages within the document), you can use the mouse in conjunction with the vertical and horizontal scroll bars to *scroll* through the document. The vertical scroll bar controls up-down scrolling; the horizontal scroll bar controls side-to-side scrolling.

Scrolling through a document changes the document display, but does *not* change the position of the insertion point. For example, if the insertion point is at the top of page 2 and you use

Figure 2.3 **Setting the default document path**

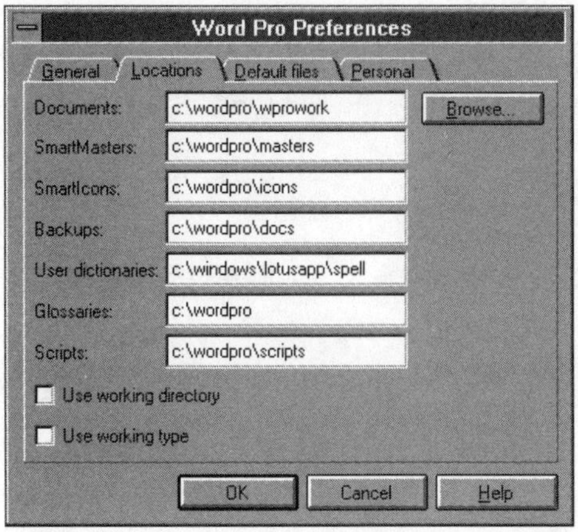

the vertical scroll bar to scroll down to page 8, Word Pro displays the contents of page 8 on the screen, but the insertion point remains at the top of page 2. If you then begin to type, your text is entered at the insertion point on page 2, not on page 8. (You'll learn how to change both the document display *and* the insertion point in the next section.)

Table 2.1 lists Word Pro's vertical and horizontal scrolling options and how to perform them. Figure 2.4 identifies screen elements used for scrolling.

Let's practice using the mouse and scroll bars to scroll through the active document:

1. Click on the **down scroll arrow** several times to scroll down through the document one line at a time. Note that the insertion point does not move.
2. Click on the **up scroll arrow** several times to scroll up through the document.
3. Drag the **vertical scroll box** to the bottom of the scroll bar to scroll to the bottom of the document.
4. Drag the **vertical scroll box** to the middle of the scroll bar to scroll to the middle of the document. (Because NAVIGATE.LWP is a two-page document, you will see the bottom of page 1, the top of page 2, or both.)

Table 2.1 **Vertical and Horizontal Scrolling Options**

To Scroll	Do This
Up or down one line	Click on up or down scroll arrow
To top, bottom, or middle of document	Drag vertical scroll box to top, bottom, or middle of vertical scroll bar
Up or down a screen	Click in vertical scroll bar above or below vertical scroll box
Left or right a column	Click on left or right scroll arrow
To left edge, right edge, or middle of a document	Drag horizontal scroll box to left, right, or middle of horizontal scroll bar
Left or right a screen	Click in horizontal scroll bar to left or right of horizontal scroll box

Figure 2.1 **The horizontal and vertical scroll bars**

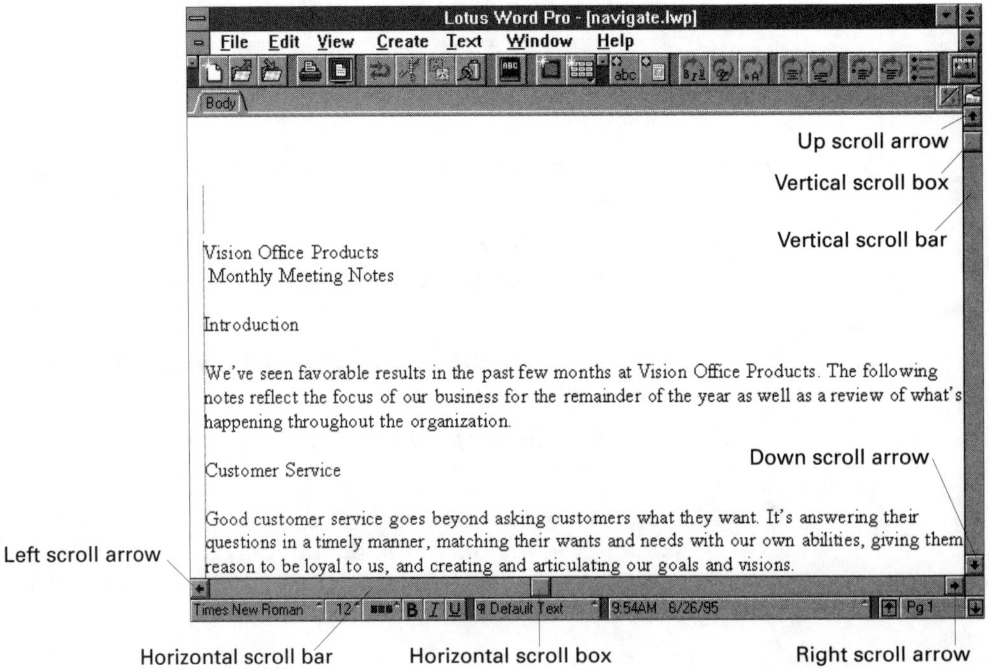

5. Drag the **vertical scroll box** to the top of the scroll bar to scroll to the top of the document. Notice that throughout all of your scrolling, the insertion point has remained at the top of the document.
6. Click in the **vertical scroll bar** below the vertical scroll box to scroll one screen length (about one-third of a page) down through the document.
7. Repeat step 6 as many times as necessary to scroll to the bottom of the document. Be careful! As you click, the vertical scroll box moves down within the scroll bar; you need to keep clicking *below* that box.
8. Click in the **vertical scroll bar** above the vertical scroll box to scroll one screen length up through the document.
9. Repeat step 8 as many times as necessary to scroll to the top of the document.

Next, take a moment to observe a common scrolling mistake. Let's say you want to type your initials at the end of the active document.

1. Drag the **vertical scroll box** to the bottom of the scroll bar to display the end of the document.
2. Type your initials. Observe that the text is inserted at the top of the document (where your insertion point is located), *not* at the end (where you had scrolled). Word Pro automatically repositions the document to display the inserted text. To avoid making such a mistake, remember these two things: Text that you type is always inserted at the insertion point, and the insertion point does not move automatically when you use the scroll bars.
3. Use **Backspace** to erase your initials.

MOVING THROUGH A DOCUMENT

When you *scroll* through a document, you change the document display but not the insertion point. Repositioning the insertion point when scrolling is a two-step process: You scroll, and then you click to position the insertion point.

Moving, on the other hand, is a one-step process: When you move through a document, you automatically change *both* the document display and the insertion point.

Generally, you should scroll when you just want to view various parts of a document, but you should move when you want to modify the document.

USING THE KEYBOARD TO MOVE THROUGH A DOCUMENT

Table 2.2 lists several keyboard techniques for moving through a document.

Table 2.2 **Keyboard Movement Techniques**

To Move	Press
Up one line	Up Arrow
Down one line	Down Arrow
Left one character	Left Arrow
Right one character	Right Arrow
To beginning of line	Home
To end of line	End
Up one screen	Page Up (or PgUp)
Down one screen	Page Down (or PgDn)
Up one page	Ctrl+Page Up (or Ctrl+PgUp)
Down one page	Ctrl+Page Down (or Ctrl+PgDn)
To top of document	Ctrl+Home
To end of document	Ctrl+End

Note: If you intend to use the PgUp and PgDn keys on your numeric keypad, rather than the Page Up and Page Down keys, make sure that Num Lock is off.

Now let's practice using the keyboard to move—rather than scroll—through the document.

1. Press **Ctrl+Home** (press and hold down the **Ctrl** key, press the **Home** key, and then release both keys) to move to the top of the document. Note that the insertion point moves to the top along with the document display.
2. Press **Page Down** twice to move two screen lengths down through the document. The insertion point moves again.
3. Press **Page Up** twice to move two screen lengths up through the document. Note that the insertion point has moved.
4. Press **Down Arrow** to move the insertion point down one line. Because you moved the insertion point within the current document display, Word Pro did not need to change the display.
5. Press **Up Arrow** to move the insertion point up one line.

Let's repeat our initials-typing task, this time using the correct method:

1. Press **Ctrl+End** to move to the end of the document.
2. Type your initials. This time they are inserted at the end of the document.
3. Press **Ctrl+Home** to return to the top of the document.

USING EDIT, *GO TO* TO MOVE TO A PAGE

You can use the Edit, Go To command to move to the top of a specific page in the active document. This technique is particularly useful when you are moving through a long (multiple-page) document.

To move to the top of a page:

- Choose *Edit, Go To* or press *Ctrl+G*.
- In the Page Number text box, type the desired page number.
- Click on *OK*.

Let's use the Edit, Go To command to move through the active document:

1. Look for the *Page Status button*, the second button from the right on the status bar. It currently displays *Pg 1*.
2. Choose **Edit, Go To** to open the Go To dialog box (see Figure 2.5).

Figure 2.4 **The Go To dialog box**

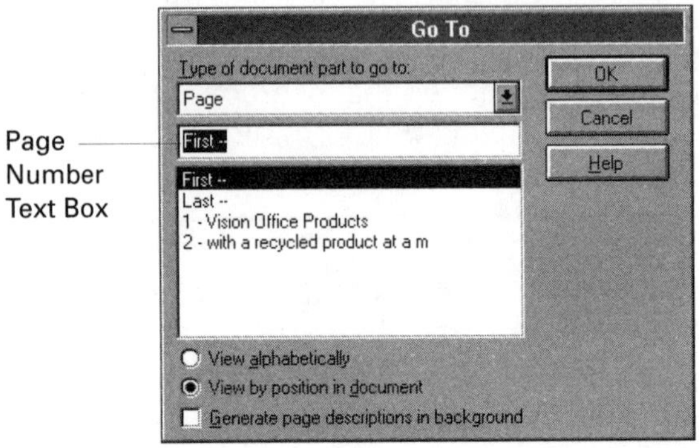

3. In the Page Number text box, type **2** to specify the destination page, and then click on **OK** to move both the document display and the insertion point to the top of page 2.
4. Observe the Page Status button. It now displays a *Pg 2*.
5. Choose **Edit, Go To**, type **1**, and then click on **OK** to move to the top of page 1.

USING THE STATUS BAR TO MOVE TO A PAGE

You can also use other buttons on the status bar to move to a different page—the Page Status button, along with the two *Page Arrow buttons* that flank the Page Status button at the right end of the status bar. The Page Status button opens the Go To dialog box; the Page Arrow buttons move the insertion point to the top of the next or previous page, without opening the Go To dialog box.

Let's use the Page Status and Page Arrow buttons now:

1. Click on the **Page Status button** (see Figure 2.6) to open the Go To dialog box.

Figure 2.5 **The Page Status and Page Arrow buttons**

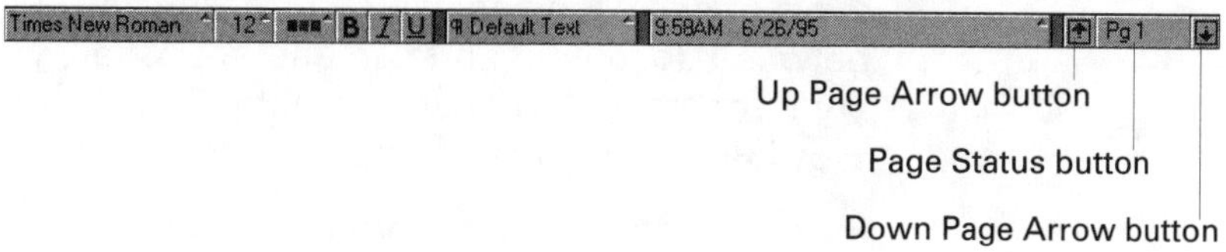

2. Type **2**, and then click on **OK** to move to the top of page 2.
3. Click on the **Up Page Arrow button** (located to the left of the Page Status button). The insertion point moves to the top of page 1.
4. Click on the **Down Page Arrow button** (located to the right of the Page Status button). The insertion point moves to the top of page 2.

PRACTICE YOUR SKILLS

Use any of the insertion-point-movement techniques you've learned to perform the following steps:

1. Move the insertion point to the bottom of the document.
2. Move the insertion point to the top of page 2.
3. Move the insertion point to the top of the document.

USING EDIT, FIND & REPLACE TEXT TO SEARCH FOR TEXT

One of Word Pro's most useful features is its ability to locate a specific word or phrase in a document. You can use this feature to move rapidly to any desired document location. For example, you can move to the phrase *we would like to establish*—even if you have no idea which page contains this phrase. To locate specific text, you use Word Pro's Edit, Find & Replace Text command. (As you might expect, you can use the Edit, Find & Replace Text command to replace text as well as search for it. You'll learn how to use Edit, Find & Replace Text's replace functions in Chapter 3.)

Sometimes having a big, clunky dialog box open in the middle of your screen is inconvenient. With that in mind, Word Pro invented *modeless bars*. Like a dialog box, a bar displays check boxes, drop-down lists, text boxes, buttons, and so on. However, unlike a dialog box, a bar is displayed at the top of your document and stays open as long as you need it. You can switch back and forth between document and bar, and best of all, you can always see your document. When you use the Find & Replace command, Word Pro opens a modeless bar.

Follow these steps when you use Edit, Find & Replace Text to search for text within a document:

- Choose *Edit, Find & Replace Text* to open the Find & Replace bar.
- In the Find text box, type your *search text* (the text that you want to find).
- Click on *Find*; Word Pro selects (highlights) the first occurrence of your search text.
- If you want to search your document beyond the first found occurrence, click on *Find* as many times as needed to search through the document. When you are ready, you can click on *Done* to end your search. When Word Pro reaches the end of your document, it opens a message box that indicates how many times your search text was found.

The Find & Replace bar provides several find options to help you refine your text searches. These options are available by selecting them from the Find Options drop-down list. They operate as follows:

- *Whole Words Only* instructs Word Pro to find only whole words that match your search text. For example, Word Pro could use the search text *rate* to find *rate* and *Rate*, but not *rates* or *operate*.
- *Words Starting With* instructs Word Pro to find words that start with your search text. For example, Word Pro could use the search text *rate* to find *rate*, and *rates*, but not *operate*.
- *Words Ending With* instructs Word Pro to find words that end with your search text. For example, Word Pro could use the search text *rate* to find *operate*, but not *rate* or *rates*.

- *Words Containing* instructs Word Pro to find words that contain your search text. For example, Word Pro could use the search text *rate* to find *rate, rates,* and *operates*.

Clicking on the Options button provides some additional options. Some of these act as follows:

- *Match Case* instructs Word Pro to find only words that exactly match the case (capitalization) of your search text. For example, Word Pro could use the search text *rate* to find *rate, rates,* and *operate*, but not *Rate*.
- *Include Properties* instructs Word Pro to find your search text only when it has certain text properties (you'll learn about text properties in Chapter 4).

Let's experiment with the Edit, Find & Replace Text command:

1. Choose **Edit, Find & Replace Text** to open the Find & Replace bar (see Figure 2.7).

Figure 2.6 **The Find & Replace bar**

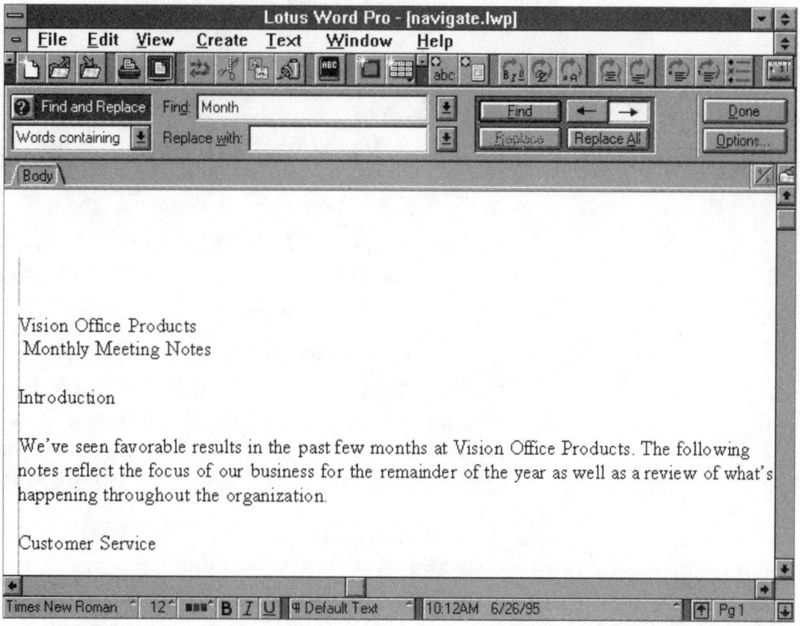

2. In the Find text box, type **Month**. Be sure to type the word with an uppercase *M*.
3. From the Find Options drop-down list, select **Words Containing** (see Figure 2.7).
4. Click on **Options** to open the Find & Replace Options dialog box (see Figure 2.8).

Figure 2.7 **The Find & Replace Options dialog box with appropriate settings**

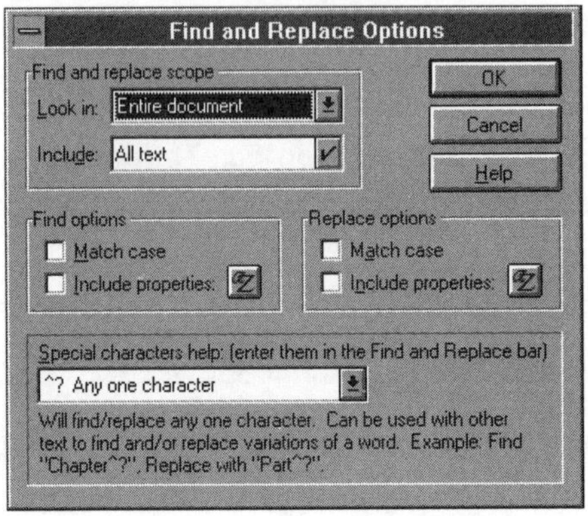

5. In the Find And Replace Scope box, verify that the Look In drop-down list is set to *Entire Document* and the Include check box is set to *All Text*.
6. Observe the Find Options box. It contains two check boxes for controlling your searches: *Match Case* and *Include Properties*. (Notice also that the Replace Options box contains the same two check boxes. Do not try to use the Replace options in this chapter; you'll learn about replace options in Chapter 8.)
7. In the Find Options box, verify that neither of the options is checked. If either is, uncheck it.
8. Click on **OK** to close the Find & Replace Options dialog box. Notice that the right arrow next to the Find button is selected. Word Pro will search from the insertion point forward.To search from the insertion point backward, click on the left arrow.

9. In the Find & Replace bar, click on **Find**. Word Pro finds the word *Monthly* in the heading *Monthly Meeting Notes*.
10. Click on **Find** four times, pausing to examine each found word. Word Pro finds *months, month, month-end,* and *month*.
11. Click on **Find** one more time. Because there are no more occurrences of your search text, Word Pro displays the search results message box shown in Figure 2.9.

Figure 2.8 **The search results message box**

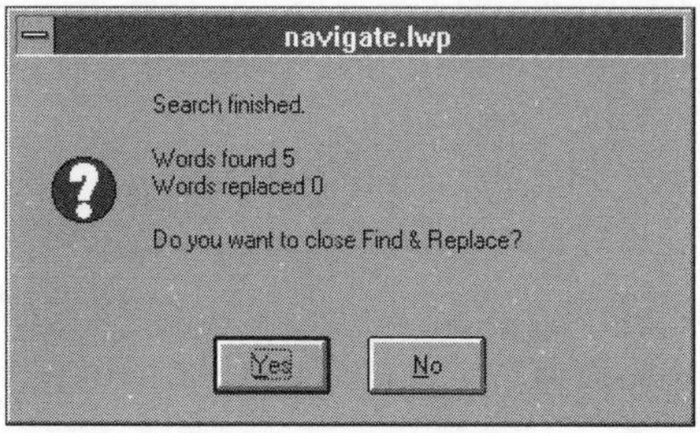

12. Click on **No** to leave the Find & Replace bar open.

Now let's refine our search by using the Whole Word Only and Exact Case options:

1. Move to the top of the document. (Click anywhere in the document and then press **Ctrl+Home**.)
2. From the Find Options list, select **Whole Words Only**.
3. Click on **Continue Find And Replace**. Word Pro finds *month*. Notice that because you selected Whole Words Only, Word Pro skipped *Monthly* in the heading *Monthly Meeting Notes* and *months* in the first paragraph.
4. Click on **Find** twice. Word Pro finds *month* and then displays the search result message box.
5. Click on **No** to close the message box without closing the Find & Replace bar.
6. Click on **Options**, and check the **Find Options Match Case** (be sure to check the Match Case option contained in the

Find Options box, not in the Replace Options box). Then click on **OK**.

7. Click on **Continue Find And Replace**. Because you checked Match Case, Word Pro skips both occurrences of *month* and displays the search results message box.
8. Click on **Yes** to close the search results message box and the Find & Replace bar.

PRACTICE YOUR SKILLS

1. Move to the top of the document.
2. Open the Find & Replace bar, replace the word *month* with the word **sales**, and then open the Find & Replace Text Options dialog box.
3. In the Find Options box, uncheck **Match Case**, click on **OK**, and then search the entire document. There are nine matches.
4. Click on **Yes** to close the Find & Replace bar.

CONTROLLING DOCUMENT MAGNIFICATION

Word Pro allows you to change the level of magnification at which your documents are displayed on the screen. By default, documents are displayed at 100 percent magnification (where the screen display matches the actual document size), but you can adjust this magnification to anywhere from 2 percent to 999 percent.

Lower magnifications (from 99 percent to 2 percent) shrink the on-screen document, allowing you to view more of a page at once. Higher magnifications (from 101 percent to 999 percent) enlarge the on-screen document, allowing you to view text and graphics close up to perform detail work.

Use the View menu to change the magnification of the active document. Word Pro provides the following magnification options:

- *Zoom to Full Page* reduces the document's magnification so that you can see an entire page at once.
- *Zoom to 100%* displays the document at full size.
- *Zoom to Margin Width* displays the document so that it fills the window from margin to margin.

- *Zoom to Page Width* displays the document so that it fills the window from the left edge of the page to the right edge.
- *Zoom to 75%* displays the document at three quarters of full size.
- *Zoom to 150%* displays the document at one and one half times full size.
- *Zoom to 200%* displays the document at double size.
- *Zoom to Custom Level* displays the document at the custom magnification level (91 percent by default).
- *Zoom to Other* allows you to set a custom magnification level.

Let's change the magnification of NAVIGATE.LWP:

1. If necessary, move the insertion point to the top of the document.
2. Display the View menu (click on **View**). Note that *Zoom to 100%* is checked, meaning that the active document is displayed at 100 percent (actual size) magnification.
3. Choose **Zoom to Full Page**. Word Pro displays a miniature view of page 1, as shown in Figure 2.10.
4. Choose **View, Zoom To 200%**. Note how much less of the text fits on-screen.
5. Choose **View, Zoom To 100%** to change the magnification back to 100%.
6. Choose **View, Zoom To, Page Width**. Note that your screen display changes. Selecting Page Width shrinks the document to the size where the width of the page fits on-screen.

PRACTICE YOUR SKILLS

Change the magnification level back to 100%.

OBTAINING ON-LINE HELP

Word Pro offers an extensive on-line Help system through its *Help window*. This Help window can provide you with "how-to" information on every aspect of the Word Pro program.

Figure 2.9 **Viewing a document in Full Page view**

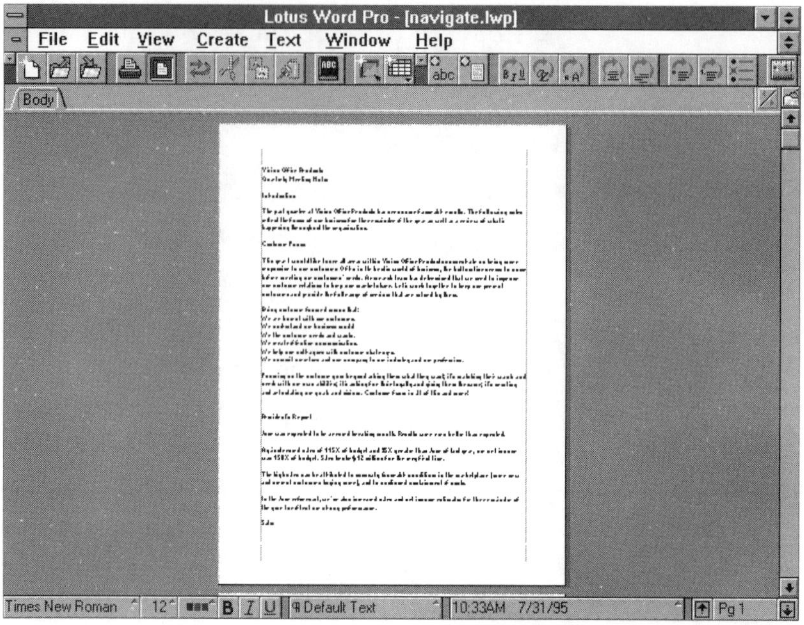

The beauty of Help is its accessibility. No matter what you are doing in Word Pro (choosing a command from the menu, editing a document, filling in a dialog box, and so on), Help is only a keystroke—or mouse click—away.

USING THE HELP TABLE OF CONTENTS

The Help window provides a table of contents that gives you an overview of available Help topics. Follow these steps when you want to use this Help table of contents:

- Choose *Help, Help Topics* to open the Help window and display the table of contents.
- To get Help for a specific topic, click on any icon. Clicking on any solid-underlined word or phrase will jump you to a new Help screen.
- To close the Lotus Word Pro Help window, either double-click on the window's *Control menu box* or choose *File, Exit.*

Let's practice using the Help table of contents:

1. Choose **Help, Help Topics** to open the Help window and display the Help table of contents.
2. Maximize the Help window (click on the window's **Maximize button**).
3. Move the mouse pointer to the icon for *Getting Started.* Notice that the mouse pointer changes to a *Help hand* (see Figure 2.11).

Figure 2.10 **Using the Help table of contents**

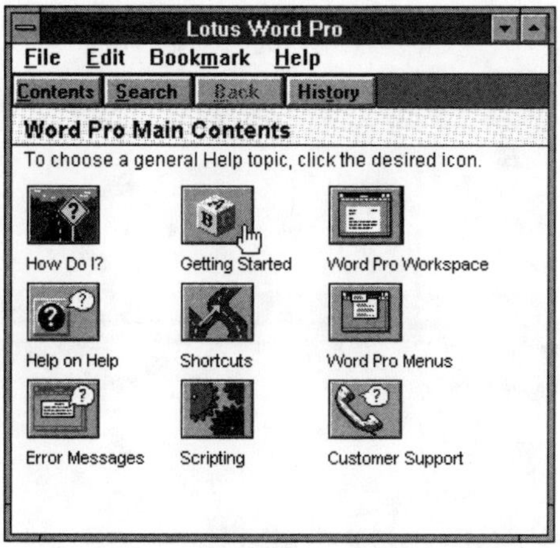

4. Use the Help hand to click on the Word Pro Workspace icon. The Help window now displays the Word Pro window with a picture of the screen. When you click on any part of the picture, Word Pro opens a pop-up window describing that part of the screen.
5. Click on the **menu bar**. Help pops up a definition window containing a description of the menu bar (see Figure 2.12).
6. Click again to close the definition window.
7. Close the Help window (double-click on the window's **Control menu box** or choose **File, Exit**).

Figure 2.11 **Viewing a definition window**

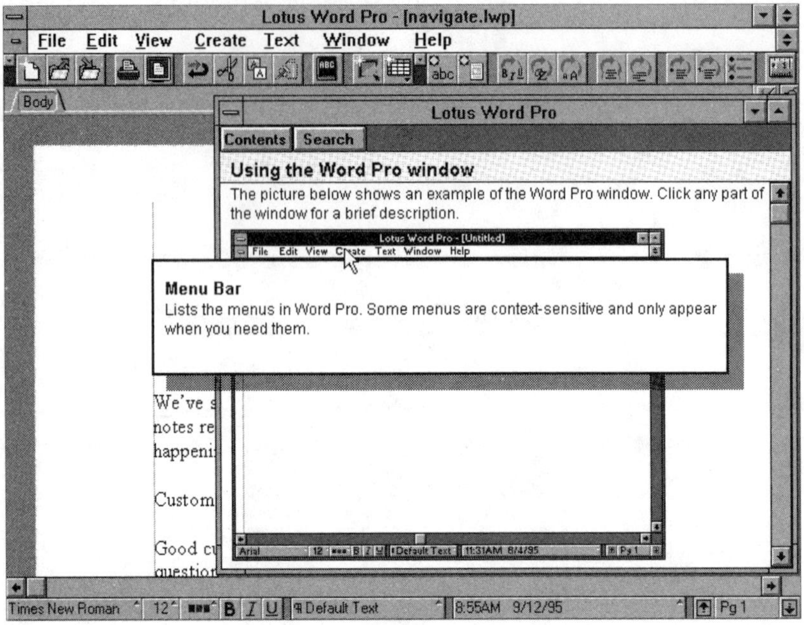

OBTAINING CONTEXT-SENSITIVE HELP

In addition to the Help table of contents, Word Pro offers you *context-sensitive Help:* information related to your current working context. For example, if a dialog box is open and you ask for context-sensitive Help, Help displays information about that dialog box. Used in this manner, Help can quickly provide information about specific dialog boxes, menu commands, or areas of the screen. This saves you the time and trouble of searching through a series of Help screens.

You can use any of the following methods to obtain context-sensitive Help:

- Press *F1.*
- From within any infobox (discussed later) or modeless bar, click on the *Help icon.*

- From within any dialog box, click on the *Help button*.

Let's use context-sensitive Help:

1. Choose **Edit, Go To** to open the Go To dialog box.
2. Press **F1**. Word Pro opens the Help window for the Edit, Go To command.
3. Close the Help window.
4. Observe the Go To dialog box. It displays a Help button. Click on the **Help button** to open once again the Help window for the Edit, Go To command.
5. Close the Help window, and then click on **Cancel** to close the Go To dialog box.
6. Choose **Edit, Find & Replace Text** to open the Find & Replace bar. Notice the question mark in the top-left corner of the bar (to the left of the bar name). This is the Help icon for the Find & Replace bar.
7. Click on the **Help icon** to open the Help window for the Find & Replace bar.
8. Close the Help window and click on **Done** to close the Find & Replace bar.
9. Choose **Text, Text Properties** to open the Text infobox (you'll learn more about infoboxes later in this book). The Text infobox displays a Help icon at the right end of its title bar (see Figure 2.13). Click on the **Help icon** to open the Help window for Text Font properties.

Figure 2.12 **Using an infobox's Help icon**

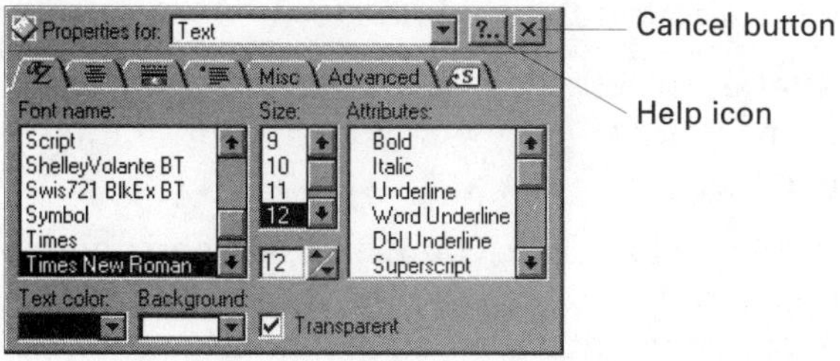

10. Close the Help window.
11. Click on the Text infobox's **Cancel** button (it displays an *X*) to close the Text Infobox.

SAVING A MODIFIED DOCUMENT

Let's end this work session by using File, Save As to rename the active document and save it to your work directory. By using the File, Save As command, you preserve the original version of the document (NAVIGATE.LWP) along with your revised version. (If you were to instead use the File, Save command to save the active document, you would preserve the revision and overwrite the original.)

1. Choose **File, Save As** to open the Save As dialog box.
2. In the File Name text box, type **mynav** as the new document name.
3. Examine the Directories line to verify that your work directory is still selected, and then click on **OK**. Word Pro saves your modified NAVIGATE.LWP document under the name MYNAV.LWP.
4. Close the document window.

PRACTICE YOUR SKILLS

You've learned a great deal about Word Pro in these first two chapters. The following two activities enable you to apply this knowledge to practical word processing tasks. Please don't think of these activities as tests, but rather as opportunities to hone your Word Pro skills. It is only through practice that you'll become more comfortable with the techniques you've learned.

After each activity step, a chapter reference (in parentheses) informs you of where we first introduced the relevant technique for that step.

In this first activity, you will create and edit the document shown in two different stages in Figures 2.14 and 2.15, to produce the final document shown in Figure 2.16.

1. Open a new document window. (Chapter 1)

Figure 2.13 **The first draft of the letter**

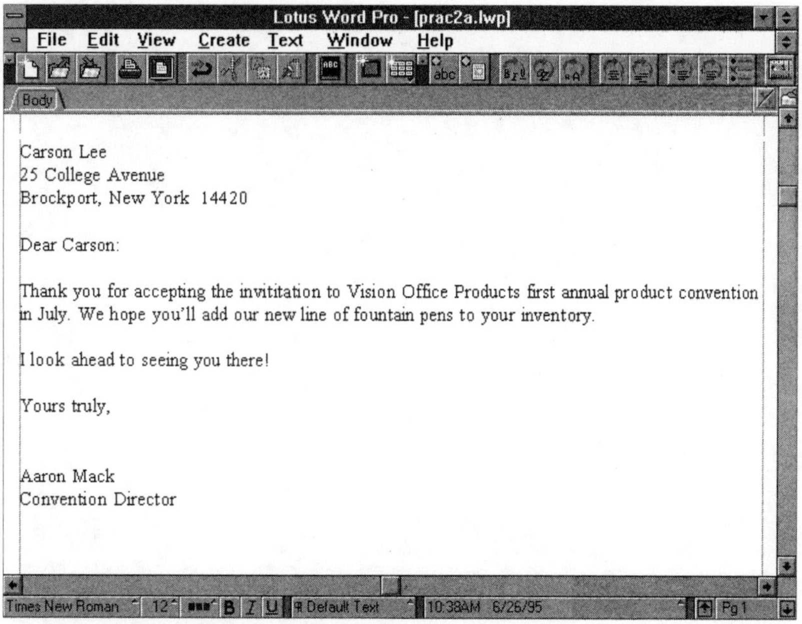

2. Enter the text shown in Figure 2.14. (Chapter 1)
3. Use **Backspace** to edit the letter as shown in Figure 2.15. (Chapter 1) (Note that the replacement text in Figure 2.15—for instance, **Street** and **our**—is in boldface for emphasis only. Do not try to enter this text in boldface; you will learn about boldface formatting in Chapter 4.)
4. Save the document in your work directory as **myprac2a**. (Chapter 1)
5. Print your document, and then compare the results to Figure 2.16. (Chapter 1)
6. Close the document window. (Chapter 1)

Figure 2.14 **Edits for the letter**

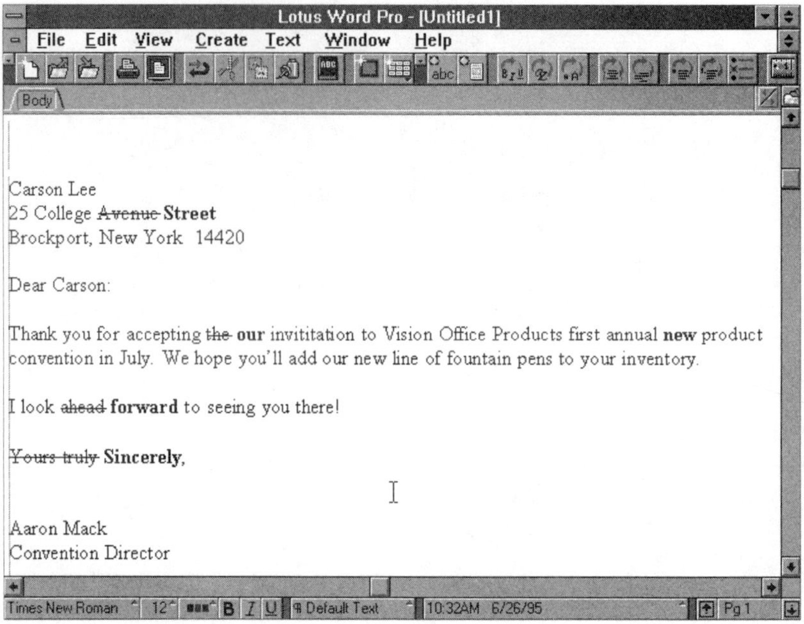

Figure 2.15 **The corrected letter**

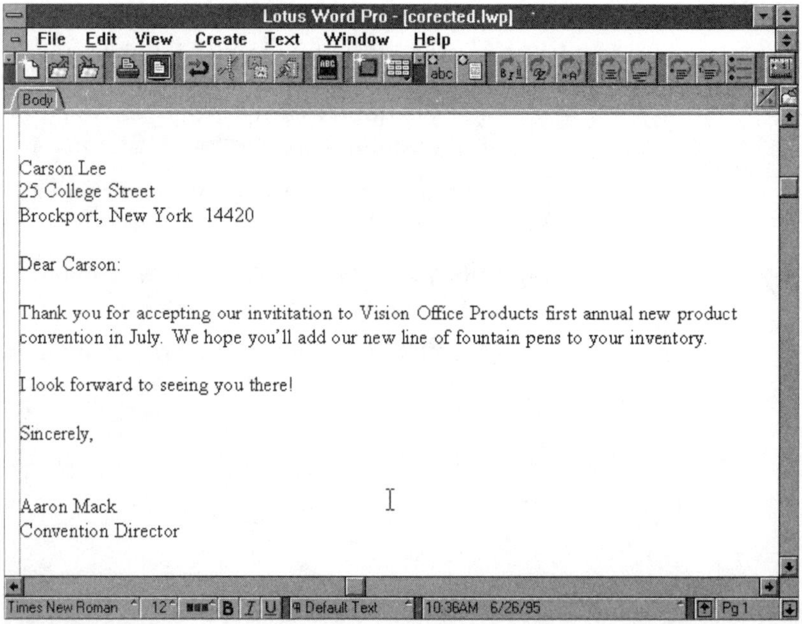

SUMMARY

In this chapter, you learned the basics of navigating in Word Pro. You now know how to open a document, set a default document path, scroll and move through a document, search for text, control document magnification, and obtain on-line help.

Here's a quick reference guide to the Word Pro features introduced in this chapter:

Desired Result	How to Do It
Open document	Choose **File, Open**; select appropriate drive and directory (if necessary); click on document's name; click on **OK** (or double-click on document's name)
Open recently opened document	Open **File** menu; click on document's name
Change default document path	Choose **File, User Setup, Word Pro Preferences**; click on **Locations**; type new path in Documents text box; click on **OK**
Scroll up or down one line	Click on **up** or **down scroll arrow**
Scroll to top, bottom, or middle of document	Drag **vertical scroll box** to top, bottom, or middle of vertical scroll bar
Scroll up or down one screen	Click in **vertical scroll bar** above or below vertical scroll box
Scroll left or right one column	Click on **left** or **right scroll arrow**
Scroll to left edge, right edge, or middle of document	Drag **horizontal scroll box** to left, right, or middle of horizontal scroll bar
Scroll to left or right one screen	Click in **horizontal scroll bar** to left or right of horizontal scroll box
Move up or down one line	Press **Up Arrow** or **Down Arrow**

Move left or right one character	Press **Left Arrow** or **Right Arrow**
Move to beginning or end of line	Press **Home** or **End**
Move up or down one screen	Press **Page Up** or **Page Down**
Move up one page	Press **Ctrl+Page Up**; or click on **Up Page Arrow button**
Move down one page	Press **Ctrl+Page Down**; or click on **Down Page Arrow button**
Move to top of document	Press **Ctrl+Home**
Move to end of document	Press **Ctrl+End**
Move to top of specific page	Choose **Edit, Go To** or click on **Page Status button**; type page number; then click on **OK**
Search for text	Choose **Edit, Find & Replace Text** and type search text; select the desired Find option in the Find options drop-down list; click on **Options** and any desired search options; click on **OK**; then click on **Find** or **Continue Find And Replace**
Change document's magnification	Open **View** menu; select Zoom To option you want
View Help table of contents	Choose **Help, Help Topics**
Jump to new Help screen	In Help window, click on any **solid underlined** word or phrase
Open definition window	In Help window, click on any **dotted-underlined** word or phrase
Get context-sensitive Help	Press **F1**; then make menu choice or click on window element; or click on infobox or dialog box's **Help icon** or **button**

In Chapter 3, you'll see how to edit text more efficiently than you can with just the Backspace key. You'll learn how to insert text; select text; delete and replace selected text; find and replace text; move and copy text; and reverse your most recent edits.

IF YOU'RE STOPPING HERE

If you need to take a break here, please exit Word Pro. (For help with this, see "Exiting Word Pro" in Chapter 1.) If you want to proceed directly to the next chapter, please do so now.

CHAPTER 3: EDITING TEXT

Basic Editing Techniques

More Techniques for Selecting Text

Using Edit, Find & Replace to Replace Found Text

Moving and Copying Text

Using Edit, Undo to Undo Your Most Recent Operation

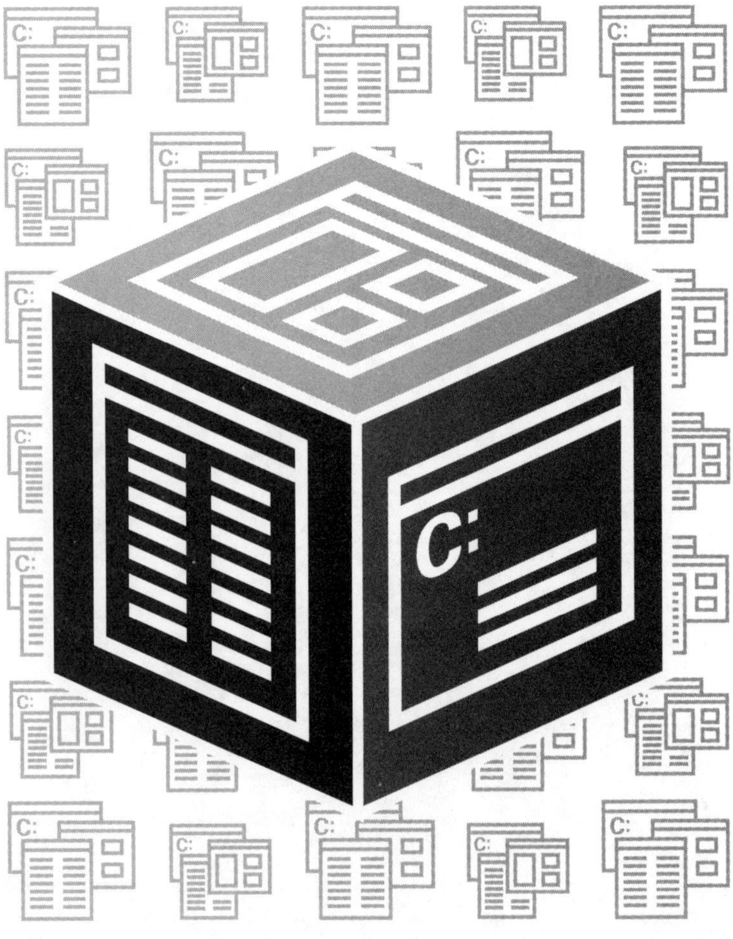

In Chapter 1, you learned the very basic way of editing text using your Backspace key. In this chapter, we'll introduce you to additional basic editing techniques, and then move on to some of Word Pro's more advanced editing techniques. You'll learn methods for deleting text with your Delete key, for selecting text, and for deleting and replacing selected text. You'll also see how to use Edit, Find & Replace Text to find and replace text, and how to move and copy text. Finally, we'll show you how to use Word Pro's Edit, Undo command to reverse your edits.

When you're done working through this chapter, you will know how to

- Delete text with the Delete key
- Select text
- Delete and replace selected text
- Use Edit, Find & Replace Text to replace found text
- Move and copy text
- Use the Edit, Undo command to reverse your last edit

BASIC EDITING TECHNIQUES

As you learned in Chapter 1, one of the best reasons for switching from a typewriter to a word processor is that the word processor makes your documents easier to edit. In the time it would take you to pencil in your desired changes to a typewritten document, you could incorporate those changes into a word-processed document and print the new version.

In the next several sections, we'll discuss the basics of editing Word Pro documents.

USING A SMARTICON TO OPEN A DOCUMENT

In Chapters 1 and 2, you learned two techniques for opening documents:

- For opening a document that you haven't opened recently, you can choose File, Open to display the Open dialog box. Within the dialog box, you then select a document location and name and click on OK (or double-click on the document's name).
- For a recently opened document, you can select the document's name from the bottom of the File menu.

You can also open a document by clicking on the *Open A Document* SmartIcon, which displays an arrow pointing out of a file folder. (Remember from Chapter 1 that SmartIcons are located directly below the menu bar.) This displays the Open dialog box; from there, you can use the dialog box just as if you had chosen the File, Open command.

Generally, a SmartIcon's appearance provides an excellent clue to its function. For example, the Open A Document SmartIcon indicates something coming out of a file folder. However, you need not depend solely on a SmartIcon's appearance to determine its function. You can also point to the SmartIcon, and Word Pro will display the SmartIcon's name in a Help bubble.

Note: If you find bubble Help annoying and want to turn it off, choose *File, User Setup, SmartIcons Setup*; uncheck *Show icon descriptions*; and click on *OK*.

If you are not running Word Pro, please start it now. (For help, see "Starting Word Pro" in Chapter 1.) Close the Welcome to Lotus Word Pro window.

Let's work now with the Open A Document SmartIcon:

1. Point to the **Open A Document** SmartIcon. Word Pro displays a Help bubble with the icon's name (see Figure 3.1).

Figure 3.1 **Displaying a SmartIcon's name**

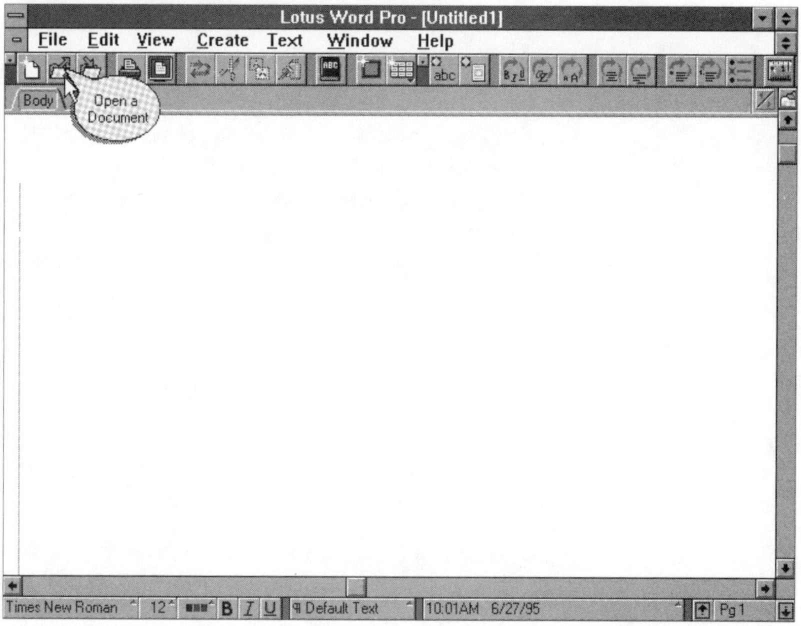

2. Click on the **Open A Document** SmartIcon. Word Pro displays the Open dialog box.
3. In the File Name list box, double-click on **editinga.lwp** to open the document. (Or, click on **editinga.lwp** and then click on **OK**.)

DELETING TEXT WITH THE DELETE KEY

In Chapter 1, you learned that you can use your Backspace key to delete one character at a time to the left of the insertion point. Your Del or Delete key does just the opposite: It deletes one character to the *right* of the insertion point.

If you have a PS/2-style Enhanced keyboard, you have access to both a Del and a Delete key. The Del key is located on the numeric keypad; the Delete key is located on the auxiliary keypad to the left of the numeric keypad. Pressing either of these keys has the same effect on the text being deleted. If you intend to use the numeric keypad's Del key to perform your deletions, be sure that Num Lock is off. (Press the Num Lock key until the Num Lock light goes out.) If Num Lock is on, Del functions as a decimal-point key; when you press it, Word Pro inserts a decimal point (.) instead of performing a deletion.

For the remainder of this book, we'll refer only to the Delete key. If you prefer to use—or only have access to—the Del key, feel free to use that key instead. Depending on your preference, as well as the location of your insertion point, you can use either the Backspace or the Delete key. Each one works equally well for deleting small amounts of text.

Let's practice deleting text with both the Backspace and Delete keys:

1. Observe EDITINGA.LWP. It needs some editing.
2. Examine Figures 3.2 and 3.3. Figure 3.2 shows edits for this document; Figure 3.3 shows the same document after those edits have been incorporated.
3. Use the I-beam to place the insertion point immediately to the right of the *e* in *Avenue* (located in the third line of the document).

Figure 3.2 **Document edits**

Ms. Cyndi Wood
Paper Supplies Unlimited
80 Queensberry ~~Avenue~~ **Circle**
Vienna, VA 22181

Dear Ms. ~~Szafranski~~ **Wood**:

Thank you for ~~calling about~~ your interest in Vision Office Products as a supplier for your business.

Vision Office Products is dedicated to manufacturing a wide range of quality office products and being responsive to our clients' needs. We offer competitive pricing, free next-day delivery, no-hassle returns, and an 800 number for customer service.

I am enclosing our corporate brochure and fall product catalog for you to look at. If you have any questions, please do not hesitate to call. You can reach me weekdays between nine and five at 1-800-555-7504. I look ~~ahead~~ **forward** to doing business with you.

~~Most truly yours~~ **Sincerely**,

Alice Mullin
Account Manager

jp
Encl.

4. Press **Backspace** six times to delete the six characters to the *left* of the insertion point.
5. Type **Circle**.
6. Place the insertion point immediately to the left of the *c* in *calling* (located in the first paragraph of the letter).
7. Press **Delete** eight times to delete the seven characters and a blank space to the *right* of the insertion point.

DELETING BLOCKS OF TEXT

Often, it is easier to work with a block of text rather than with single characters. For example, if you need to delete a paragraph, you probably will not want to delete each character individually (a multiple-step, tedious task); rather, you will want to delete the entire paragraph at once (a single-step, straightforward task).

Figure 3.3 **The edited document**

Ms. Cyndi Wood
Paper Supplies Unlimited
80 Queensberry Circle
Vienna, VA 22181

Dear Ms. Wood:

Thank you for your interest in Vision Office Products as a supplier for your business.

Vision Office Products is dedicated to manufacturing a wide range of quality office products and being responsive to our clients' needs. We offer competitive pricing, free next-day delivery, no-hassle returns, and an 800 number for customer service.

I am enclosing our corporate brochure and fall product catalog for you to look at. If you have any questions, please do not hesitate to call. You can reach me weekdays between nine and five at 1-800-555-7504. I look forward to doing business with you.

Sincerely,

Alice Mullin
Account Manager

jp
Encl.

To specify a block of text for deletion, you must first *select* it. One method of selecting is called *dragging* (you'll learn about other selection techniques later in this chapter). To select text by dragging:

- Use the I-beam to point to the first (or final) character of the text you want to select.
- Press and hold the mouse button.
- Drag forward (or backward) across the text to the final (or first) character. As you drag, the selected text is displayed in reverse video.
- Release the mouse button.

You can select text from the first to the last character, or from the last to the first character. Both methods are equally effective; use whichever method you find more comfortable.

Once you've selected a block of text, you can delete it by simply pressing Delete.

Let's select and delete a couple blocks of text:

1. Position the I-beam to the left of the *a* in *about* (located in the first sentence of the paragraph beginning *Thank you for*).
2. Press and hold the mouse button; then, drag forward over the word **about** to select the text. As you drag, notice how the characters and the space appear in reverse video (see Figure 3.4). If you drag too far or not far enough, just keep holding down the mouse button and moving the I-beam until you have highlighted exactly the text you want selected.

Figure 3.4 **Selected text**

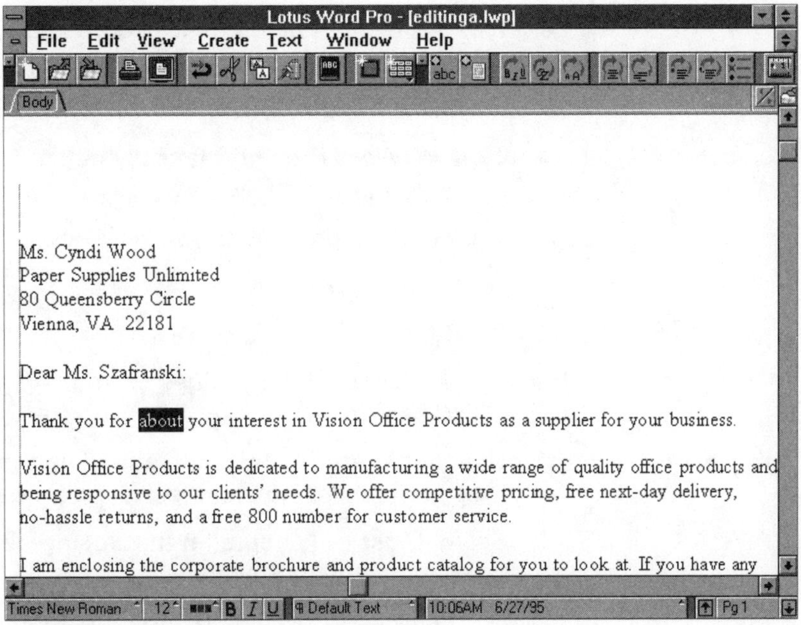

3. Release the mouse button.
4. Press **Delete** to delete the selected text. Note that Word Pro automatically deletes the space following *about* even though you didn't select it.

REPLACING TEXT

To replace text, you can use the skills you've already learned to first select and delete the existing text and then insert new text in its place. For example, if you want to replace the standard letter closing, *Yours truly,* with *Sincerely,* you can select and delete *Yours truly* and then type *Sincerely* in its place. However, this three-step method is inefficient—particularly when you are replacing many blocks of text. Fortunately, Word Pro provides a more convenient solution.

Here is a two-step method to replace existing text with new text:

- Select the existing text you want to replace.
- Type the new text.

As soon as you start typing your new text, Word Pro automatically deletes your selected text. You do not have to press Delete.

Let's use this technique to replace some text:

1. In the salutation *Dear Ms. Szafranski*, select *Szafranski* (but not the colon that follows).
2. Type **W**. Word Pro automatically deletes your selected text and replaces it with *W*.
3. Type **ood** to complete the word *Wood*.

PRACTICE YOUR SKILLS

Use Figures 3.2 and 3.3 as guides for making the remaining edits to EDITINGA.LWP.

1. Use the Delete key to delete **ahead** (in the paragraph beginning *I am enclosing*), and then type **forward**.
2. Select **Most truly yours** (in the closing), and then replace the selected text with **Sincerely**.
3. Compare your revised document with Figure 3.3.
4. Save the document as **myeditsa** (use the **File, Save As** command).
5. Close the document.

MORE TECHNIQUES FOR SELECTING TEXT

As you'll see throughout this book, selecting text is often a crucial first step to editing and formatting that text. For this reason, Word Pro provides numerous text selection techniques besides dragging. Table 3.1 lists a variety of these techniques.

Don't be concerned about learning all of these techniques at once. Rather, be sure to learn some of the most basic methods (for example, dragging, selecting a word, and selecting a paragraph); then, as you become more familiar with Word Pro, you can add new techniques to your repertoire. Before long, you'll find that you are using all of these techniques, or perhaps only a chosen few that work best for you.

Table 3.1 **Text Selection Techniques**

To Use This Technique	Follow These Steps
Drag	Use I-beam to point at one end of text you want to select; press and hold mouse button; drag I-beam to other end of text; release mouse button
Select word	Point anywhere inside word; double-click mouse button
Select sentence	Point anywhere inside sentence; press and hold Ctrl; click mouse button; release Ctrl. Word Pro automatically selects, along with the sentence, its end punctuation (period, question mark, or exclamation point). (Word Pro considers any text that ends with a period, question mark, or exclamation point to be a sentence.)
Select paragraph	Point anywhere inside paragraph; press and hold Ctrl; double-click mouse button; release Ctrl. Word Pro automatically selects the return that ends the paragraph, along with the paragraph. (Word Pro considers any text between two returns to be a paragraph.)

Table 3.1 Text Selection Techniques (Continued)

To Use This Technique	Follow These Steps
Select multiple words, sentences, or paragraphs	Use word, sentence, or paragraph selection technique to select single word, sentence, or paragraph. Hold mouse button down on last click; then drag
Select using Shift and mouse	Place insertion point at one end of text; press and hold Shift; click at other end of text you want to select; release Shift. Word Pro automatically selects the text in between.
Select using Shift and keyboard	Place insertion point at one end of text; press and hold Shift; use any keyboard movement technique (from Chapter 2) to move to other end of text; release Shift. Word Pro automatically selects the text in between. (The "Select an entire document" method in this table is an example of this type of technique.)
Extend existing selection	Press and hold Shift; click beyond existing selection; release Shift
Shorten existing selection	Press and hold Shift; click inside existing selection; release Shift
Select entire document	Place insertion point at top of document and press Shift+Ctrl+End; or place insertion point at bottom of document and press Shift+Ctrl+Home
Deselect	Make another selection; or click mouse button in typing area

Let's open a document and practice the dragging technique first:

1. Open **editingb.lwp**. Feel free to use either **File, Open** or the **Open A Document** SmartIcon.

2. Point to the left of the *I* in *Introduction* (the third line of text in the document).
3. Drag to the right to select **Introduction**, and then release the mouse button.

Now let's use the whole-word selection technique:

1. Use the I-beam to point to the word *favorable* in the first multiple-line paragraph of the document (the paragraph beginning *We've seen favorable*).
2. Double-click to select the entire word **favorable**. Notice that by selecting *favorable*, you automatically deselected *Introduction*.

Try selecting a sentence and a paragraph:

1. Point to the sentence beginning *Good customer service* (in the document's second multiple-line paragraph).
2. Press and hold **Ctrl**, click once, and then release **Ctrl**. Word Pro selects the entire sentence, including the period (see Figure 3.5).
3. Point to the document's first multiple-line paragraph.
4. Press and hold **Ctrl**, double-click, and then release **Ctrl**. Word Pro selects the entire paragraph.

Now practice selecting multiple words and paragraphs:

1. Point to *Good* (in the document's second multiple-line paragraph).
2. Double-click to select **Good**, and hold the mouse button down on the second click.
3. Observe the selection as you drag to the right. Word Pro adds entire words at a time to the selection. This feature is called *SmartSelect*. (**Note**: To disable SmartSelect, choose **File, User SetUp, Word Pro Preferences**; select **SmartSelect** in the Disable drop-down check list; and click on **OK**.)
4. Release the mouse button.
5. Point to the document's first multiple-line paragraph.
6. Press and hold **Ctrl**, and then double-click, holding down the mouse button on the second click. Then release **Ctrl**.

Figure 3.5 **Selecting a sentence**

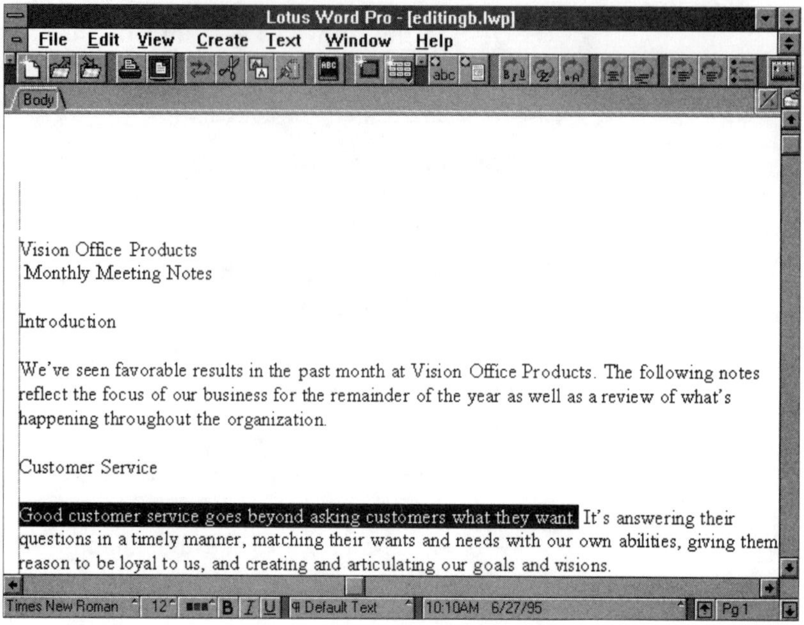

7. Drag downward, observing the selection as you drag. Word Pro adds entire paragraphs at a time to the selection.
8. Release the mouse button.
9. Click anywhere in the typing area to deselect the text.

Now use the Shift key to select a block of text, and then extend and shorten this selection:

1. Place the insertion point before the *I* in *Introduction* (in the document's third line of text).
2. Press and hold **Shift**, click in the space after *favorable* (in the document's first multiple-line paragraph), and then release **Shift**. Word Pro selects all of the text from *Introduction* through *favorable*.
3. Point to *business* (in the next line down from *favorable*).
4. Press and hold **Shift**, click the mouse button, and then release **Shift**. Word Pro extends the selection through to the end of *business* (see Figure 3.6).

Figure 3.6 **Extending a selection**

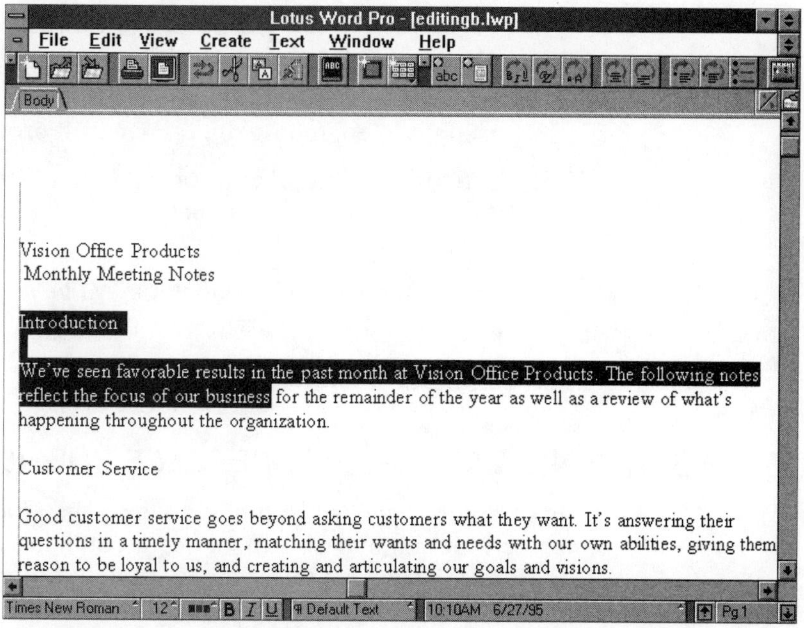

5. Point to the left of the *V* in *Vision* (one line up from *business*), press and hold **Shift**, click the mouse button, and then release **Shift**. Word Pro shortens the selection.

Finally, select the entire document:

1. Move to the top of the document (press **Ctrl+Home**).
2. Press **Shift+Ctrl+End**. This combination of Shift with the keyboard movement technique Ctrl+End selects the entire document from beginning to end.
3. Click anywhere in the typing area to deselect the document.

PRACTICE YOUR SKILLS

1. Move to the top of the document.
2. Use the dragging technique to select the first sentence of the paragraph beginning *We've seen favorable*.
3. Deselect.

4. Select the same sentence as in step 2, this time using the mouse in conjunction with **Ctrl** to select the entire sentence without dragging. (For help, refer back to Table 3.1.)
5. Use the double-clicking technique to select each of the following words in the document's first multiple-line paragraph: **Vision**, **following**, **reflect**, and **organization**.
6. Use the multiple-paragraph selection technique to select the document's first four lines (*Vision Office Products* through *Introduction*).
7. Extend the selection to include *We've seen favorable* (in the first multiple-line paragraph).
8. Shorten the selection to include only the first two lines.

USING EDIT, FIND & REPLACE TO REPLACE FOUND TEXT

In Chapter 2, you learned how to use Edit, Find & Replace Text to search for text in a document. Here you'll learn how to use Edit, Find & Replace Text to search for text and then to replace that text with new text.

Edit, Find & Replace Text is one of Word Pro's most powerful commands. Let's say you typed a 100-page document that made frequent reference to a woman named Gerta Sitauskus. Later, you found out that the correct spelling was *Sitauskis*. You could manually find each occurrence of *Sitauskus* and retype it—a tedious task, considering the length of the document. With Edit, Find & Replace Text, however, you could use Word Pro to help you rapidly replace every occurrence of *Sitauskus* with *Sitauskis*.

To use Edit, Find & Replace Text to replace found text in a document:

- Place the insertion point where you wish to begin the find-and-replace operation.
- Choose *Edit, Find & Replace Text* to open the Find & Replace bar.
- In the Find text box, type the *search text* (the text you want to find).
- In the Replace With text box, type the *replacement* text (the text you want to use instead of the search text).
- If necessary, select an option from the Search Options list.

- If necessary, click on *Options* to open the Find And Replace Text Options dialog box. Then select the appropriate find-and-replace options and click on *OK*.
- Click on *Find*; Word Pro selects the first occurrence of your search text. (If you prefer to have Word Pro automatically replace every occurrence, without asking you for confirmation, you can instead click on *Replace All*. However, this can be risky.)
- To replace the found text and then search again for the next occurrence, click on *Replace*. To leave the found text unchanged and search for the next occurrence, click on *Find*. To replace all occurrences of the search text throughout the rest of the document, without verifying the replacements (another risky choice), click on *Replace All*. To stop the find-and-replace operation, click on *Done*.
- Repeat the previous step as many times as necessary until you have searched through the entire document, or end your search at any time by clicking on *Done*.

Once Word Pro has searched the entire document, it displays the search results message box. To close the message box and the Find & Replace bar, click on *Yes*. To close only the message box, click on *No*.

Let's use the procedure just described to find and replace some text:

1. In preparation for searching the entire document, move the insertion point to the top of the document.
2. Choose **Edit, Find & Replace Text** to open the Find & Replace bar. (The Find text box might still contain your earlier search text.)
3. In the Find text box, type **20**. This is the text you will search for and replace.
4. Press **Tab** to move to the Replace With text box, and then type **50**. This is the text that will replace the search text (see Figure 3.7).

Figure 3.7 **Specifying search and replacement text**

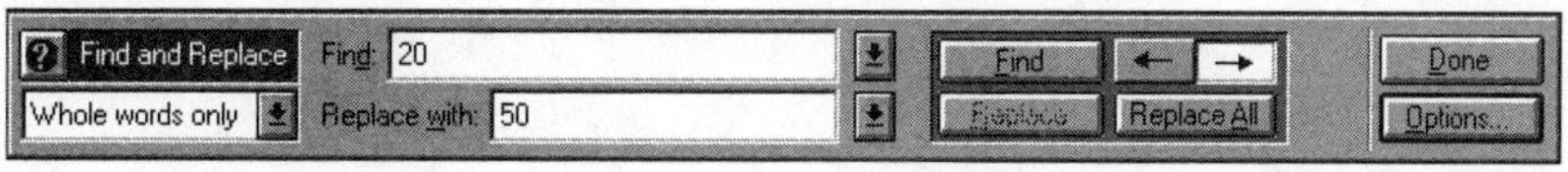

5. Click on **Options** to open the Find And Replace Text Options dialog box, and then observe the Replace Options box (on the right side of the dialog box). Just as you can tell Word Pro to find text that meets certain conditions (Match Case, IncludeProperties), so can you set conditions for the replacement text (Match Case, Include Properties).
6. In both the Find Options and Replace Options boxes, uncheck any checked options, and then click on **OK**. (You'll learn how to use some of these options in Chapter 8.)
7. Click on **Find**. In the document window, Word Pro selects the first occurrence of *20*.
8. Click on **Replace** to replace *20* with *50* and search for the next occurrence of *20*.
9. Examine the selected text in the document window. Replacing *20* with *50* here wouldn't make sense (50–30% higher?). This shows why it's risky to use the Replace All button; Word Pro would have changed this text blindly.
10. Click on **Find** to leave *20–30%* unchanged and search for the next occurrence of *20*.
11. Click on **Yes** to close the message box and the Find & Replace bar.
12. Save your revised document as **myeditsb**.

MOVING AND COPYING TEXT

Another of Word Pro's powerful editing features is its ability to move and copy existing text. You can, for example, quickly and easily move entire paragraphs from the top of the fifth page of a business report to the bottom of the 11th page, or copy a four-line address to several locations within the body of a letter.

One way to move and copy text is to use a combination of the *Edit, Cut*, the *Edit, Copy*, and the *Edit, Paste* commands. Word Pro also provides three SmartIcons (described later) that you can use as replacements for those three Edit commands.

UNDERSTANDING THE WINDOWS CLIPBOARD

Windows provides a temporary storage area called the *Clipboard* that is useful for moving and copying text. When selected text is cut (removed) by using Edit, Cut or copied by using Edit, Copy, Word Pro places a copy of that text on the Clipboard. When you paste by using Edit, Paste, Word Pro inserts a copy of the Clipboard contents at the insertion point. Pasting does not empty the Clipboard. Barring computer problems (such as a power loss), entries remain on the Clipboard until you cut or copy another entry to it or until you exit from Windows.

MOVING TEXT

To move text within a document:

- Select the text to be moved.
- Choose *Edit, Cut* or click on the *Cut To The Clipboard SmartIcon* (it displays a pair of scissors). This cuts the selected text from the document and places a copy on the Clipboard.
- Place the insertion point where you want to move the text.
- Choose *Edit, Paste* or click on the *Paste The Clipboard Contents SmartIcon* (it displays a paste jar). This pastes the cut text at the insertion point.

Let's practice moving text from one location to another within a document:

1. Move to the top of the document.
2. Select both the paragraph beginning *In an increasingly competitive* and the blank line that follows (the second multiline paragraph after the Customer Service heading).
3. Choose **Edit, Cut** to remove the selected text from the document and place it on the Windows Clipboard.
4. Place the insertion point before the *G* in *Good customer service goes.*
5. Choose **Edit, Paste** to paste a copy of the Clipboard contents at the insertion point (see Figure 3.8).

Figure 3.8 **Page 1 of EDITINGB.LWP, after moving text**

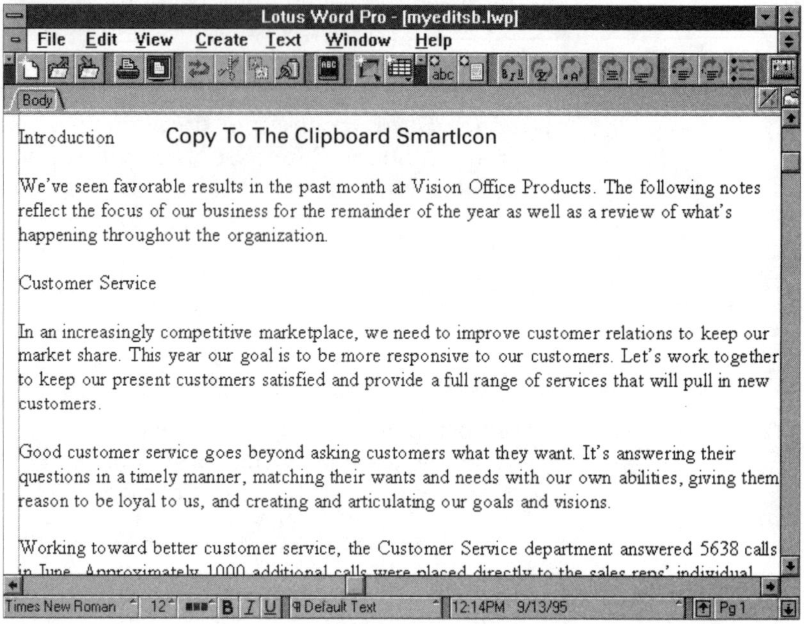

COPYING TEXT

Follow these steps when you want to copy text within a document:

- Select the text to be copied.
- Choose *Edit, Copy* or click on the *Copy To The Clipboard SmartIcon* (it displays two overlapping squares, each containing a capital *A*). This copies the selected text to the Clipboard.
- Place the insertion point where you want to copy the text.
- Choose *Edit, Paste* or click on the *Paste The Clipboard Contents* SmartIcon to paste the Clipboard text at the insertion point.

Let's copy some text:

1. Select the first three lines of the document (the two-line page heading and the blank line following).
2. Choose **Edit, Copy** to place a copy of the selected text on the Clipboard. Notice that Word Pro does not remove the selected text from the document, as it did when you chose Edit, Cut.
3. Move the insertion point to the top of page 2 (click on the **Down Page Arrow button**).
4. Choose **Edit, Paste** to paste a copy of the Clipboard contents at the insertion point (see Figure 3.9).

Figure 3.9 **Page 2 of MYEDITS.LWP, after copying text**

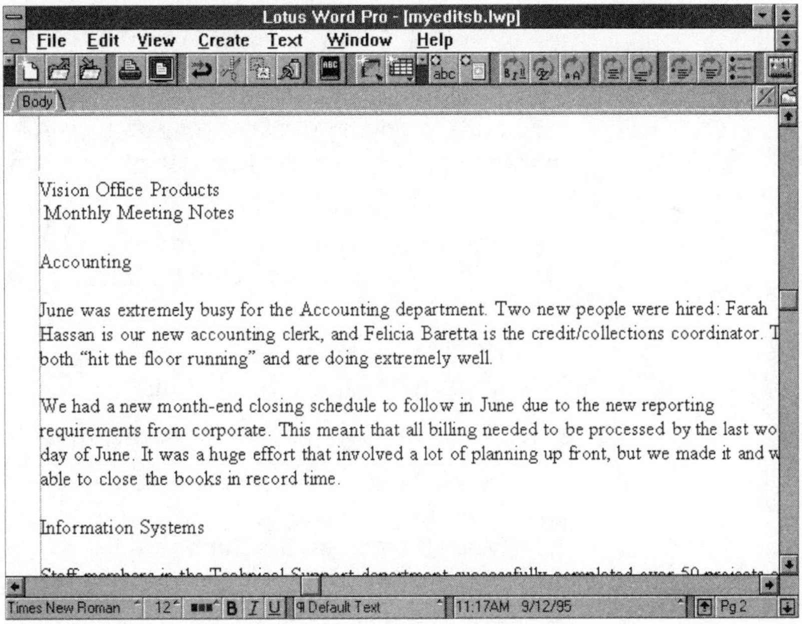

As you learned earlier, you can also use the Paste The Clipboard Contents SmartIcon to paste text from the Clipboard.

Try this out:

1. Move the insertion point to the top of page 3.

2. Click on the **Paste The Clipboard Contents SmartIcon**. (Because a copy of the text is still on the Clipboard from the last activity, you do not need to copy the text again before pasting.)
3. Choose **File, Save** to save your revised document. (Because you specified a document name and location earlier, you don't need to use File, Save As.)

USING EDIT, UNDO TO UNDO YOUR MOST RECENT OPERATION

Word Pro provides an *Edit, Undo* command that enables you to reverse (undo) an operation you have just completed. You can set Edit, Undo to reverse as many or as few operations as you like. The default setting is the last 100 operations you performed. Since Edit, Undo undoes operations in reverse, it is a good idea to use Edit, Undo as soon as possible after performing the operation.

As we said above, you *can* increase or decrease the number of Undo levels (by using the File, User Setup, Word Pro Preferences command). Refer to your Word Pro documentation for information on using the File, User Setup, Word Pro Preferences command to change the number of Undo levels.

Here are two methods for reversing an operation immediately after you've completed it: either choose Edit, Undo, or click on the *Undo The Last Command Or Action SmartIcon* (it displays two arrows making a U-turn).

Let's delete a block of text from your document, and then use Edit, Undo to reverse the deletion:

1. Select the paragraph *Accounting* (near the top of page 2).
2. Press **Delete** to delete the selected text. (When you use Delete rather than Edit, Cut or Edit, Copy, Word Pro does *not* place the text on the Clipboard.)
3. Choose **Edit, Undo-Text Deletion**. Word Pro restores your deleted text. (**Note**: Edit, Undo changes to reflect your last action. If your last action had been to paste text, it would say *Undo-Paste*.)
4. Save your document.

Now let's use the Undo The Last Command Or Action SmartIcon to reverse a potentially catastrophic text-replacement mistake:

1. Move the insertion point to the end of the document (press **Ctrl+End**) and press **Shift+Ctrl+Home** to select the entire document.
2. Type your first initial. Oops! All that's left in the document window is a single character!
3. Click on the **Undo The Last Command Or Action** SmartIcon. Whew! Word Pro restores the entire document.
4. To avoid deleting the entire document again, deselect it.
5. Save your document.
6. Close the document.

PRACTICE YOUR SKILLS

In this chapter, you have learned how to select, delete, and replace text; how to move and copy text; and how to undo edits. The following two Practice Your Skills activities give you the opportunity to practice some of these techniques. After each activity step, we've provided a chapter reference (in parentheses) to inform you of where we introduced the relevant technique for that step.

Follow these steps to produce the final document shown in Figure 3.10 from the original document PRAC3A.LWP:

1. Open **prac3a.lwp**. (Chapter 2)
2. Replace all seven occurrences of *Mayco* with **Macco**. (Select *Words Containing* from the Find options drop-down list.) (Chapter 3)
3. Cut the document's second multiple-line paragraph (beginning with *Congratulations to all*) and the following blank line, and paste them before the document's first multiple-line paragraph (beginning with *As we expected*). (Chapter 3)
4. Copy the three-line heading and the following blank line on the top of page 1 to the top of page 2. (Chapter 3)
5. Save the document as **myprac3a**. (Chapter 1)
6. Print your document, and then compare it to Figure 3.10. (Chapter 1)
7. Close the document window. (Chapter 1)

Figure 3.10 The completed document MYPRAC3A

Macco Plastics Inc.
Quarterly Sales Report
First Quarter

1. Introduction

Congratulations to all of you! An initial review of the sales figures for the nation reveals a surge in sales in all of Macco's sales areas. Major new clients have been added and many new products are on the way.

As we expected when we entered the field, computer-related products, such as keyboard housings and protective carrying cases, are accounting for a major portion of this upswing.

2. Regional Updates

Midwestern Territory

After several years of falling sales due to the slump in the auto industry, Blair Williams and his folks have something to celebrate. The recent boom in auto manufacturing has led to renewed demand of Macco Products in Detroit.

Northeastern Territory

John Martinson and his group are doing a great job in Nashua. They have secured major contracts for a wide range of new and existing products. Much of this business is coming from Computer Equipment Corporation, a major client of Macco's.

Southern Territory

Mark Daley and his group have done a fine job of maintaining relations with Becker's Product Development Division in Boca Raton. They have been working closely with Becker to decrease manufacturing costs.

3. Computer Study

A companywide study will begin in March, under the direction of Cathy Donaldson and Bill Schuster in data processing, to determine how to most effectively implement automation in our firm. We will be making a large commitment to productivity gains via computerization sometime late this year.

Figure 3.10 The completed document MYPRAC3A (Continued)

Macco Plastics Inc.
Quarterly Sales Report
First Quarter

4. Quarterly Meeting

The quarterly meeting will take place in Memphis this time. You will find the agenda attached to this report.

5. Conclusion

If the recovery continues at the current pace, this year should be a banner year for all of us at Macco. We want to thank all of you for the outstanding jobs you have done and, most important, for standing by Macco in hard times. Keep up the good work!

John Smith
Regional Coordinator
Macco Plastics Inc.

Follow these steps to produce the final document shown in Figure 3.11, using the original document PRAC3B.LWP:

1. Open **prac3b.lwp**. (Chapter 2)
2. Replace all three occurrences of *Territory* with **Region**. (Chapter 3)
3. Cut the heading *3. Computer Study* and the remaining three paragraphs on page 1 (one multiple-line paragraph and two blank lines) and paste them before the heading *2. Regional Updates*. (Chapter 3)
4. Change *3. Computer Study* to **2. Computer Study**. (Chapter 3)
5. Change 2*. Regional Updates* to **3. Regional Updates**. (Chapter 3)
6. Add your name as a fourth line to the three-line heading on the top of page 1. (Chapter 1)
7. Copy your name as a fourth line into the heading on the top of page 2. (Chapter 3)
8. Save the document as **myprac3b**. (Chapter 1)
9. Print your revised document and compare it to Figure 3.11. (Chapter 1)
10. Close the document. (Chapter 1)

SUMMARY

In this chapter, you learned how to delete text with your Delete key, select text, delete and replace selected text, replace found text, move and copy text, and undo operations.

Here's a quick reference guide to the Word Pro features introduced in this chapter:

Desired Result	**How to Do It**
Open document with SmartIcon	Click on **Open A Document** SmartIcon; select document location and name; click on **OK** (or double-click on document's name)
Display SmartIcon's name in bubble help	Point to SmartIcon

Figure 3.11 The completed document MYPRAC3B

Macco Plastics Inc.
Quarterly Sales Report
First Quarter
(your name)

1. Introduction

Congratulations to all of you! An initial review of the sales figures for the nation reveals a surge in sales in all of Macco's sales regions. Major new clients have been added and many new products are on the way.

As we expected when we entered the field, computer-related products, such as keyboard housings and protective carrying cases, are accounting for a major portion of this upswing.

2. Computer Study

A companywide study will begin in March, under the direction of Cathy Donaldson and Bill Schuster in data processing, to determine how to most effectively implement automation in our firm. We will be making a large commitment to productivity gains via computerization sometime late this year.

3. Regional Updates

Midwestern Region

After several years of falling sales due to the slump in the auto industry, Blair Williams and his folks have something to celebrate. The recent boom in auto manufacturing has led to renewed demand of Macco Products in Detroit.

Northeastern Region

John Martinson and his group are doing a great job in Nashua. They have secured major contracts for a wide range of new and existing products. Much of this business is coming from Computer Equipment Corporation, a major client of Macco's.

Southern Region

Mark Daley and his group have done a fine job of maintaining relations with Becker's Product Development Division in Boca Raton. They have been working closely with Becker to decrease manufacturing costs.

Figure 3.11 The completed document MYPRAC3B (Continued)

Macco Plastics Inc.
Quarterly Sales Report
First Quarter
(your name)

4. Quarterly Meeting

The quarterly meeting will take place in Memphis this time. You will find the agenda attached to this report.

5. Conclusion

If the recovery continues at the current pace, this year should be a banner year for all of us at Macco. We want to thank all of you for the outstanding jobs you have done and, most important, for standing by Macco in hard times. Keep up the good work!

John Smith
Regional Coordinator
Macco Plastics Inc.

Desired Result	**How to Do It**
Delete single character with Delete key	Place insertion point to left of character; press **Delete**
Select text by dragging	Point at one end of text; press and hold mouse button; drag I-beam to other end of text; release mouse button
Select word	Point inside word; double-click
Select sentence	Hold down **Ctrl**; click
Select paragraph	Hold down **Ctrl**; double-click
Select multiple words, sentences, or paragraphs	Use word, sentence, or paragraph selection technique to select single word, sentence, or paragraph, holding down mouse button on last click; drag
Select text using Shift and mouse	Place insertion point at one end of text; press and hold **Shift**; click at other end of text; release **Shift**
Select text using Shift and keyboard	Place insertion point at one end of text; press and hold **Shift**; use any keyboard movement technique to move to other end of text; release **Shift**
Extend existing selection	While holding down **Shift**, click beyond existing selection
Shorten existing selection	While holding down **Shift**, click inside existing selection
Select existing document	Move to top of document; press **Shift+Ctrl+End.** Or move to end of document; press **Shift+Ctrl+Home**
Deselect text	Make another selection, or click outside existing selection
Delete selected text	Press **Delete**
Replace selected text	Type new text over selection

Desired Result	**How to Do It**
Find and replace text	Place insertion point where you want to start searching; choose **Edit, Find & Replace Text**; in Find text box, type your search text; in Replace With text box, type your replacement text; click on **Find** or **Replace All**. For found text, click on **Find, Replace** or **Replace All**
Move text	Select text; choose **Edit, Cut** or click on **Cut To The Clipboard SmartIcon**; place insertion point where you want to move text; choose **Edit, Paste** or click on **Paste The Clipboard Contents SmartIcon**
Copy text	Select text; choose **Edit, Copy** or click on **Copy To The Clipboard SmartIcon**; place insertion point where you want to insert copy; choose **Edit, Paste** or click on **Paste The Clipboard Contents SmartIcon**
Reverse last operation	Choose **Edit, Undo**; or click on **Undo The Last Command Or Action SmartIcon**

In Chapter 4, you'll learn the basics of text formatting—how to apply and remove text attributes (such as boldface and italic); how to change fonts; and how to use Word Pro's Fast Format feature to copy and apply text formatting quickly.

IF YOU'RE STOPPING HERE

If you need to take a break here, please exit Word Pro. If you want to proceed directly to the next chapter, please do so now.

CHAPTER 4: TEXT FORMATTING

Understanding Text Formatting

Applying Text Attributes

Changing Fonts

Using Fast Format to Copy Text Formatting

The way a document looks has a direct relationship to its overall effectiveness. The impact of a brilliantly written business report, for example, can be severely undermined by an inappropriate typeface, text that is too small to read comfortably, a dizzying barrage of italics or underlining, tables with columns that don't line up, an overly busy page layout, and so on.

We have devoted the next three chapters to controlling a document's appearance. We'll proceed logically: This chapter covers *text formatting,* which controls the appearance of Word Pro's smallest appearance units: characters. Chapter 5 covers *text enhancements,* which control Word Pro's intermediate units: paragraphs. And Chapter 6 covers *page layouts,* which control Word Pro's largest units: pages.

When you're done working through this chapter, you will know how to

- Apply and remove text attributes
- Change fonts
- Use Word Pro's *Fast Format* feature to copy text formatting

UNDERSTANDING TEXT FORMATTING

Text formatting controls a document's appearance at the character level. This means you can give every letter on a page a different look, if you'd like. (However, we don't advise it; too much text formatting can make a document hard to read and amateurish-looking.)

Word Pro supports the following types of text formatting:

- *Text attributes.* These include bold, italic, underline, and double underline—for example, **bold**, *italic*, underline, and double underline.
- *Fonts.* In Word Pro a font consists of a *typeface* (the overall shape of characters), a *point size* (the overall height of characters), and a *color.* For example, the text you are reading is printed in a Universe 10-point black font: Universe is the typeface, 10-point is the point size, and black is the color.
- *Color.* You can change the color of the text itself, or of the background. By default, text is black and the background is white.

In this chapter, we'll show you how to apply and change two types of text formatting: text attributes and fonts.

APPLYING TEXT ATTRIBUTES

Text attributes help you to emphasize specific text. In this book, for example, we chose to use bold for certain headings, such as **Desired Result** and **How to Do It** (which appear in each chapter's Summary), and to italicize new terms, such as *text formatting.*

Word Pro provides three methods for applying and removing text attributes: the Text menu, SmartIcons, and keyboard shortcuts. Here we'll show you how to apply text attributes with the Text menu and SmartIcons; for information on Word Pro's keyboard shortcuts, see Appendix B.

USING THE TEXT INFOBOX TO APPLY AND REMOVE TEXT ATTRIBUTES

To use the Text infobox to apply text attributes:

- Select the desired text.
- Choose *Text, Text Properties.*
- Select your desired text attribute: Bold, Italic, Underline, Word Underline, and so on.

Follow these steps when you want to use the Text infobox to remove text attributes:

- Select the text that displays the text attribute you wish to remove.
- Choose *Text, Text Properties.*
- Click on the name of the text attribute you want to remove.

You can also remove *all* text attributes by choosing *Text, Normal.*

If you are not running Word Pro, please start it now. Close the Welcome to Lotus WordPro window.

Let's begin by opening a new document and applying some text attributes:

1. Open **attribut.lwp**.
2. Select **Introduction** (near the top of the document).
3. Choose **Text, Text Properties.** The Text infobox opens (see Figure 4.1). You can use the tabs on the Text infobox to change the appearance of text.
4. In the Attributes list box, select **Bold.**
5. Deselect **Introduction**, and then observe the text. (You can see text attributes better when the text is deselected.) *Introduction* is now displayed bolder (darker) than the surrounding text. Notice that the Text infobox is still open. It stays open on-screen until you close it.
6. Select **Office Products** (the next heading on page 1).
7. Select **Bold** in the Text infobox to display *Office Products* in boldface.

Figure 4.1 **The Text infobox**

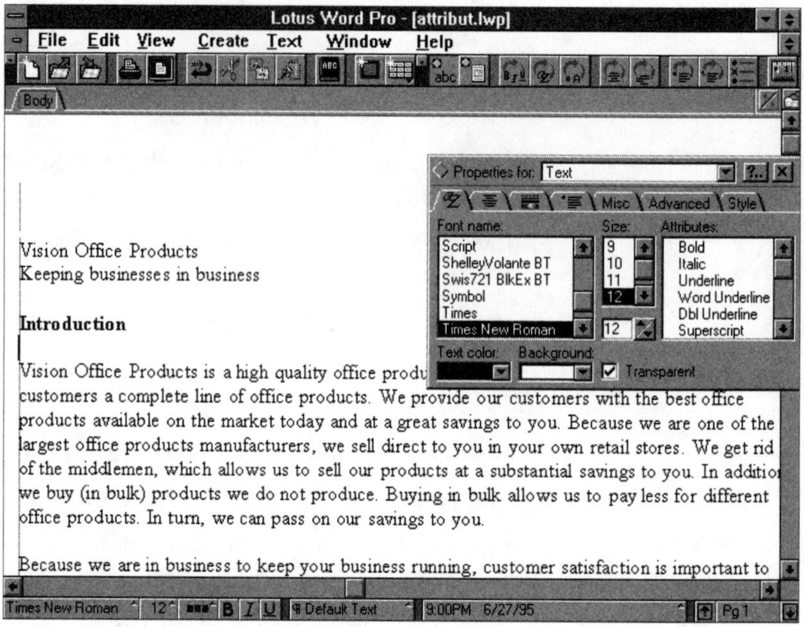

Now let's remove the text attribute that you just applied, and then restore it:

1. If it is not already selected, select **Office Products.**
2. Observe the Attributes list box in the Text infobox. A check mark is displayed next to *Bold.*
3. Click on **Bold,** and then observe your selected text. *Office Products* is no longer in boldface.
4. Click on the **Undo The Last Command Or Action SmartIcon** (or choose **Edit, Undo**) to restore the Bold text attribute.

Now let's use the Text infobox to apply multiple text attributes:

1. Select **Vision Office Products** (the document's first line).
2. In the Attributes list box, select **Italic**. The selected text is now italicized.
3. Select **Underline**. The selected text is now italicized *and* underlined.

4. Deselect **Vision Office Products** in order to see the multiple text attributes more clearly (see Figure 4.2).

Figure 4.2 **Italicized and underlined text**

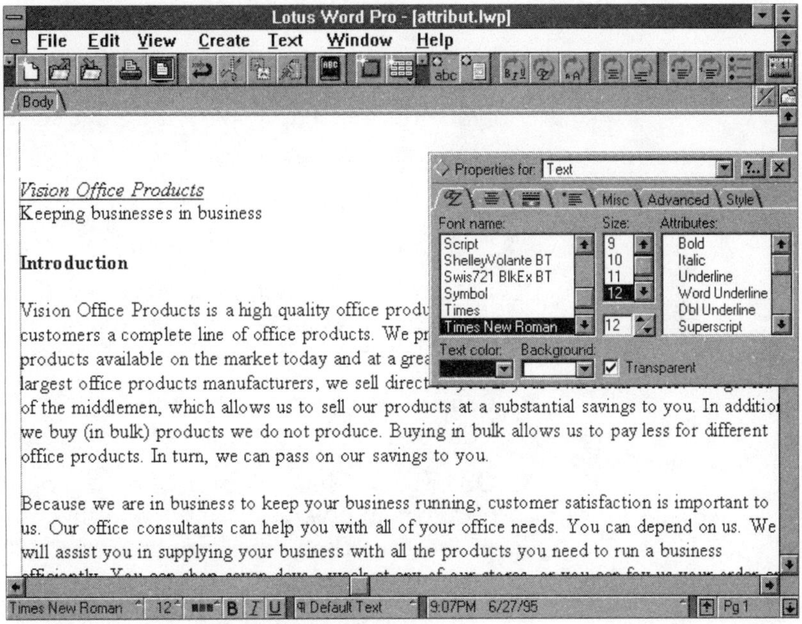

5. Select **Vision Office Products** again.
6. Select **Italic**.
7. Deselect, and observe the text. You have removed the italic, but not the underlining.

USING THE STATUS BAR BUTTONS TO APPLY AND REMOVE TEXT ATTRIBUTES

The following status bar buttons provide quick access to the Bold, Italic, and Underline text attributes:

- The *Bold Text button* displays a boldface **B**.
- The *Italicize Text button* displays an italicized *I*.

- The *Underline Text button* displays an underlined U.

To use a button to apply a text attribute:

- Select the desired text.
- Click on the appropriate button.

To use a button to remove a text attribute:

- Select the text that displays the text attribute you wish to remove.
- Click on the appropriate button.

Let's practice using buttons to apply text attributes:

1. Select the first multiple-line paragraph beginning *Vision Office Products is a high quality* (while holding **Ctrl**, double-click on the paragraph).
2. Click on the **Bold Text button** on the status bar to apply the Bold text attribute to the entire paragraph.
3. Observe the Text infobox. The Bold option is checked. Regardless of how you apply text attributes—by using buttons or the Text infobox—Word Pro reflects the selected text's attributes in the Text infobox.
4. Select **Bold** in the Text infobox to remove the Bold text attribute.
5. Click on the **Bold Text button** again to reapply the Bold text attribute.
6. Click on the **Italicize Text button** to italicize the text.
7. Click on the **Underline Text button**. Your selected text now displays three text attributes: Bold, Italic, and Underline (see Figure 4.3).

Now let's use the Text, Normal command to remove *all* text attributes from your selected text:

1. If it is not already selected, select the paragraph beginning *Vision Office Products is a high quality.*
2. Observe the Text infobox. *Bold, Italic,* and *Underline* are all checked.
3. Choose **Text, Normal** to remove all three of these text attributes from the selected text.

Figure 4.3 **Selected text, with three text attributes applied**

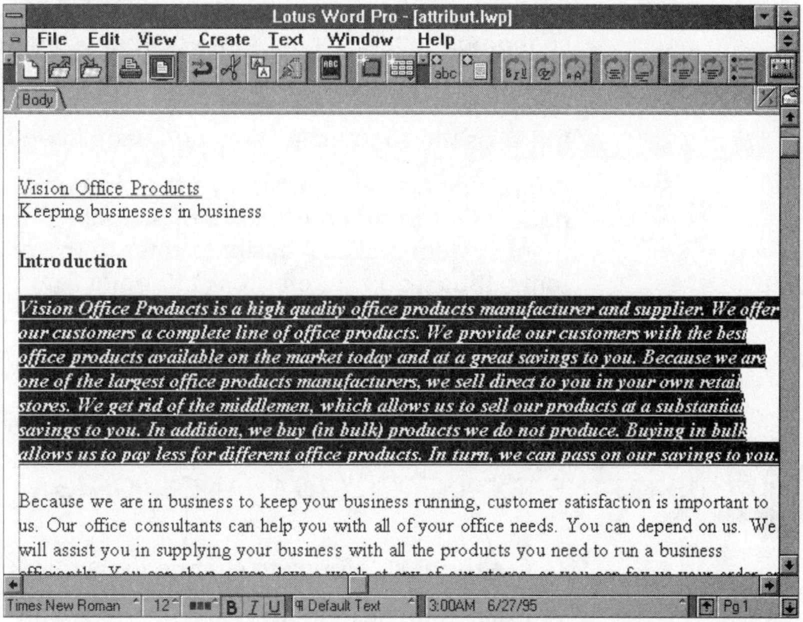

4. Observe the Text infobox. All of the check marks are gone.
5. Click on the **Cancel** button in the Text infobox (in the upper-right corner of the box, it displays an *X*) to close the Text infobox.

PRACTICE YOUR SKILLS

1. Remove the underlining from the document's first line, *Vision Office Products*, and then apply the Bold and Italic attributes to it.
2. Move to the top of page 2.
3. Add Bold and Italic to the second page's first line, *Vision Office Products.*
4. Save your document as **myattrib**.

CHANGING FONTS

You can change the shape, size, and color of your selected text by changing the text's font. Some people use different fonts for various elements of their documents. For example, this book uses a small black Univers font for body text, and larger blue Tekton fonts for the chapter, section, and page headings.

A font's size, as suggested by the term *point size*, is measured in points. One point equals 1/ 72 of an inch. The points measurement system makes it easier to refer to the relatively small size of fonts; thus, you can refer to a "10-point font" rather than a "10/72" font."

In Word Pro, you can apply fonts through the Text infobox or by using the status bar.

USING THE TEXT INFOBOX TO CHANGE FONTS

To use the Text infobox to change fonts:

- Select the desired text.
- Choose *Text, Text Properties* to open the Text infobox to the Color & Font tab.
- Select your desired font name, point size, and/or color.

Let's select some text and use the Font dialog box to change the font:

1. In the heading at the top of page 1, select the line *Keeping businesses in business.*
2. Choose **Text, Text Properties** to open the Text infobox.
3. Observe the Font Name list box. It lists your available typefaces in alphabetical order, and indicates your selected text's current typeface, *Times New Roman* (or, perhaps, *Times* or *Tms Rmn*).
4. Scroll up in the Font Name list box (if necessary), and select **Arial** (or, if Arial is not available, select **Helvetica** or **Helv**). The text changes immediately to the new typeface.
5. Observe the Size list box and the Points text box (see Figure 4.4). You can use either box to change your font's point size.

Figure 4.4 The Text infobox

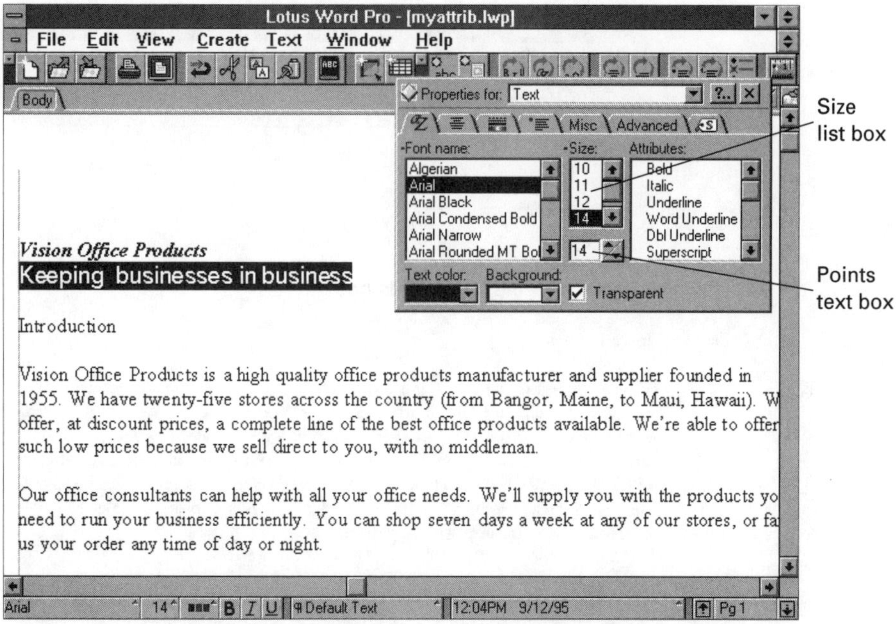

6. In the Size list box, click on **14** (or, if 14 is not available in the Size list box, use the Points text box's increment arrows to change the number in that box to **14**). Note that when you change the number in the Size list box, the number in the Points box also changes.
7. Observe the selected text. It now displays a larger font.
8. Close the Text infobox (click on the **Cancel** button).
9. Deselect the text and compare your screen to Figure 4.5.

PRACTICE YOUR SKILLS

1. Select the document's first line, **Vision Office Products.**
2. Change the selected text's font to **Arial** (or **Helvetica** or **Helv**) **18**-point.
3. Save your document.

Figure 4.5 **Line 2 of the heading, after changing the font**

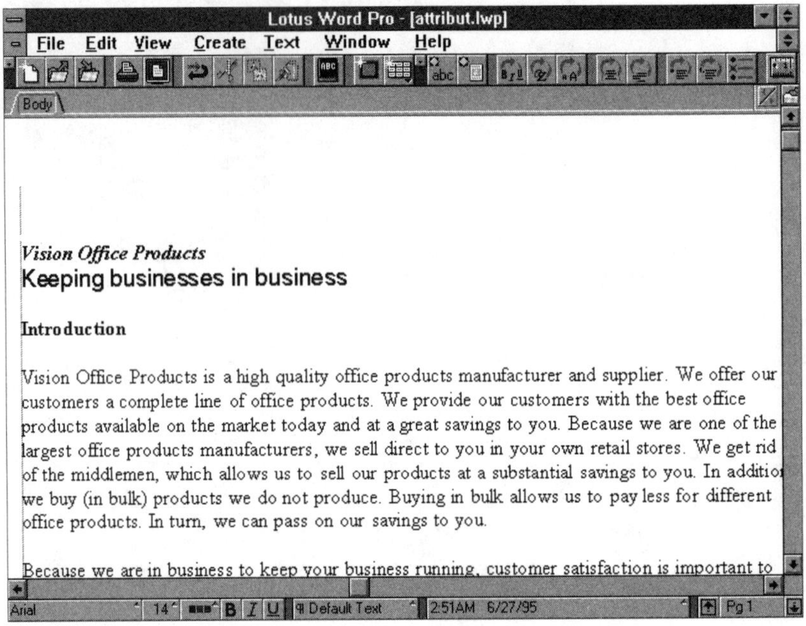

USING THE STATUS BAR TO CHANGE FONTS

In addition to the Text infobox, you can also use the status bar's *Font Name button, Point Size button,* and *Color button* to change fonts. The Font Name button is the first button from the left on the status bar; the Point Size button is the second button; the Color button is the third.

To use the status bar buttons to change fonts:

- Select the desired text.
- Click on the *Font Name button* and/or the *Point Size button* to open the list of available typefaces and/or point sizes.
- Select your desired typeface and/or point size.

Let's use the status bar to change a typeface and point size:

1. Move to the top of page 2, and select the page's first line, **Vision Office Products**.
2. Observe the status bar's Font Name and Point Size buttons. They display *Times New Roman* and *12*, respectively—the typeface and point size of the currently selected text.
3. Click on the **Font Name button** to open the list of available typefaces (see Figure 4.6). (**Note**: Your screen may not exactly match ours, depending upon the fonts you have available.)

Figure 4.6 **Using the status bar's Font Name button**

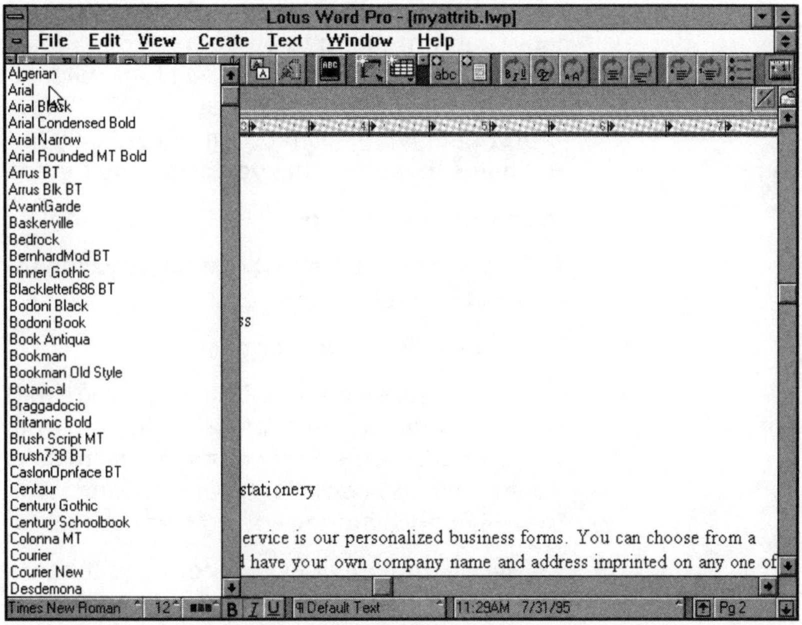

4. From the list, select **Arial** (or **Helvetica** or **Helv**). Your selected text is displayed in the new typeface.
5. Click on the **Point Size button** to open the list of available point sizes, and then select **18** (or the closest available size). The selected text's point size increases.

PRACTICE YOUR SKILLS

1. Select the second line on page 2, **Keeping businesses in business.**
2. Change the selected text's font to **Arial 14**-point (or the closest equivalent).
3. Save the document.

USING FAST FORMAT TO COPY TEXT FORMATTING

Once you have applied one or more text formats to some of your document's text, you can use Word Pro's *Fast Format* feature to copy that formatting to other text. For example, if you've applied the Bold, Italic, Arial, and 18-point formats, you can use Fast Format to copy all four formats at once. This saves you the time and effort of applying each format individually for each text selection, and helps to ensure that you apply the formats consistently.

To use Fast Format to copy text formatting:

- Drag to select the text that displays the text formatting you wish to copy.
- Choose *Text, Fast Format.*
- Your mouse pointer will change from an I-beam to a *Fast Format shape*, which appears as an I-beam with a paintbrush attached. Use the *Fast Format shape* to select the text to which you want to copy the text formatting. Word Pro immediately will apply all of the copied text formats to the text you select.
- Repeat the previous step for all of the text to which you want to apply the same text formatting.
- When you're done copying text formats, choose *Text, Fast Format* to exit the Fast Format mode.

You'll find that Fast Format works much like a paintbrush. You "dip" the paintbrush into text containing the text formatting you want, and then "paint" that formatting across other text.

Let's use Fast Format to copy text formatting:

1. Drag to select the first line on page 2, **Vision Office Products**.

2. Examine the selected text. It displays the Bold, Italic, Arial, and 18-point text formats.
3. Choose **Text, Fast Format**.
4. Observe your mouse pointer. It has changed to a Fast Format shape.
5. Move to the top of page 3, and then select the page's first line, **Vision Office Products**. The text immediately changes to bold, italic, Arial, and 18-point (see Figure 4.7).

Figure 4.7 **Using Fast Format to apply text formatting**

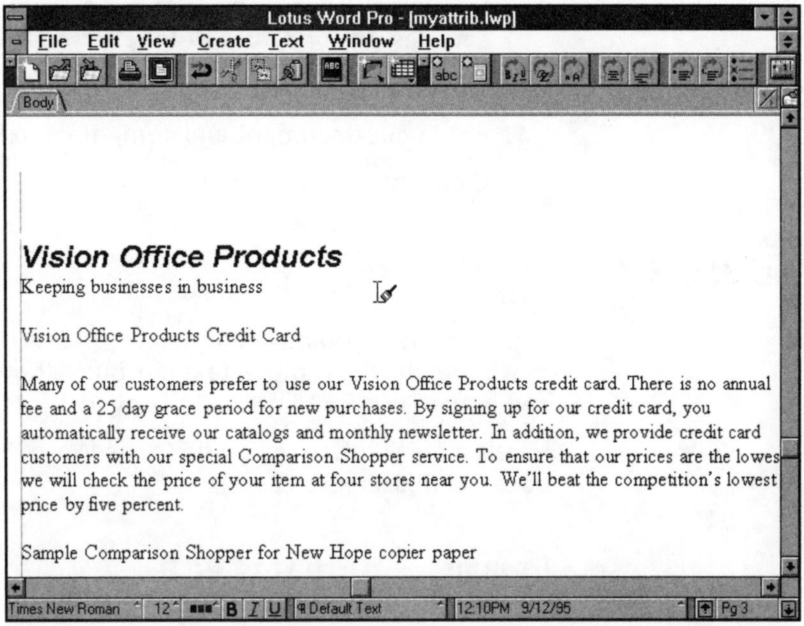

6. Choose **Text, Fast Format** again to exit Fast Format mode. Your mouse pointer changes back to an I-beam.
7. Return to the top of page 2, and then drag to select **Keeping** in the page's second line, *Keeping businesses in business.*
8. Choose **Text, Fast Format**.

9. Move to the top of page 3, and then select the page's second line, **Keeping businesses in business**. The text changes to match the text formatting on page 2.
10. Choose **Text, Fast Format** to exit Fast Format mode.

PRACTICE YOUR SKILLS

1. Move to the top of the document.
2. Use Fast Format to copy the text formatting of the word *Introduction* (the document's fourth line) to the following headings throughout the document: **Customer satisfaction, Printing and copying services, Fax services, Business repair services, Vision Office Products credit card.**
3. Save the document.
4. Print your document and compare it to Figure 4.8.
5. Close the documents.

SUMMARY

In this chapter, you have learned the basics of text formatting: how to apply and remove text attributes, how to change fonts, and how to use Fast Format to copy text formatting.

Here's a quick reference guide to the Word Pro features introduced in this chapter:

Desired Result	How to Do It
Open Text infobox	Choose **Text, Text Properties** or click right mouse button on typing area and select **Text Properties**
Apply or remove Bold text attribute	Select text; open Text infobox and select **Bold** or click on status bar's **Bold Text** button

Figure 4.8 **MYATTRIB.LWP, after copying text formatting**

Vision Office Products

Keeping businesses in business

Introduction

Vision Office Products is a high quality office products manufacturer and supplier founded in 1955. We have twenty-five stores across the country (from Bangor, Maine, to Maui, Hawaii). We offer, at discount prices, a complete line of the best office products available. We're able to offer such low prices because we sell direct to you, with no middleman.

Our office consultants can help with all your office needs. We'll supply you with the products you need to run your business efficiently. You can shop seven days a week at any of our stores, or fax us your order any time of day or night.

Office products

Our office products inventory is one of the largest in the country. We carry a variety of products at guaranteed low prices.

* Office supplies
* Business machines
* Furniture
* Computer equipment

You can shop at any of our stores or from one of our catalogs and either phone or fax your order to us. In either case, whether you shop in person or by phone, you can count on a staff that will assist you. Our staff is experienced and knowledgeable in the office products industry. They are specially trained to help you find the best product to fit your specific needs.

Customer satisfaction

We are committed to making your business work. Our expert staff focuses beyond just asking you what you want. We take the guess work out of running a business by matching your needs and wants with products that help run your business. We'll help you set up a system so the office materials you need are always available. When you are ready to expand your business, our special trade-in program can help you reduce the pains of a growing business.

Figure 4.8 MYATTRIB.LWP (continued)

Vision Office Products

Keeping businesses in business

Printing and copying services

At our retail stores, we also offer printing and copying services. You can come to us whether your printing job is large or small. Using our own business machines to produce your documents means we can keep our printing and copying costs down. We promise you speedy service at any of our stores. Let our staff become your staff by using our printing and copying services.

A new printing and copying service is our personalized business forms. You can choose from a wide assortment of forms and have your company name and address imprinted them. This helps your business look professional, and enables you to easily meet the standards set in today's competitive market.

You can choose below from any of our standard font options or come in to the store and let our staff assist you in creating your professional stamps and stationery.

Available Font Type and Style Options

A	B	C
Treasures and Traditions 13201 Seventeenth Street Santa Ana, CA 92705 (714) 744-2343	*Power Mowers Landscaping* 1234 *Jefferson Road* *Rochester, New York* 14610 (716) 248-0001	Sheltered Storage 15678 Pine Avenue Orange, CA 92667 (714) 538-9999

Fax services

Vision Office Products also offers fax services at any of our stores. You can send or receive faxes. Think of us as your second office. We are committed to helping you get the job done right. Our fax services include domestic transmissions, international transmissions, and receptions.

Unlike some major office supplies stores, our fax prices do not vary depending upon the location of the transmission or reception. We have a set standard price. So, you don't need to worry about figuring out how the location will affect the price of your fax.

Business repair services

When our business machines need to be repaired, we're happy to come to you. If you choose, you can also bring the machine into our store. If you purchased your equipment from us, then we offer you an optional extended service warranty. This warranty will always be offered to you when you purchase equipment from us. You are automatically covered by the manufacturer's warranty, but our hassle-free plan can keep you up and running when your machine is not. When your equipment needs repair, you will be given a similar product on loan while we fix your machine.

Figure 4.8 MYATTRIB.LWP (continued)

Vision Office Products
Keeping businesses in business

Vision Office Products credit card

Many of our customers prefer to use our Vision Office Products credit card. There is no annual fee and a 25 day grace period for new purchases. By signing up for our credit card, you automatically receive our catalogs and monthly newsletter. In addition, we provide credit card customers with our special Comparison Shopper service. To ensure that our prices are the lowest, we will check the price of your item at four stores near you. We'll beat the competition's lowest price by five percent.

Sample Comparison Shopper for New Hope copier paper

Store	Location	Price
Big Al's	North Chili	35.09
Office Supplies Unlimited	Churchville	37.90
Office Works	Scottsville	36.60
Paper, Paper, Paper	Mumford	34.99

Desired Result	How to Do It
Apply or remove Italic text attribute	Select text; open Text infobox and select **Italic** or click on status bar's **Italic Text** button
Apply or remove Underline text attribute	Select text; open Text infobox and select **Underline** or click on status bar's **Underline Text** button
Remove all text attributes	Select text; choose **Text, Normal**
Change typeface	Select text; open Text infobox; select new typeface from Font Name list box. Or, select text; click on status bar's **Font Name** button; select new typeface
Change point size	Select text; open the Text infobox; select new point size from Size list box or specify new point size in Points box. Or select text; click on status bar's **Point Size** button; select new point size
Copy text formats using Fast Format	Drag to select text containing text formats you want to copy; choose **Text, Fast Format** or press **Ctrl+T**; select every piece of text to which you want to copy text formats; choose **Text, Fast Format** or press **Ctrl+T**

In the next chapter, you will learn the basics of text enhancements. You'll see how to work with tabs and paragraph indents, create new lines within a paragraph, align paragraphs, and set line spacing.

IF YOU'RE STOPPING HERE

If you need to take a break here, please exit Word Pro. If you want to proceed directly to the next chapter, please do so now.

CHAPTER 5: TEXT ENHANCEMENTS

Displaying the Ruler

Working with Tabs

Setting Indents and Line Breaks

Changing Paragraph Alignment

Changing Line Spacing

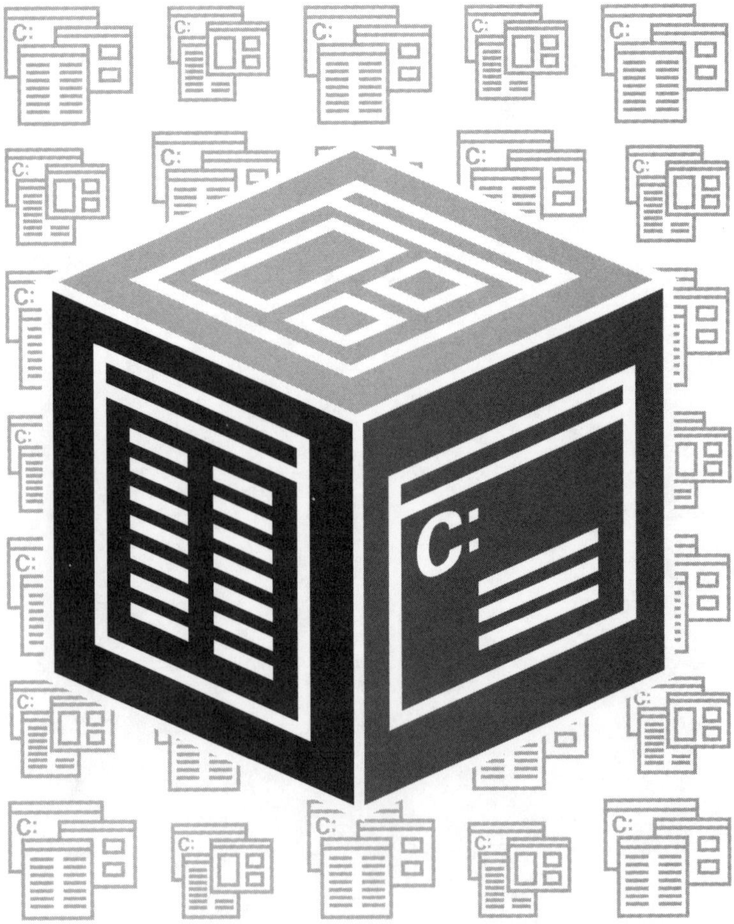

In Chapter 4, you learned how to use text formatting to control the appearance of individual characters in your documents. In this chapter, you'll learn about *text enhancements*, which control Word Pro's intermediate unit of appearance—the paragraph. You can control many important paragraph appearance features through text enhancements; text enhancements include tabs, indents, paragraph alignment, and line spacing.

When you're done working through this chapter, you will know how to

- Display and hide the ruler
- Clear, set, and change tabs
- Set indents
- Create new lines within a paragraph
- Change paragraph alignment
- Change line spacing

DISPLAYING THE RULER

To help you control tabs and indents, Word Pro supplies an on-screen ruler. Word Pro's ruler looks like its physical counterpart, complete with tick marks that mark inches and fractions of inches. Word Pro does not display the ruler by default, but it is a simple matter to display it. Use either of these methods to display the ruler:

- Choose *View, Show/Hide, Ruler.*
- Click on the *Show/Hide Ruler SmartIcon*; it displays one end of a ruler.

To hide the ruler when you are finished using it, use one of these methods:

- Choose *View, Show/Hide, Ruler.*
- Click on the *Show/Hide Ruler SmartIcon*. (This SmartIcon acts as a toggle; click on it once to display the ruler, click on it again to hide the ruler.)

If you are not running Word Pro, please start it now. Let's practice showing and hiding the ruler:

1. Open **enhance.lwp**. (You can choose to hide and display the ruler only when a document window is open.)
2. Choose **View, Show/Hide, Ruler**. Word Pro displays the ruler at the top of the document window, directly below the Smart-Icons (see Figure 5.1).
3. Choose **View, Show/Hide, Ruler**. Word Pro hides the ruler again.

Figure 5.1 The current ruler

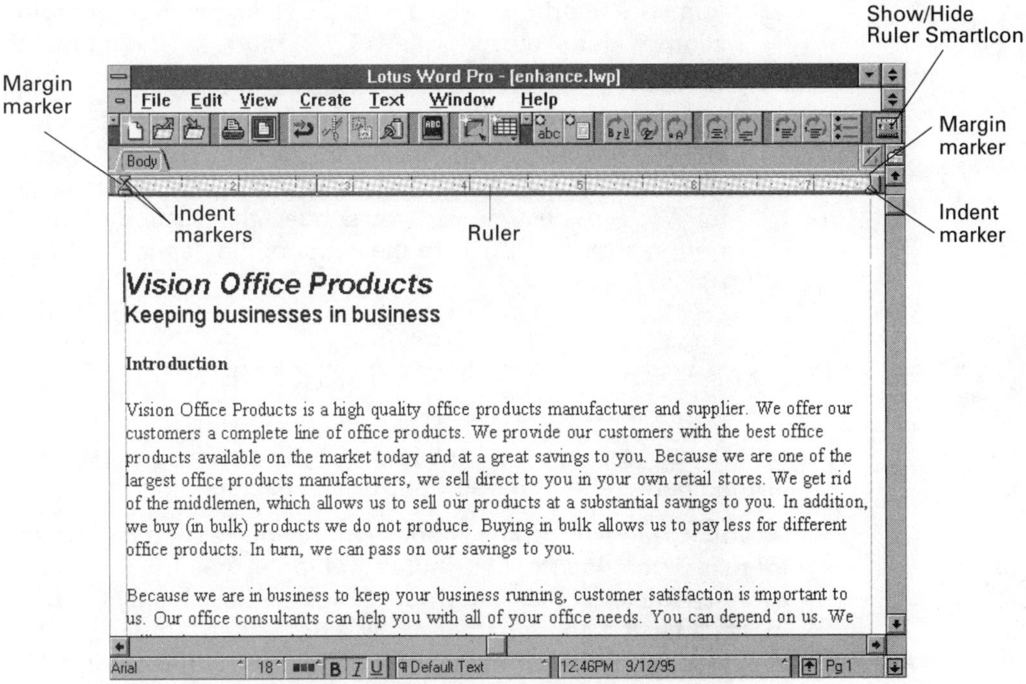

4. Now click on the **Show/Hide Ruler SmartIcon**. Once again, Word Pro displays the ruler.
5. Observe the ruler. It looks like a physical ruler, complete with tick marks that divide the ruler into inches, and inches into 8ths of an inch. It contains the elements you use for controlling text enhancements, including *indent markers* at the 1" and 7 1/2" marks. (You'll learn how to use indent markers later in this chapter.)
6. Click on the **left scroll arrow** a few times and examine the left end of the ruler. Notice that the ruler does not start at 0" at the left margin. Word Pro measures the ruler's tick marks from the *left edge of the current page*, not the left margin.
7. Compare the left margin with the ruler. The left margin aligns with the ruler's 1" mark, indicating that this document's left margin is 1" wide.

8. Click on the **right scroll arrow** until you can see the right margin of the document on-screen.
9. Compare the right margin with the ruler. The right margin aligns with the current ruler's 7 1/2" mark, indicating that the document's right margin is 1" wide.

   (Calculating the right margin requires a bit of math. Because this document is set up for an 8 1/2-by-11-inch piece of paper—the standard size for business paper and the default paper size for Word Pro documents—you subtract the location of the right margin, 7 1/2", from the width of the paper, 8 1/2", to arrive at 1".)

SELECTING PARAGRAPHS FOR TEXT ENHANCEMENTS

Before you apply or change text enhancements, you must first select the paragraph or paragraphs to be affected.

As you learned in the last chapter, when you select a paragraph for text formatting (text attributes and fonts), you must select every character in the paragraph. However, because text enhancements affect an entire paragraph at a time (for example, you can't single-space half a paragraph and double-space the other half), you do not have to select the *entire* paragraph when you select for text enhancements.

- To select a *single* paragraph for text enhancements, all you need to do is place the insertion point anywhere within the paragraph; you do not have to select any characters.
- To select *multiple* paragraphs for text enhancements, you only need to select a portion of each paragraph. (As with any multiple-paragraph selection technique, you can select only contiguous paragraphs—that is, paragraphs that immediately precede or follow one another.)

Throughout the rest of this book, we'll refer to these partial-paragraph selection techniques as *paragraph selection shortcuts.* If you feel more comfortable selecting entire paragraphs for text enhancements, please feel free to do so whenever we instruct you to use the paragraph selection shortcuts.

WORKING WITH TABS

You learned in Chapter 1 that you can use Word Pro's default tabs to align text across the page. This type of alignment is particularly important in tabbed tables, where several categories of information must line up in precise columns. Word Pro's default tabs, however, do not fit every purpose; sometimes, it's much better to set your own, *custom* tabs.

In this part of the chapter, you'll learn how to clear Word Pro's default tabs, and how to set and change your own custom tabs.

TAB TYPES

Word Pro provides four basic types of tabs: left, centered, right, and numeric, and two quick tabs: center and right. Word Pro's default tabs are left tabs set at half-inch increments.

Figure 5.2 illustrates how the four basic tab types align text; Table 5.1 defines each of the tab types.

Figure 5.2 **The four tab types**

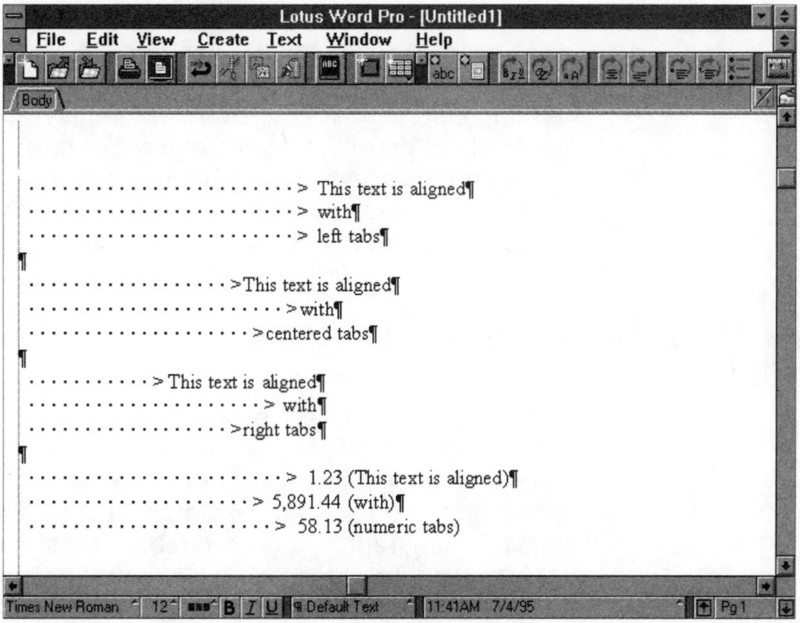

Table 5.1 **Types of Tabs**

Type	How Tab Affects Text
Left	The left edge of the text aligns against the tab, and then flows to the right.
Centered	Text centers on the tab.
Right	The right edge of the text aligns against the tab, and then flows to the left.
Numeric	Text aligns on decimal points. (Numeric tabs are useful for aligning columns of numbers.)
Quick Center	Text centers between the margins.
Quick Right	The right edge of the text aligns with the right margin.

USING SHORT CUT MENUS

There are often many ways to issue commands in Word Pro. We've already seen that the SmartIcons bar offers buttons that act as shortcuts for menu commands. Another useful feature for issuing commands is the *shortcut menu*. When you point to many parts of the Word Pro screen and click the *right* mouse button, Word Pro displays a menu containing commands that are appropriate to the part of the screen on which you click. You then choose the commands as you would in any menu.

SETTING CUSTOM TABS IN THE RULER

For each tab character you want to have in each selected paragraph, you should set one and only one tab in the ruler. (You set *tabs* in the ruler; you insert *tab characters* in the typing area by pressing the Tab key.) For example, if you have two tab characters in each paragraph of a tabbed table, you should select those paragraphs, and then set two tabs in the ruler. These two tabs will then instruct each of the tab characters where to align the text in the tabbed table. If, on the other hand, you set too many or too few tabs, your text might not align properly.

To clear any tabs you have set:

- Select the paragraph(s) from which you want to clear tabs. You can select entire paragraphs, or use a paragraph selection shortcut.
- Click the *right mouse button* on the ruler to display the ruler's shortcut menu. The shortcut menu gives you access to all commands you can perform using the ruler.
- Select *Clear All Tabs.* (See Figure 5.3, which displays the ruler's shortcut menu.)

Figure 5.3 **The ruler's shortcut menu**

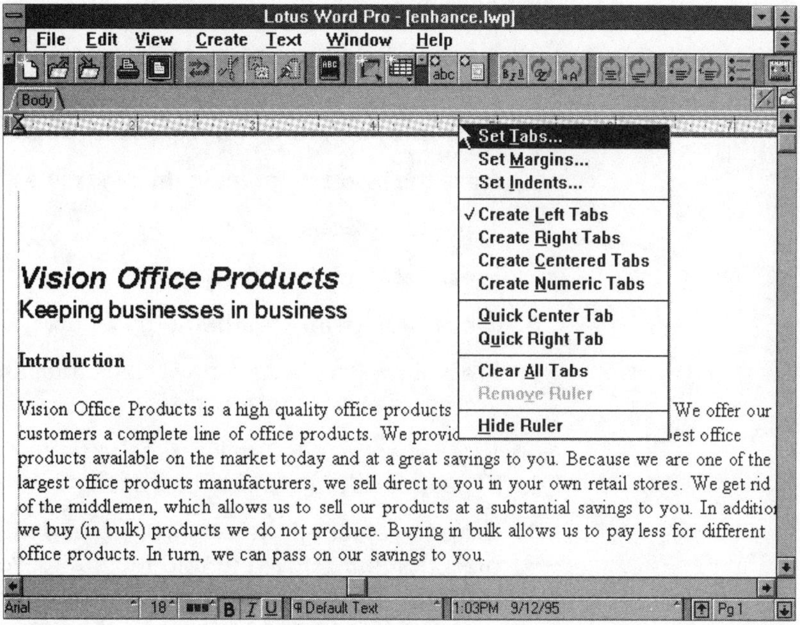

To set custom tabs:

- Select the paragraph(s) for which you want to set custom tabs.

- Click the *right mouse button* on the ruler to display the ruler's quick menu.
- Select the desired tab type.
- Point to the desired tab position in the ruler, and then click the *left mouse button*.
- Repeat the previous three steps as necessary to set every tab that you want.

Note: In Chapter 1, you saw the symbols for tab characters displayed on-screen as ·····>. However, as you'll see in this chapter, Word Pro expands or contracts the tab symbol to fill the available space. For example, when there's very little room between words, tab characters appear as >; when there's more room, they might look like ············>. Regardless of their length, each tab symbol represents a single tab character.

Let's begin our exploration of tabs by adding a line of text to an existing tabbed table:

1. Move to the top of page 3.
2. Observe the tabbed table for Fax Service Prices. The First Page and Additional Pages prices are misaligned.
3. Place the insertion point in the blank line after the tabbed table.
4. Type **Receptions**.
5. Press **Tab** and then type **$1.50**.
6. Press **Tab** again, and then type **$1.00**.
7. Press **Enter** to create a new blank line, and then compare your screen to Figure 5.4.

Now let's set some custom left tabs to fix the misalignment of the First Page and Additional Pages prices:

1. Drag to select all the text from *First Page* (in the tabbed table's first line) down to and including *Receptions* (in the last line). Even though you've only partially selected the first and last lines of the table, the paragraphs between are fully selected for applying text enhancements; this is the multiple-paragraph selection shortcut. Any text enhancements you make now will apply equally to all four lines.

Figure 5.4 **Adding a line to a tabbed table**

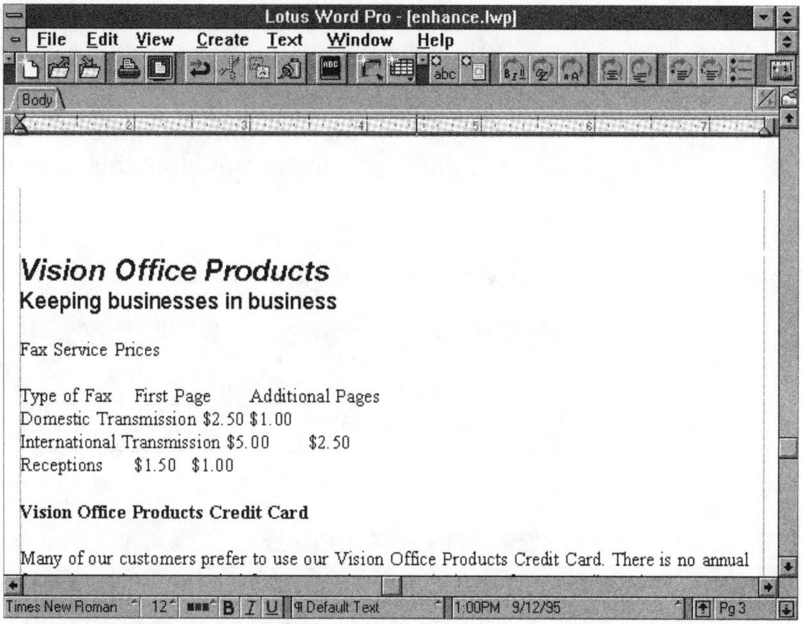

2. Click the **right mouse button** on the ruler to display the ruler's shortcut menu. (**Note:** If you don't click on the ruler, Word Pro displays a different shortcut menu. If your shortcut menu doesn't match that shown in Figure 5.3, press **Esc** to close the shortcut menu, and then reselect the text in step 1 and try again. Make sure the mouse pointer is on the ruler before you click the right mouse button.)
3. Observe the shortcut menu. You use the first three commands to set tabs, margins, and indents. The next six commands allow you to select tab types. You use the last three commands to clear all tabs from the ruler, reset the ruler with default tabs, and hide the ruler.
4. Verify that Create Left Tabs is selected (a check mark indicates that it is selected). The currently selected tab type determines the alignment of the next tab you set. (**Note**: If necessary, select **Create Left Tabs**.)
5. Press **Esc** to close the shortcut menu without making another selection.

6. Point to the ruler's 3" mark. Word Pro displays a vertical line in the ruler to indicate the exact ruler position to which you are pointing and a left tab marker attached to the mouse pointer to indicate that you are pointing to the ruler (see Figure 5.5).
7. Click the **left mouse button** to set a left tab at **3"**. (Don't worry if the tab isn't exactly at the 3" mark. You'll learn how to adjust tab positions later in this chapter.)

Figure 5.5 **Setting a left-aligned tab**

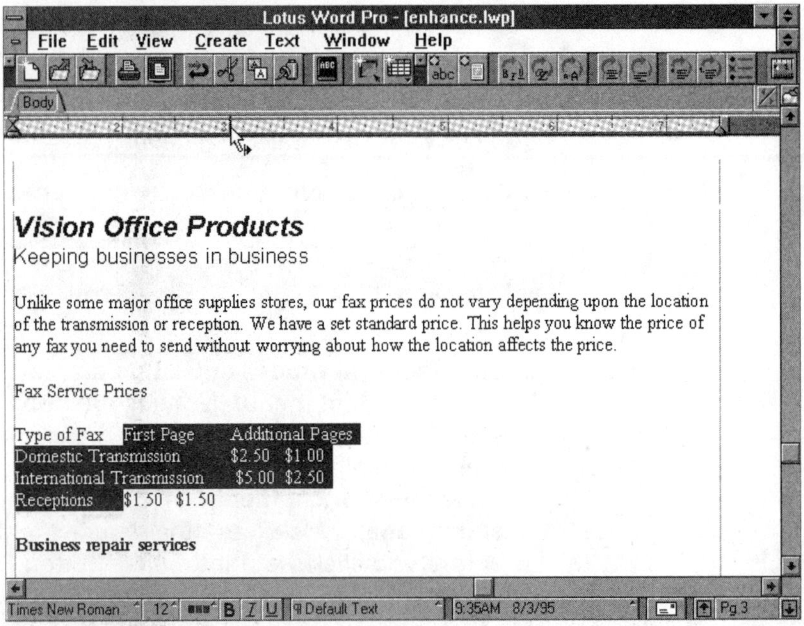

8. Observe the tabbed table. The table's second column is now left-aligned under the ruler's 3" mark.
9. Click at the ruler's 4" mark to set another left tab. Word Pro aligns the table's third column (see Figure 5.6).

Figure 5.6 **The tabbed table, after setting two tabs**

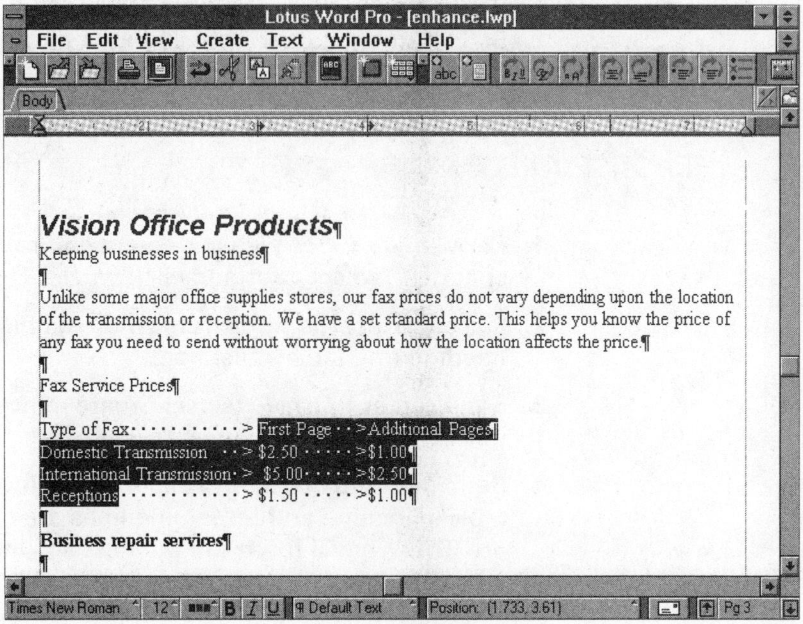

SETTING VARIOUS TYPES OF TABS

Now that you've had a chance to work with left tabs, let's set some other types of tabs:

1. Scroll down to the tabbed table following the heading *Vision Office Products credit card,* near the bottom of page 3.
2. Use the multiple-paragraph selection shortcut to select the body (the lower four lines) of the tabbed table.
3. Display the ruler's shortcut menu (click the **right mouse button** on the ruler) and select **Create Right Tabs** to make the next tab you set a right tab.
4. Click at the ruler's **4 1/2"** mark to set a right tab at 4 1/2".
5. Look at your tabbed table. The right edges of the locations now align at 4 1/2".

6. Display the ruler's shortcut menu and select **Create Numeric Tabs** to make the next tab you set a numeric tab.
7. Set a numeric tab at **7"** to align the numbers in the *Price* column by each number's decimal point.

PRACTICE YOUR SKILLS

1. Choose *View, Set View, Preferences*. From the Show Marks checklist , select *Tabs* and click on *OK*.
2. Place the insertion point anywhere within the tabbed table's heading (the table's first line).
3. Set a center tab at **4"** (select **Create Center Tabs** from the quick menu).
4. Set a right tab at **6 1/2"**. Notice that columns for the tabbed table's first line and remaining lines are misaligned (see Figure 5.7). We will fix this in the next activity.

Figure 5.7 **The Comparison Shopper tabbed table, misaligned**

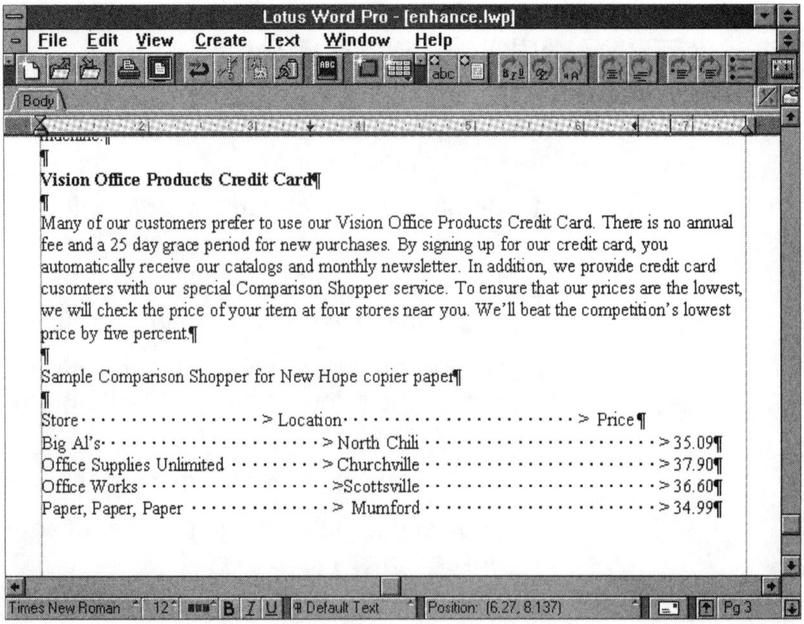

MOVING CUSTOM TABS

Once you've set custom tabs, Word Pro enables you to change their positions quickly and easily. Follow these steps when you want to move custom tabs:

- Select the desired paragraph(s).
- Drag the custom tab to a new position.

Note: Even though you can drag to change the *position* of a custom tab (for example, from 2" to 3"), you cannot drag to change a custom tab's *type* (for example, from a left tab to a center tab). Instead, you must clear the existing tab, and then set a new tab with the desired tab type. You'll learn how to clear individual tabs next.

CLEARING INDIVIDUAL TABS

You've learned that you can clear *all* tabs by selecting Clear All Tabs from the shortcut menu. However, if you already have set up a number of custom tabs for a paragraph or paragraphs, you might wish to delete one or more *individual* tabs. To clear individual tabs:

- Select the desired paragraph(s).
- Drag the custom tab down into the typing area, and then release the mouse button.

Let's fix the tabbed table's misalignment by changing and clearing individual tabs:

1. Select the body (the last four lines) of the tabbed table.
2. Drag the numeric tab at 7" over to **6 1/4"**, to adjust the position of all the table's numbers.
3. Place a center tab at **4"**. Notice that this causes a severe misalignment, because there is now an unnecessary tab in the ruler (the right tab at 4 1/2"). This prevents the Price column from moving to its intended numeric tab location at 6 1/4".
4. Drag the unnecessary right tab at 4 1/2" down off the ruler into the typing area, and then release the mouse button to

clear this tab. This corrects the tabbed table's misalignment problem.

5. Deselect the text, and then compare your screen to Figure 5.8.
6. Save your document as **myenhanc**.

Figure 5.8 **The Comparison Shopper tabbed table, properly aligned**

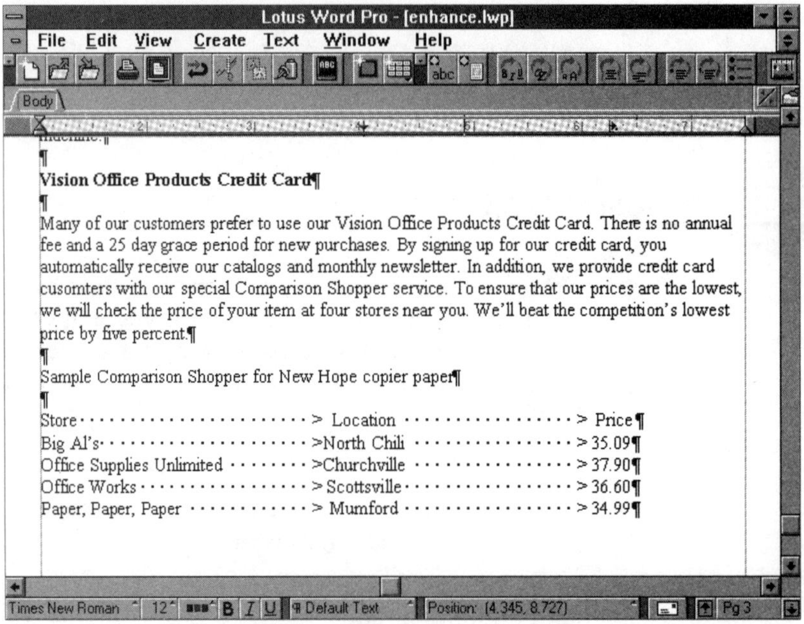

SETTING INDENTS AND LINE BREAKS

Margins define the top, bottom, left, and right page-boundaries of an entire document. (You'll learn more about margins in Chapter 6.) *Indents,* on the other hand, define the left and right boundaries for each paragraph within a document.

By default, Word Pro sets a paragraph's left and right indents equal to the document's left and right margins. By modifying indentions, however, you can set left and right paragraph boundaries that are different from the overall document's boundaries. Figure 5.9 illustrates the relationship between margins and indentions.

Word Pro enables you to set indents using either the ruler's indent markers or the Indent tab in the Text infobox. Because the indent markers are more visually intuitive, we'll show you how to use the indent markers first. Then we'll proceed to the Indent tab in the Text infobox.

Figure 5.9 **Margins and indents**

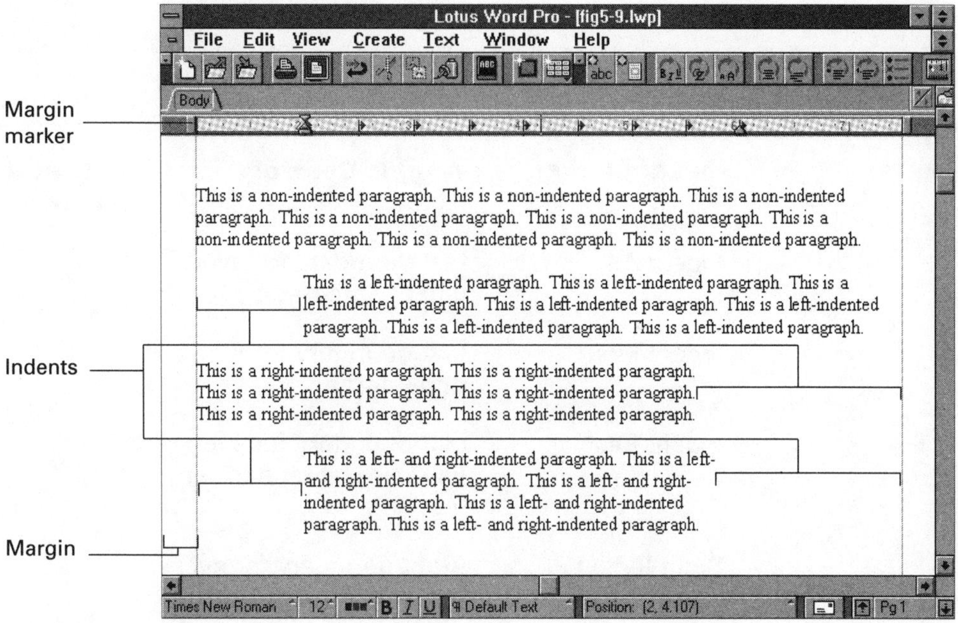

THE RULER'S INDENT MARKERS

The ruler contains four indent markers that you can use to control indents. Table 5.2 defines the indent markers and their functions; Figure 5.10 shows the location and appearance of these indent markers.

Figure 5.10 **The location and appearance of indent markers on the ruler**

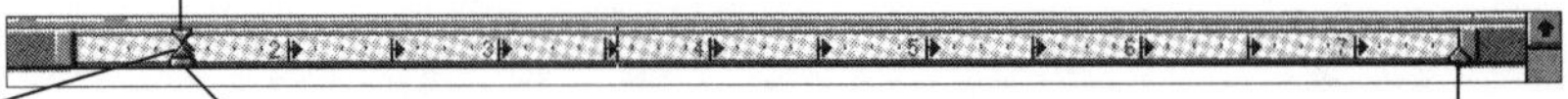

Table 5.2 **The Ruler's Indent Markers**

Indent Marker	What It Controls	What It Looks Like
Indent All	Left boundary for every line of paragraph	
Indent First	Left boundary for first line of paragraph	
Indent Rest	Left boundary for every line in paragraph except first line	
Right Indent	Right boundary for every line in paragraph	

SETTING INDENTS WITH THE RULER

As it is for changing custom tabs, the procedure for setting indents with the ruler's indent markers is simply a matter of dragging. To set indents with the ruler:

- Select the paragraph(s) you want to indent.
- Drag the appropriate indent marker(s) to new position(s) in the current ruler.

Let's use the indent markers to set some indents in MYENHANC.LWP:

1. Move to the top of page 2.
2. Scroll down, and then place the insertion point in the heading *Copying* under the heading *Printing and copying services*. This heading is indented 1/2" from the left margin.
3. Observe the ruler's indent markers, located at both ends of the ruler. At the left end, the Indent All marker (the horizontal bar), the Indent First marker (the upper triangle), and the Indent Rest marker (the lower triangle) are all clustered at the 1 1/2" mark, a half-inch in from the left margin. At the right end, the Right Indent marker (the single triangle) is at the 7" mark, a half-inch in from the right margin (see Figure 5.11).

Figure 5.11 **Indent markers for a left- and right-indented paragraph**

The mouse pointer with Indent All selected

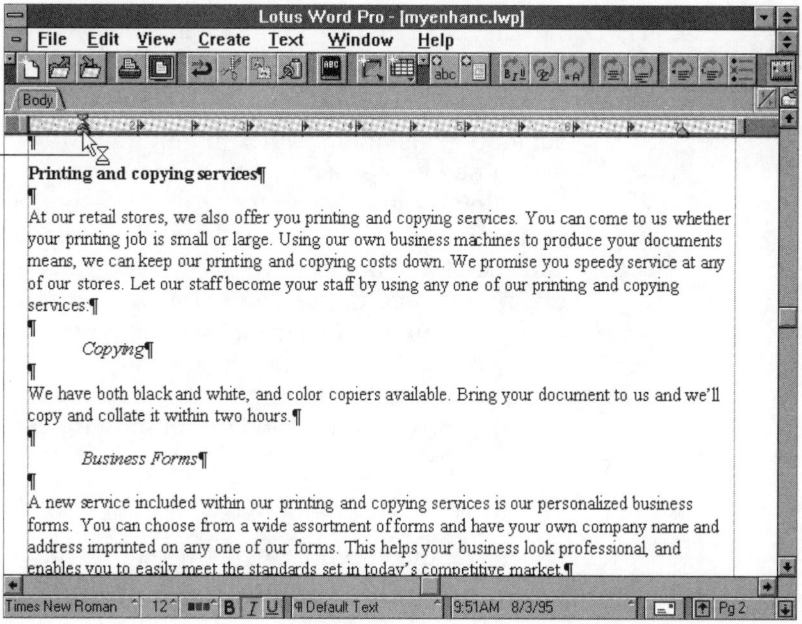

4. Place the insertion point in the paragraph beginning *We have both black and white*. This paragraph is not indented. On the ruler, you can see that the three indent markers at the left end are set even with the left margin at 1", and the Right Indent marker is set even with the right margin at 7 1/2".
5. Drag the **Right Indent marker** to **7"**. (Align the indent marker's flat side with the ruler's 7" mark. This new right indent creates a different right-hand boundary for the selected paragraph. **Note**: You might need to scroll to see the right indent marker.
6. Drag the **Indent All marker** to the **1 1/2"** mark to change the left-hand boundary of the selected paragraph. Notice that as you drag the Indent All marker, the Indent First and Indent Rest markers move along with it. (If you accidentally drag only the Indent First or only the Indent Rest marker, use **Edit, Undo** to reverse your change, and then try again.) **Note**: You can tell you've selected the Indent All marker when your mousepointer looks like that shown in Figure 5.11.

SETTING INDENTS USING THE TEXT INFOBOX

If you are not comfortable with the mouse, you might prefer to set indents using the Quick Indent buttons or the Indent Options dialog box in the Text infobox. Using the Indent Options dialog box allows you to be very precise in setting indents, even if your mousing skills aren't the greatest. The disadvantage is that you can't see the indents you set until you close the dialog box, so you might need to use some trial and error to find the settings that give you the results you want. If you use the Quick Indent buttons, you can set indents and see the results instantly. However, if you want to set a different left and right indent (for example, a 1/2-inch left indent and a 1-inch right indent), you must use the Indent Options dialog box.

To use the Quick Indent buttons to set indents:

- Select the paragraph(s) you want to indent.
- Open the ruler's quick menu and select *Set Indents*.

- Click on the Quick Indent button you want to use. There are four:
    - All lines from left
    - First line of paragraph
    - Rest of paragraph
    - All lines from both left and right
- Set the desired indent in the Indent From Margin text box.
- Close the Text infobox.

To use the Indent Options dialog box to set indents:

- Select the paragraph(s) you want to indent.
- Open the ruler's quick menu and select *Set Indents* to open the Text infobox.
- Click on *Options*.
- Use any of the Indent boxes to set the desired indents.
- Click on *OK* to close the dialog box.
- Close the Text infobox.

Let's use the Text infobox to set some indents:

1. Verify that the insertion point is still in the paragraph beginning *We have both black and white*, and then open the ruler's shortcut menu (click the **right mouse button** on the ruler).
2. Select **Set Indents** to open the Text infobox. In Chapter 4, we used the Font and Color tab in this infobox to change the font and attributes of our text. Note that because you chose Set Indents, Word Pro opened the Text infobox to the Alignment tab. Notice that the fourth Quick Indent button is selected and the Indent From Margin text box is set to 0.5 (one-half inch) as shown in Figure 5.12. (**Note:** If necessary, click on the fourth Quick Indent button to select it, and type **.5** in the Indent From Margin text box now.)
3. Place the insertion point in the paragraph beginning *A new service included* (the next multiple-line paragraph on page 2).
4. In the Text infobox, click on the **Indent All** quick indent button (see Figure 5.12).

Figure 5.12 The Indent tab in the Text infobox

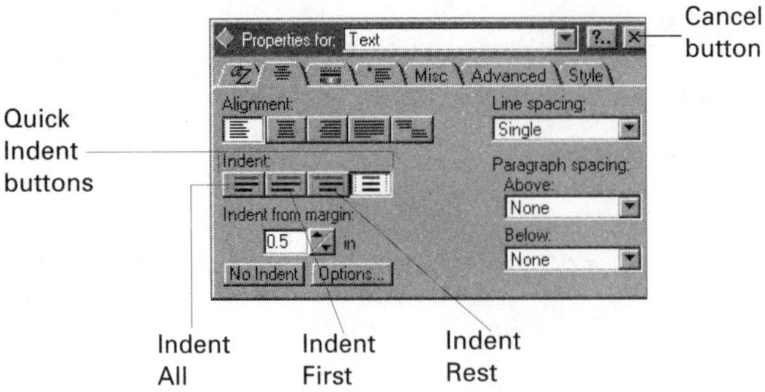

5. Observe the Indent From Margin text box. When you use a quick indent button to set an indent, Word Pro automatically sets the indent at .5".
6. Click on the **Indent Both** quick indent button (see Figure 5.12) to indent both the left and the right margins one-half inch.
7. Observe the current paragraph. It is now indented one-half inch from both sides, just like the previous paragraph.
8. Observe the ruler. All four indent markers reflect the indents you set in the Text infobox.
9. Click on the Text infobox's **Cancel** button to close the infobox.

PRACTICE YOUR SKILLS

1. Scroll down, if necessary, and then place the insertion point in the paragraph beginning *You can choose from any.*
2. Use either the indent markers or the Text infobox to indent the paragraph one-half inch in from both the left and right margins.
3. If you used the Text infobox in step 2, close it.
4. Compare your screen to Figure 5.13.

Figure 5.13 **MYENHANC.LWP, after indenting three paragraphs**

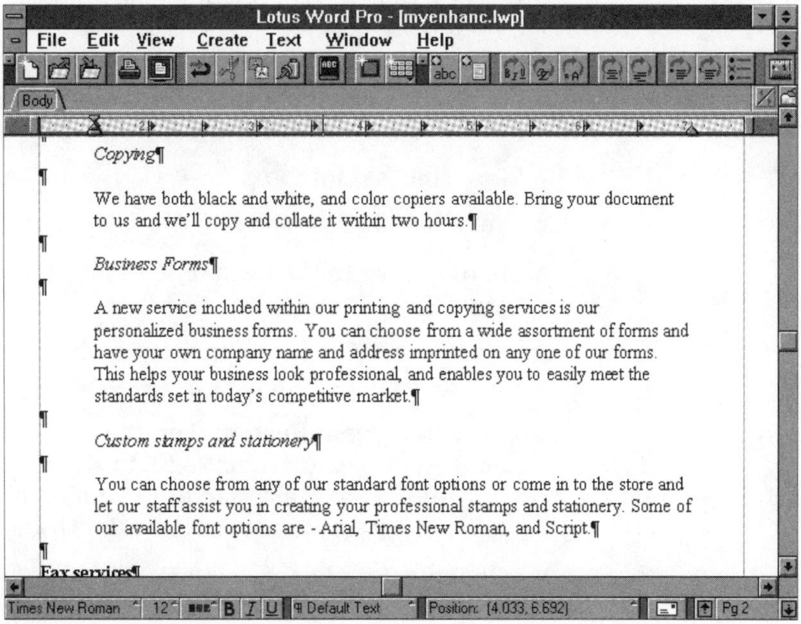

SETTING HANGING INDENTS

Paragraphs with *hanging indents* are paragraphs where the first line is left-indented less than all of its subsequent lines. In effect, the first line *hangs* to the left over the rest of the lines. People commonly use hanging indents for bulleted or numbered lists, like the lists throughout this book.

As with all indents in Word Pro, you can create hanging indents by using either the ruler's indent markers and/or the Alignment tab in the Text infobox.

To set a hanging indent with the ruler:

- Select the paragraph(s) for which you want to set a hanging indent.
- Drag the *Indent Rest marker* so that it is farther from the left margin than the Indent First marker.

To set a hanging indent using the Text infobox:

- Select the paragraph(s) for which you want to set a hanging indent.
- Open the ruler's shortcut menu and choose *Set Indents*.
- Click on the *Indent Rest* quick indent button.
- Close the Text infobox.

Let's set a hanging indent with the ruler:

1. Scroll down to the heading *Catalogs* (near the bottom of page 3).
2. Place the insertion point in the paragraph beginning *1. Special deals*.
3. Drag the **Indent Rest marker** (the lower of the two triangles on the current ruler's left end) to **1 1/2"**. Be careful to drag *only* the Indent Rest marker! If you inadvertently drag the other indent markers, choose **Edit, Undo**, and then try again.
4. Observe your hanging indent. The second line of the paragraph is indented one-half inch, and the first line remains unindented at the left margin (see Figure 5.14).

Now let's use the Text infobox to set a hanging indent:

1. Verify that the insertion point is still in the paragraph beginning *1. Special deals*.
2. Open the ruler's quick menu, select **Set Indents**, and then observe the Indent tab. The Indent Rest button is selected and the Indent From Margin text box is set to 0.5.
3. Place the insertion point in the paragraph beginning *2. Office supplies*.
4. Click on the **Indent Rest button**. The current paragraph's hanging indent now matches the hanging indent above it.
5. Close the Text infobox.

PRACTICE YOUR SKILLS

1. Place the insertion point in the paragraph beginning *3. Office furniture*.

Figure 5.14 **A paragraph with a hanging indent**

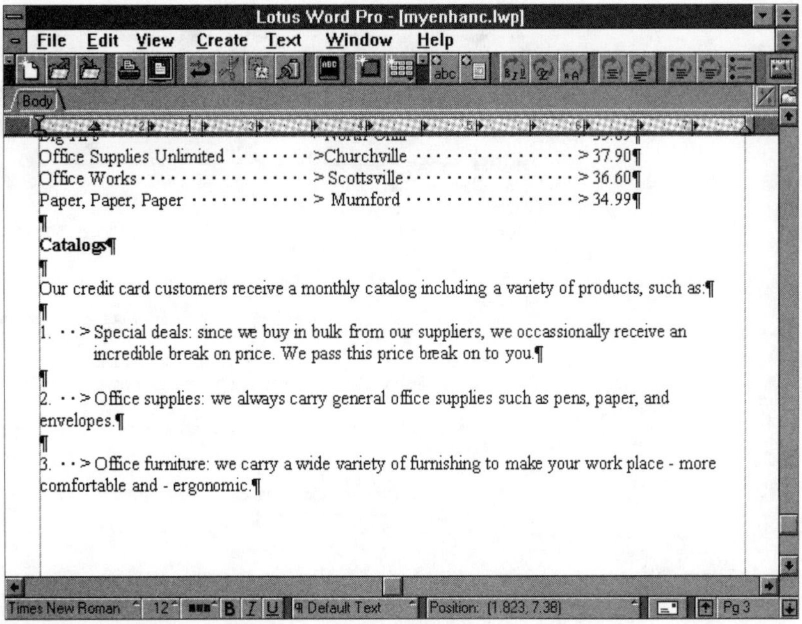

2. Use either the ruler or the Text infobox to set a half-inch hanging indent.
3. If you used the Text infobox in step 2, close it.
4. Compare your screen to Figure 5.15.

USING SHIFT+ENTER TO CREATE A NEW LINE

You learned in Chapter 1 that when you press Enter to begin a new line, you also create a new paragraph. (Remember—in Word Pro, a paragraph is any amount of text between two returns.) To save you some formatting effort, Word Pro automatically carries down into your new paragraph any text enhancements that you set in the previous paragraph. For example, if you apply a 1-inch left indent to a paragraph, and then press Enter anywhere within that paragraph in order to create a new paragraph, your new paragraph will also have a 1-inch left indent.

Figure 5.15 MYENHANC.LWP, after creating three paragraphs with hanging indents

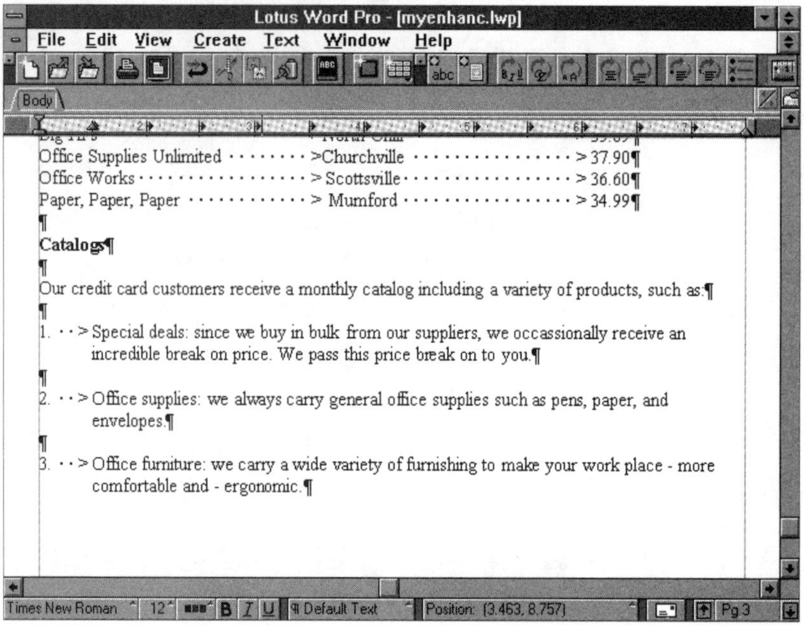

This carrying down of text enhancements is convenient for many paragraphs, but may not work well for maintaining hanging indents. For example, let's say you want to insert a new line in the middle of a list that is within a hanging-indent paragraph. When you press Enter after adding the list item, you lose your hanging indent. Why? It's because you've created a new hanging-indent paragraph, and the first line of that new paragraph aligns itself with the Indent First marker, rather than with the Indent Rest marker.

To remedy this situation, Word Pro lets you use Shift+Enter to insert a *line break*. A line break creates a new line *without* creating a new paragraph. In this way, the new line, not being a new paragraph, aligns with the Indent Rest marker and maintains the hanging indent.

To create a new line within a paragraph without creating a new paragraph:

- Place the insertion point at the place where you want to end the current line and create a new line.
- Press Shift+Enter to insert a line break.

Let's see how Shift+Enter works to maintain a hanging indent:

1. In the paragraph beginning *3. Office furniture*, place the insertion point immediately to the left of the hyphen (-) before *more comfortable and.*
2. Press **Enter** to create a new paragraph. Word Pro moves all the text that is to the right of the insertion point onto the next line. Because you've created a new paragraph, the first (and in this case, the only) line loses the hanging indent and moves back flush with the left margin.
3. Press **Backspace** to delete the return you just inserted and bring the text back up to its original position.
4. Now press **Shift+Enter** to enter a line break and create a new line without creating a new paragraph. You maintain your hanging indent (see Figure 5.16). Pressing **Shift+Enter** ends the line with a soft return instead of with a regular (hard) return.

Figure 5.16 **Maintaining a hanging indent**

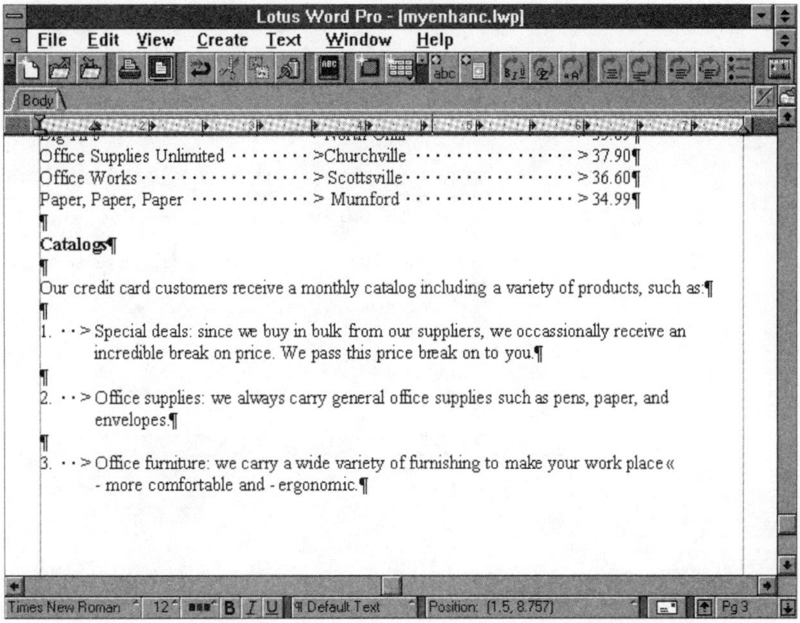

5. Press **Shift+Enter** again to create a blank line while still maintaining the hanging indent.
6. Place the insertion point to the left of the second hyphen in the same paragraph, before - *ergonomic.*
7. Press **Shift+Enter** twice to create two new lines while maintaining the hanging indent.

CHANGING PARAGRAPH ALIGNMENT

Paragraph alignment determines how Word Pro positions a paragraph between the left and right indents. Word Pro provides four options for paragraph alignment. Figure 5.17 illustrates how the various paragraph alignments appear on your computer screen; Table 5.3 defines each paragraph alignment option.

Figure 5.17 **Paragraph alignment**

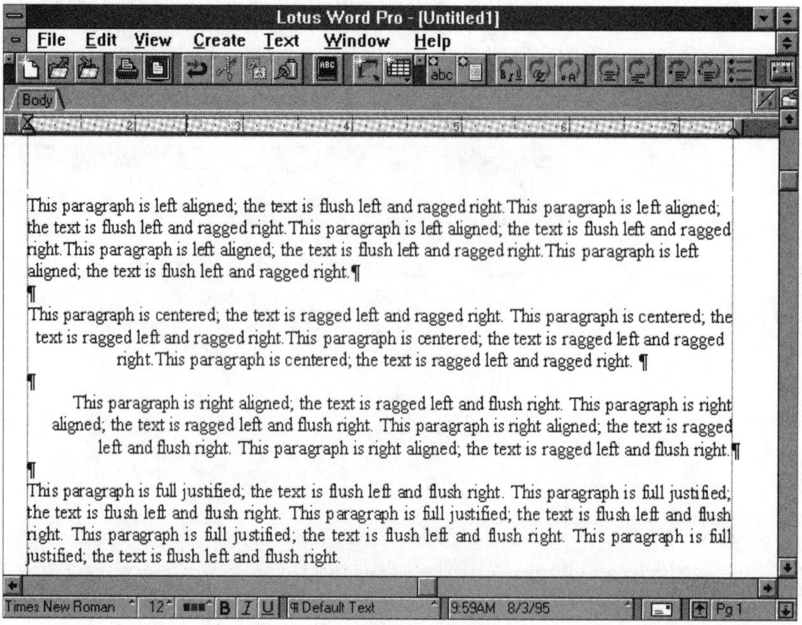

Table 5.3 **Paragraph Alignment Options**

Alignment Option	How It Affects Text
Left	Lines of text *flush left* (aligned evenly along left indent) and *ragged right* (aligned unevenly near right indent)—Word Pro's default paragraph alignment setting
Center	Lines of text centered between left and right indents; both left and right sides of centered paragraph are ragged
Right	Lines of text flush right (aligned evenly along right indent) and ragged left (aligned unevenly near the indent)
Full Justify	Lines of text are both flush left and flush right; Word Pro adjusts spacing between words so that each line stretches from left indent to right indent. On last line of paragraph, Word Pro usually does not attempt to justify; it leaves line flush left

The Text menu enables you to select any of the four paragraph alignment options. To use the Text menu to align paragraphs:

- Select the paragraph(s) you wish to align.
- Choose *Text, Alignment* to open the Text, Alignment *submenu.* (A submenu is displayed as a menu extension off to the side of the open menu.)
- Click on any of the submenu's four alignment options: *Left, Center, Right,* or *Full Justify.*

To align paragraphs, you can also use the Cycle Through Alignment Options ("Alignment Cycle") SmartIcon. As you click on the Alignment Cycle SmartIcon, it cycles through the alignment options. To use the Alignment Cycle SmartIcon to align paragraphs:

- Select the paragraph(s) you wish to align.
- Click on the *Cycle Through Alignment Options SmartIcon.*

Note: Word Pro has several other cycle SmartIcons that you might like to try. For more information, see your Word Pro documentation.

Let's use both the Text menu and the SmartIcon to center some paragraphs:

1. Move to the top of the document, placing the insertion point in the document's first line, *Vision Office Products*.
2. Choose **Text, Alignment**. A submenu opens to display Word Pro's paragraph alignment options (see Figure 5.18).

Figure 5.18 **The Text, Alignment submenu**

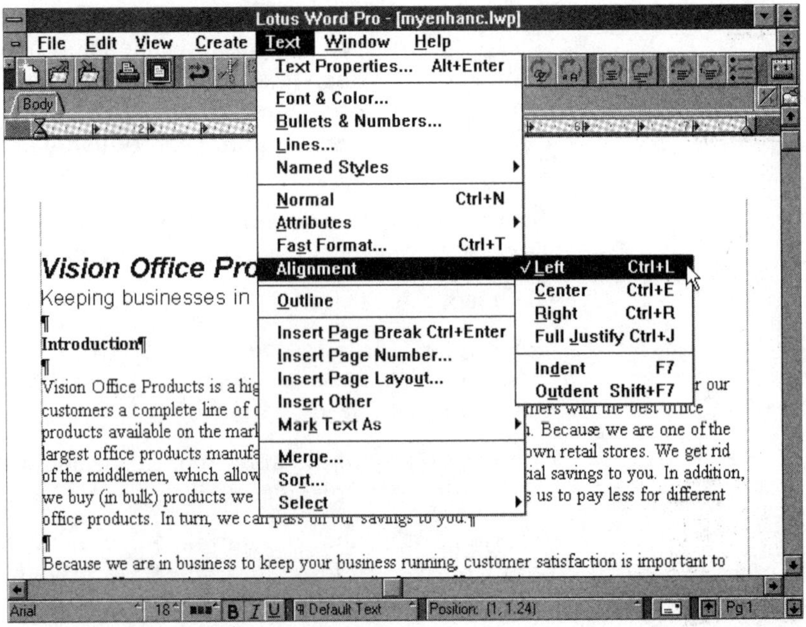

3. Click on **Center** to center the current paragraph between the left and right indents.
4. Select line 2 of the heading.

5. Click on the **Cycle Through Alignment Options SmartIcon** to center the paragraph, and then compare your screen with Figure 5.19.

Figure 5.19 **Centered paragraphs**

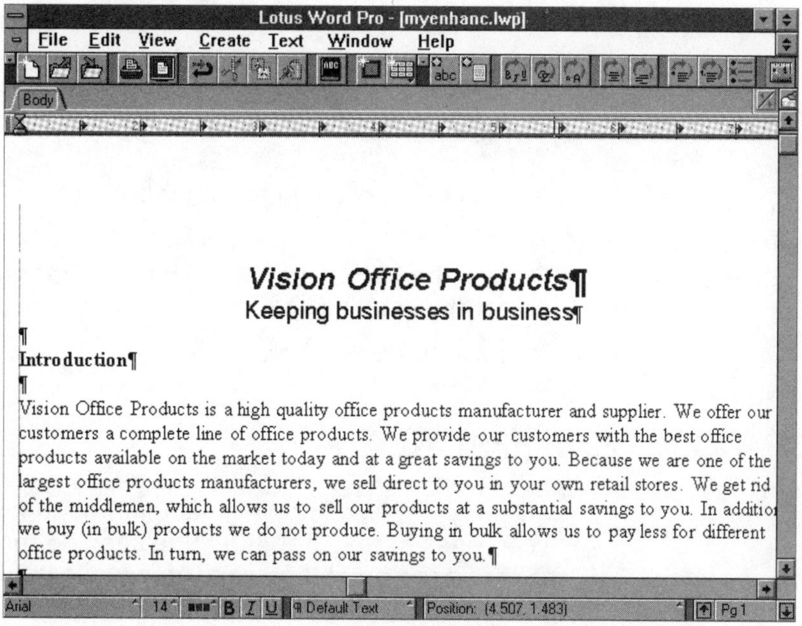

Now let's try the other paragraph alignments:

1. Place the insertion point in the paragraph beginning *Vision Office Products is a high quality* (the first multiple-line paragraph on page 1).
2. Choose *View, Zoom To, Margin Width.*
3. Look at the last word in each line of the selected paragraph. Because the paragraph is left-aligned, text is ragged right and does not always reach the right indent before wrapping to the next line.
4. Choose **Text, Alignment**, and then select **Full Justify**.
5. Look again at the last word in each line. Word Pro has increased the spacing between words in the current paragraph to fill each line (except the last one) so that the text is even with both the left and right indents (flush left and flush right).

6. Choose **Text, Alignment, Right** (that is, choose **Text, Alignment**, and then select **Right**), and then observe your document. Text in the current paragraph is now aligned only with the Right Indent marker; the left edge of the paragraph is now ragged.
7. Click on the **Cycle Through Alignment Options SmartIcon** until you return the paragraph to its original left alignment.

PRACTICE YOUR SKILLS

1. Use the **Text** menu to center both lines of the heading on the top of page 2.
2. Use the **Cycle Through Alignment Options SmartIcon** to center the two-line heading on the top of page 3.
3. Save the document.

CHANGING LINE SPACING

Line spacing (also known as *leading*) is the vertical distance between lines of text. Too little line spacing makes text difficult to read, and too much line spacing can waste paper by making documents unnecessarily long. Word Pro provides seven line-spacing options:

- *Single* (the default setting) sets the line spacing to one single line; Single always maintains a minimum of 12-point (1/6") spacing.
- *1/2* sets the line spacing to 1/2 line.
- *1 1/2* sets the line spacing to 1 1/2 lines.
- *Double* sets the line spacing to two lines.
- *Multiple* sets the line spacing to accommodate more than one line.
- *Leading* allows you to set line spacing as it relates to the point size of your text.
- *Custom* allows you to set any line spacing you want in inches, picas, points, or centimeters.

Note: The first five line-spacing options—Single, 1/2, 1 1/ 2, Double, and Multiple—provide spacing that is *relative* to the point size of the largest character in a line; that is, the larger the font, the greater the line spacing, and vice versa. (You might have noticed in Chapter 4 that when you increased the point size of selected text, Word Pro automatically increased the line spacing for that text.) When you use the other options, Word Pro uses an *exact and unchanging* value for line spacing, regardless of the text's point size. For this reason, it's a good idea to avoid using Leading and Custom line spacing unless you absolutely need them.

To change line spacing in a document:

- Select the paragraph(s) for which you want to change line spacing.
- Choose *Text, Text Properties*.
- Click on the *Alignment* tab (the second tab).
- Select the desired line-spacing option.
- Close the Text infobox.

Let's use the above procedure to change the line spacing for every paragraph in MYENHANC.LWP:

1. Select the entire document. (Move to the top of the document, and then press **Shift+Ctrl+End**.)
2. Choose **Text, Text Properties** to open the Text infobox, and click on the **Alignment** tab. This is the tab you used to set indents earlier in this chapter (it is the second tab and displays a center-aligned paragraph).
3. From the Line Spacing drop-down list, select **1 1/2** (see Figure 5.20).
4. Deselect the text, move to the top of the document, and then observe the text. The line spacing has increased from 1 to 1 1/2 lines (see Figure 5.20).
5. Select the entire document again.
6. Select **Double** from the Line Spacing drop-down list.
7. Deselect and return to the top of the document and examine the text. The entire document is now double-spaced.
8. Select the entire document one more time.

Figure 5.20 **Setting line spacing**

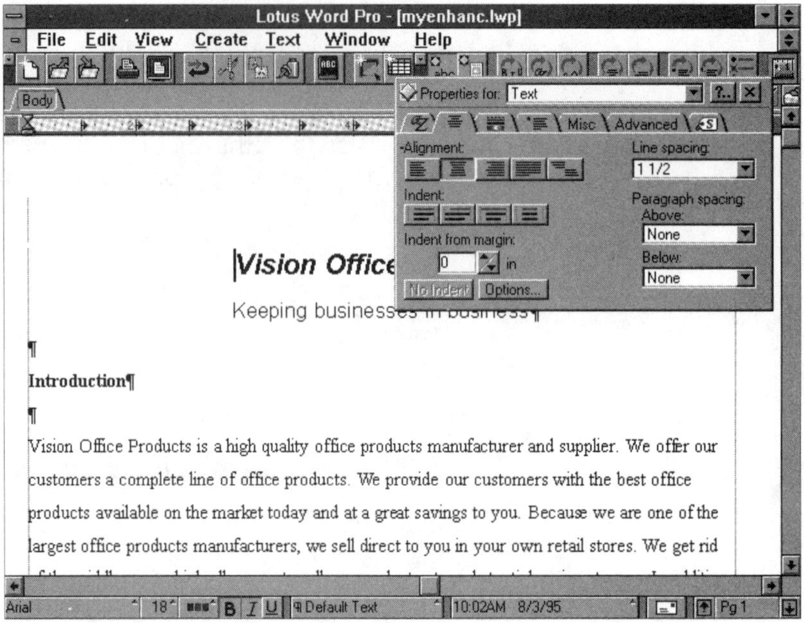

9. Select **Single** and then close the Text infobox. The document returns to single spacing.
10. Deselect to avoid inadvertently deleting the entire document.

Up to now, you've always saved the changes you made to your active document before closing it. However, you can also close a document *without* saving the changes. This might be helpful should you open a document and make so many mistakes you don't want to use the Edit, Undo command to reverse them. By closing the document without saving changes, you effectively reverse any changes you made since the last time you saved the document.

Let's close a document without saving changes:

1. Choose **File, Close**. Word Pro prompts:

   `MYENHANC.LWP has changed. Save changes?`

2. Click on **No** to close the document without saving your latest changes. (Don't worry; it's safe to do this now because all you have done since the last time you saved is increase the document's line spacing and then return it to single spacing.)

PRACTICE YOUR SKILLS

In Chapters 4 and 5, you have learned how to use text formatting to control character appearance, and how to use text enhancements to control paragraph appearance. The following two "Practice Your Skills" activities give you the opportunity to practice some of these techniques. After each activity step, we've provided a chapter reference (in parentheses) to inform you of where we introduced the relevant technique for that step.

Follow these steps to produce the final document shown in Figure 5.21 from the original document PRAC5A.LWP:

1. Open **prac5a.lwp**. (Chapter 2)
2. Select the entire document, and then remove all text attributes. (Chapters 3 and 4) (**Hint:** Use the **Text, Normal** command.)
3. Change the following headings to boldface. (Chapter 4)

   ```
   1. Introduction
   2. Computer Study
   3. Regional Updates
   4. Quarterly Meeting
   5. Conclusion
   ```

4. Change the font of the three-line heading on the top of page 2 to **Arial 14-point** (or the closest available equivalent). (Chapter 4)
5. Use Fast Format to copy the text formatting you applied in step 4 to the three-line heading on the top of page 1. (Chapter 4)
6. Scroll to the bottom of page 1. (Chapter 2)
7. For the 11 paragraphs (including blank lines) under the heading *3. Regional Updates*—beginning with *Midwestern Region* and ending with *manufacturing costs*—set left and right indents of one-half inch. (Chapter 5)
8. Center the three-line headings on the top of pages 1 and 2. (Chapter 5)
9. Save the document as **myprac5a**. (Chapter 2)
10. Print the document, and then compare it to Figure 5.21. (Chapter 1)

Figure 5.21 The completed document MYPRAC5A

Macco Plastics Inc.
Quarterly Sales Report
First Quarter

1. Introduction

Congratulations to all of you! An initial review of the sales figures for the nation reveals a surge in sales in all of Macco's sales regions. Major new clients have been added and many new products are on the way.

As we expected when we entered the field, computer-related products, such as keyboard housings and protective carrying cases, are accounting for a major portion of this upswing.

2. Computer Study

A companywide study will begin in March, under the direction of Cathy Donaldson and Bill Schuster in data processing, to determine how to most effectively implement automation in our firm. We will be making a large commitment to productivity gains via computerization sometime late this year.

3. Regional Updates

Midwestern Region

After several years of falling sales due to the slump in the auto industry, Blair Williams and his folks have something to celebrate. The recent boom in auto manufacturing has led to renewed demand of Macco Products in Detroit.

Northeastern Region

John Martinson and his group are doing a great job in Nashua. They have secured major contracts for a wide range of new and existing products. Much of this business is coming from Computer Equipment Corporation, a major client of Macco's.

Southern Region

Mark Daley and his group have done a fine job of maintaining relations with Becker's Product Development Division in Boca Raton. They have been working closely with Becker to decrease manufacturing costs.

Figure 5.21 The completed document MYPRAC5A (Continued)

Macco Plastics Inc.
Quarterly Sales Report
First Quarter

4. Quarterly Meeting

The quarterly meeting will take place in Memphis this time. You will find the agenda attached to this report.

5. Conclusion

The following items will be discussed at the next managers' meeting:

A. Marketing and sales strategies for the introduction of the new System 400 and System 500 product lines.

B. Current available positions resulting from the early retirement program and normal attrition of personnel.

C. Development of the new expense form to facilitate the prompt payment of - travel reimbursements - other out-of-pocket expenses and - commissions.

If the recovery continues at the current pace, this year should be a banner year for all of us at Macco. We want to thank all of you for the outstanding jobs you have done and, most important, for standing by Macco in hard times. Keep up the good work!

John Smith
Regional Coordinator
Macco Plastics Inc.

11. Close the document. (Chapter 1)

Follow these steps to produce the final document shown in Figure 5.22 from the original document PRAC5B.LWP:

1. Open **prac5b.lwp**. (Chapter 2)
2. Italicize the first line on page 1, *Macco Plastics Inc.*, and then change the point size to **24**. (Chapter 4)
3. Use Fast Format to copy the text formatting you applied in step 2 to the first line on page 2. (Chapter 4)
4. Underline the following subheadings (near the bottom of page 1). (Chapter 4)

```
Midwestern Region
Northeastern Region
Southern Region
```

5. Add a left tab at **1 1/2"** for the paragraph that begins *B. Current available positions* (near the top of page 2). (Chapter 5)
6. Set half-inch hanging indents for the five paragraphs (including blank lines) from the paragraph beginning with *A. Marketing and sales* through the paragraph ending *and - commissions.* (Chapter 5)
7. In the paragraph beginning *C. Development of the,* maintain the paragraph's hanging indent while creating three new lines for the following text. (Chapter 5)

```
- travel reimbursements
- other out-of-pocket expenses and
- commissions.
```

8. Save the document as **myprac5b**. (Chapter 1)
9. Print the document and compare it to Figure 5.22. (Chapter 1)
10. Close the document. (Chapter 1)

Figure 5.22 The completed document MYPRAC5B

Macco Plastics Inc.

Quarterly Sales Report
First Quarter

1. Introduction

Congratulations to all of you! An initial review of the sales figures for the nation reveals a surge in sales in all of Macco's sales regions. Major new clients have been added and many new products are on the way.

As we expected when we entered the field, computer-related products, such as keyboard housings and protective carrying cases, are accounting for a major portion of this upswing.

2. Computer Study

A companywide study will begin in March, under the direction of Cathy Donaldson and Bill Schuster in data processing, to determine how to most effectively implement automation in our firm. We will be making a large commitment to productivity gains via computerization sometime late this year.

3. Regional Updates

Midwestern Region

After several years of falling sales due to the slump in the auto industry, Blair Williams and his folks have something to celebrate. The recent boom in auto manufacturing has led to renewed demand of Macco Products in Detroit.

Northeastern Region

John Martinson and his group are doing a great job in Nashua. They have secured major contracts for a wide range of new and existing products. Much of this business is coming from Computer Equipment Corporation, a major client of Macco's.

Southern Region

Mark Daley and his group have done a fine job of maintaining relations with Becker's Product Development Division in Boca Raton. They have been working closely with Becker to decrease manufacturing costs.

Figure 5.22 The completed document MYPRAC5B (Continued)

Macco Plastics Inc.

Quarterly Sales Report
First Quarter

4. Quarterly Meeting

The quarterly meeting will take place in Memphis this time. You will find the agenda attached to this report.

5. Conclusion

The following items will be discussed at the next managers' meeting:

A. Marketing and sales strategies for the introduction of the new System 400 and System 500 product lines.

B. Current available positions resulting from the early retirement program and normal attrition of personnel.

C. Development of the new expense form to facilitate the prompt payment of
- travel reimbursements
- other out-of-pocket expenses and
- commissions.

If the recovery continues at the current pace, this year should be a banner year for all of us at Macco. We want to thank all of you for the outstanding jobs you have done and, most important, for standing by Macco in hard times. Keep up the good work!

John Smith
Regional Coordinator
Macco Plastics Inc.

SUMMARY

In this chapter, you learned how to use text enhancements. You learned how to display and hide the ruler; how to clear, set, and change tabs; how to set indentions; how to create new lines without creating new paragraphs; how to align paragraphs; and how to change line spacing.

Here's a quick reference guide to the Word Pro features introduced in this chapter:

Desired Result	How to Do It
Display current ruler	Choose **View, Show/Hide, Ruler**, or click on **Show/Hide Ruler SmartIcon**
Hide current ruler	Choose **View, Show/Hide, Ruler**, or click on **Show/Hide Ruler SmartIcon**
Select single paragraph for text enhancements	Place insertion point anywhere in paragraph
Select multiple paragraphs for text enhancements	Select at least portions of each paragraph
Open ruler shortcut menu	Click **right mouse button** on ruler
Set custom tab	Select paragraph(s); open ruler shortcut menu; select tab type; click at desired tab position in ruler
Clear all tabs	Select paragraph(s); open ruler's shortcut menu; select **Clear All Tabs**
Clear single tab	Select paragraph(s); drag tab down into typing area
Move tab	Select paragraph(s); drag tab to new position
Set indents using ruler	Select paragraph(s); drag appropriate indent marker(s) to new position(s) on ruler

Desired Result	How to Do It
Set indents using Text infobox	Select paragraph(s); open ruler's shortcut menu and select **Set Indents**; click on desired Quick Indent button; close Text infobox
Set hanging indent using ruler	Select paragraph(s); drag **Indent Rest marker** to right of Indent First marker
Create new line without creating new paragraph	Press **Shift+Enter**
Change paragraph alignment using menu	Select paragraph(s); choose **Text, Alignment**; select desired alignment option
Align paragraph(s) using SmartIcon	Select paragraph(s); click on **Cycle Through Alignment Options SmartIcon**
Change line spacing	Select paragraph(s); choose **Text, Text Properties**; click on **Alignment tab**; select line spacing option; close Text infobox
Close document without saving changes	Choose **File, Close**; click on **No**

In the next chapter, you will learn about page layouts. You'll see how to work with headers and footers, add today's date, add page numbers, change margins, and control your document printing.

IF YOU'RE STOPPING HERE

If you need to take a break here, please exit Word Pro. If you want to proceed directly to the next chapter, please do so now.

CHAPTER 6: PAGE LAYOUTS

Creating Headers and Footers

Setting Margins

Paginating a Document

Controlling the Printing of Your Documents

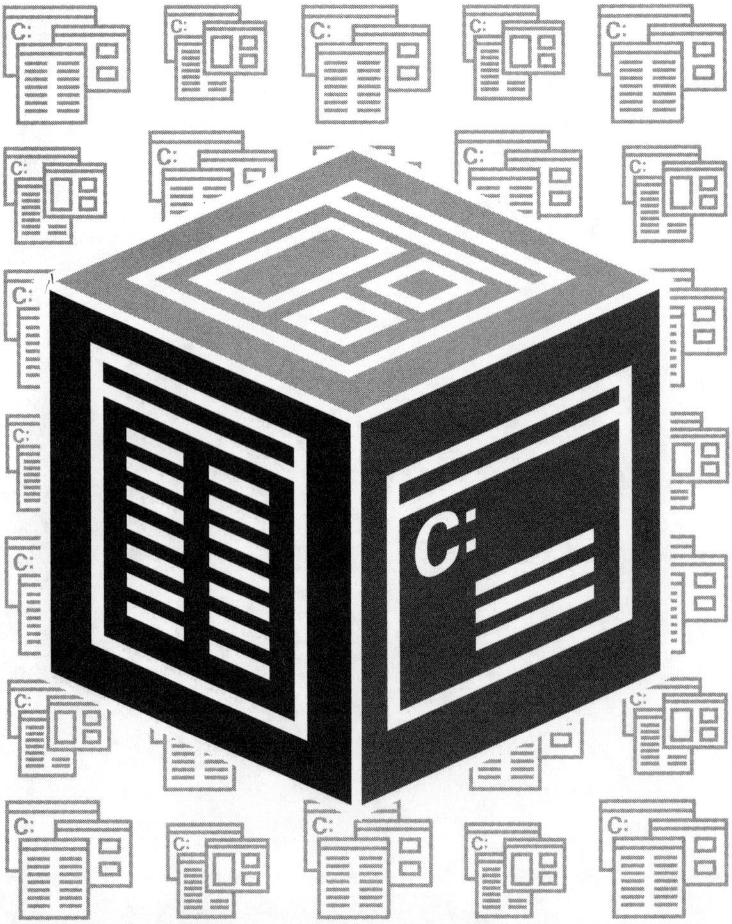

In Chapters 4 and 5, you learned how to control document appearance at the character level with text formatting and at the paragraph level with text enhancements. In this chapter, we'll introduce you to *page layouts*, which control a document's appearance at the page level. Page layouts include headers and footers, margins, and page breaks.

When you're done working through this chapter, you will know how to

- Create and edit headers and footers
- Add today's date and page numbers to a footer
- Change margins
- Use manual page breaks to paginate a document
- Control document printing

CREATING HEADERS AND FOOTERS

A *header* is text that prints at the top of every page in a document; a *footer* is text that prints at the bottom of every page. People commonly use headers and footers to repeatedly print information such as a document's title and/or author name, the current date, page numbers, and so on. Anytime you want certain text to appear on every page, you'll probably find that a header or footer is the best tool for the job.

Word Pro offers you two types of headers and footers: *fixed* and *floating*. Fixed headers and footers enable you to print the same header and footer throughout a document, with options for omitting them from the document's first page, and for alternating them on the document's left and right pages. (For instance, this book uses left and right alternating headers; the header text on the left-hand pages is different from that on the right-hand pages.) Floating headers and footers are even more flexible; they enable you to change the headers and footers throughout a document. For example, you can have one header print on pages 1 through 10, and another header on pages 11 through 20.

Because most people only need the basic features of fixed headers and footers, we will not cover the more advanced floating headers and footers in this chapter. For more information on creating and using floating headers and footers, refer to your Word Pro documentation.

Note: For easier reading, we will refer to fixed headers and footers in this chapter simply as headers and footers.

To create a header or footer:

- Click in any page's top or bottom margin to place the insertion point.
- Type your header or footer text.
- Press *Esc* or click inside the typing area to move out of the header or footer.

CREATING A HEADER

If you are not running Word Pro, please start it now. Let's open a document and create a header:

1. Open **layout.lwp**.
2. Click above *Vision Office Products* (the first line of the document) to place the insertion point in the header. Notice that when the header is active, Word Pro displays the Header SmartIcons bar (see Figure 6.1). Likewise, when the footer is active, Word Pro displays the Footer SmartIcons bar.

Figure 6.1 **The Header SmartIcons bar**

3. Type **Vision Office Products**, press **Tab** twice, and then type **Office Supplies Store** (see Figure 6.2).
4. Observe the header text. Notice that *Office Supplies Store* is flush right.
5. Display and observe the ruler (choose *View, Show/Hide, Ruler)*. For headers and footers, Word Pro automatically sets a center tab halfway between the left and right margins (at 4 1/4" in this case) and a right tab flush right. Using these preset tabs helps you to quickly and easily center your header text and/or align it with the right margin.
6. Click inside the typing area, scroll to the top of page 2, and then examine the top margin there. By adding a header to page 1, you automatically added a header to every page in the document.

Figure 6.2 **Adding a header**

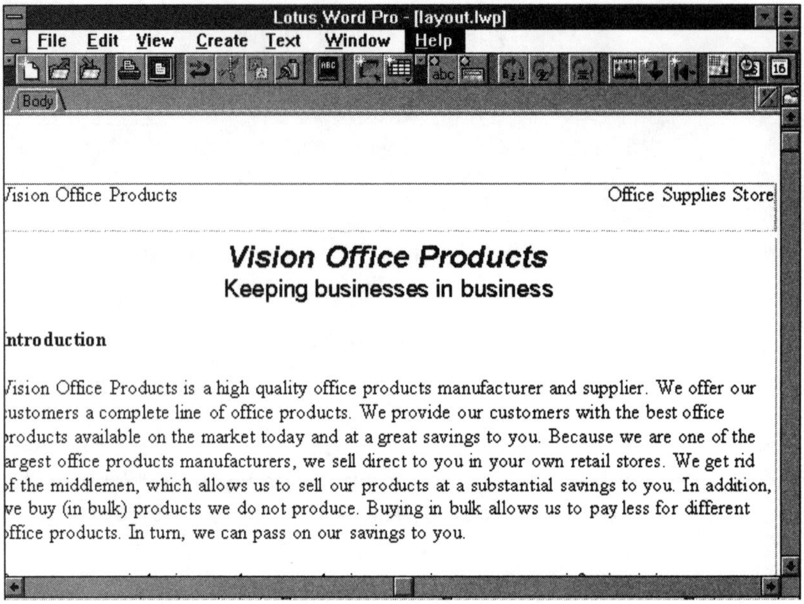

7. Save your document as **mylayout**.

CREATING A FOOTER

Now let's create a footer:

1. Scroll up to the bottom of page 1 until you can see the page's bottom margin.
2. Click in the bottom margin to place the insertion point in the page's footer.
3. Type your name.

ADDING A DATE

If you want to date- or time-stamp your document, headers and footers are often the ideal place to do so. Word Pro provides several options for inserting dates and times. There are seven date options:

- *Today's Date (system),* which displays and prints your computer system's current date
- *Today's Date (static),* which always displays and prints the day when you inserted the date
- *Yesterday's Date,* which displays and prints the previous day's date
- *Tomorrow's Date,* which displays and prints the next day's date
- *Date Created,* which displays the date you first created the document
- *Date of Last Save,* which displays and prints the date you last saved the document
- *Date of Last Version,* which displays and prints the date you last saved the last version of the document

For each date option, Word Pro offers 21 *date styles.* Here are four examples of date styles for the same date:

```
October 10, 1995
10 October, 1995
10/10/95
OCTOBER 10 1995
```

There are four time options:

- *Current Time,* which displays and prints your computer system's current time
- *Time Created,* which displays the time you first created the document
- *Time of Last Save,* which displays and prints the time you last saved the document
- *Time of Last Version,* which displays and prints the time you last saved the last version of the document

For each time option, Word Pro offers ten *time styles.* For example, 1:37:29 PM.

(**Note:** We do not cover versions in this book. For more information, see your Word Pro User's Guide.)

To insert a date or time:

- Place the insertion point where you want to insert the date or time.
- Choose *Text, Insert Other, Date/Time* to open the Insert Date/Time dialog box.
- Select the desired date or time option.
- If you selected one of the date options, pick a date format. If you selected one of the time options, pick a time format.
- Click on *OK*. Word Pro inserts the appropriate date or time at the insertion point.

Note: For Word Pro to insert the correct dates and times, your computer's internal clock must be set correctly. Whenever you insert a date or time, double-check to make sure that Word Pro inserts the correct information. If it doesn't, refer to your DOS or Windows documentation for information on resetting your computer's clock.

Let's insert today's date in the footer:

1. Verify that the insertion point is still in the footer.
2. Press **Tab** to center the insertion point.
3. Choose **Text, Insert Other**, and select **Date/Time** to open the Insert Date/Time dialog box, shown in Figure 6.3. (The date listed in *your* dialog box should reflect *your* computer's current date. Therefore, your dialog box will probably differ somewhat from Figure 6.3.)
4. Notice the options available in the dialog box's Insert box. You can insert one of the Date or Time options.
5. Observe the Date Format list box. It provides a list of different date styles.
6. In the Insert box, if necessary, select the **Date** radio button and **Today's Date (system)** from the Date drop-down list. Choose the first option in the Date Format list box. Then click on **OK**. Your footer now displays today's date.

Figure 6.3 **The Insert Date/Time dialog box**

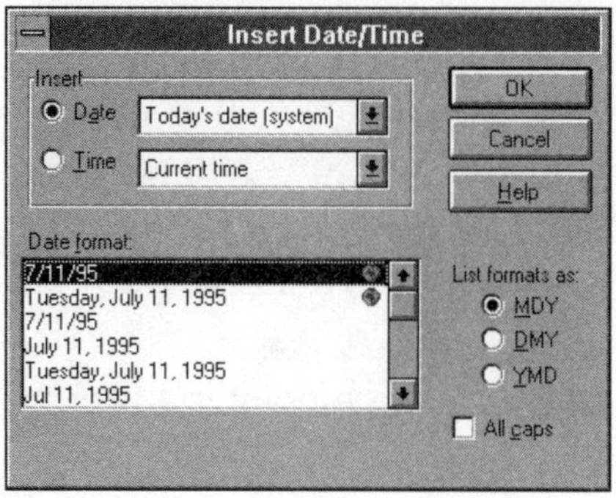

ADDING PAGE NUMBERS

Like dates, page numbers are useful elements to include in headers and footers, particularly if the document is longer than a couple of pages. When page numbers are placed in a header or footer, Word Pro automatically provides the correct number on each page.

To insert page numbers:

- Place the insertion point where you want to insert the page number. If you want page numbers to appear on every page, place the insertion point in either the header or footer.
- Choose *Text, Insert Page Number* (or click on the Insert A Page Number SmartIcon) to open the Insert Page Number Otions dialog box.
- If desired, choose a *number style* from the Number drop-down list box. Word Pro offers arabic numerals (1, 2, 3), uppercase roman numerals (I, II, III), lowercase roman numerals (i, ii, iii), uppercase letters (A, B, C), or lowercase letters (a, b, c).
- If you want *leading text* before your page numbers (for example, if you want your first page number to read *Page 1*, rather than just *1*), type that text in the Text Before text box. Be sure to include a space at the end of your leading text, so that your page numbers don't display as *Page1, Page2*, and so on.
- Click on OK.

By default, Word Pro starts page numbering on your document's first page, and starts with the number *1* (or *I, i, A,* or *a,* as appropriate). If you want your page numbers to start on a page other than the first one, or if you want to start with a page number other than 1, you can override the defaults for the Start At Page and Begin Numbering on Page options available through the Page Number Options dialog box.

Let's add page numbers to your document, using Word Pro's defaults:

1. Verify that the insertion point is still in the footer.
2. Press **Tab** to move the insertion point to the right margin.
3. Choose **Text, Insert Page Number**, and then observe the Insert Page Number dialog box. Word Pro is set by default to number your pages with arabic numerals and to use 1 as the first page number (see Figure 6.4).

Figure 6.4 **The Insert Page Number dialog box**

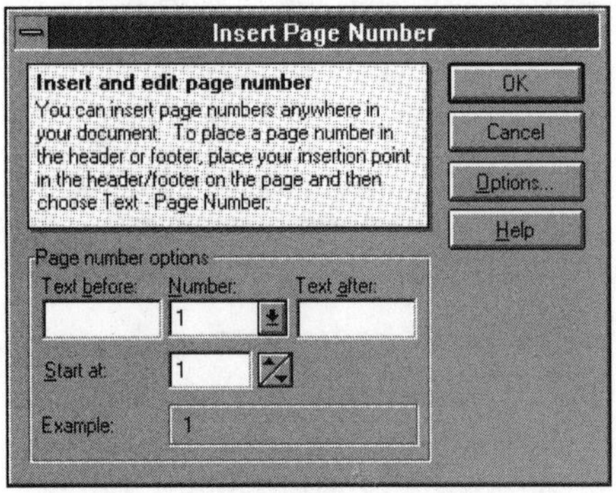

4. Click on **Options** to open the Page Number Optons dialog box. Note that Word Pro is set by default to begin numbering on page 1 (see Figure 6.5).
5. Click on **Cancel** to return to the Insert Page Number dialog box.
6. Place the insertion point in the Text Before text box, type **Page**, and then press **Spacebar**. This provides leading text for your page numbers.

Figure 6.5 **The Page Number Options dialog box**

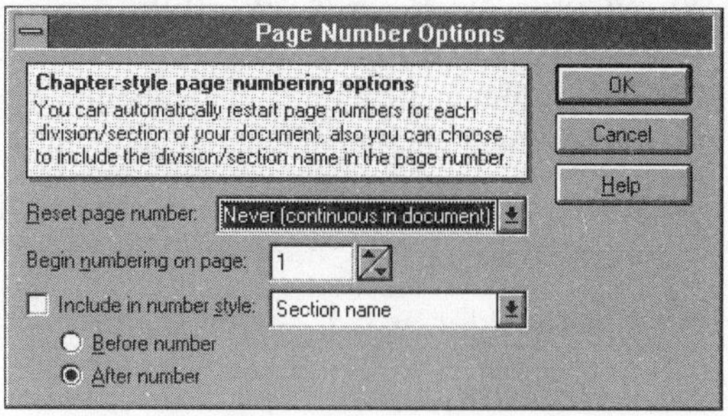

7. Click on **OK** to insert your leading text, *Page*, and the current page number, *1*, in the footer (see Figure 6.6).

Figure 6.6 **The completed footer**

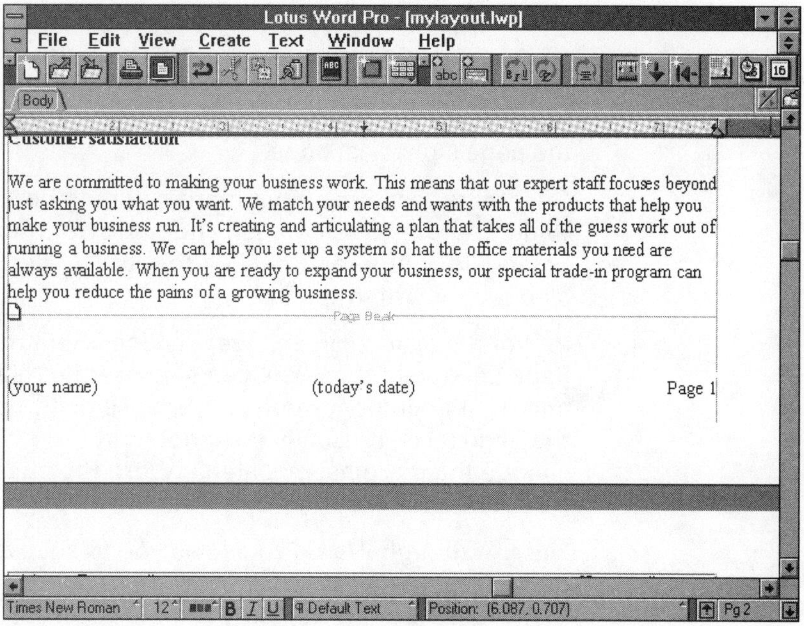

8. Scroll down to the bottom of page 2, and look at the footer there. Word Pro displays the correct page number, *2*.

EDITING HEADERS AND FOOTERS

Once you've created headers and footers, you can edit them as you would any other text. By default, Word Pro will incorporate any edits you make in one header or footer into every one of the document's headers or footers.

If you wish to completely remove a header or footer from the entire document, select the header or footer text, and then press Del.

Let's edit your header now by adding a word:

1. Scroll down to the top of page 3.
2. Place the insertion point in the header, immediately before the *O* in *Office Supplies Store*.
3. Type **Your**, and then press **Spacebar**.
4. Scroll up and observe the headers on pages 1 and 2. Word Pro has incorporated on both pages the header edit you made on page 3.

SETTING MARGINS

Margins determine the space between your document's text and the page's physical edge.

Generally, each document margin should be 1 to 1 1/2" wide. Wider margins waste paper, and narrower margins can make documents look busy and difficult to read. By default, Word Pro sets all document margins to 1".

In Word Pro, you can change any document margin through the Page Layout infobox. You can also use the ruler to change the left and right document margins. Because document margins work at the page level, it usually does not matter on which page you change the margins; by default, Word Pro changes document margins for entire documents, not for single pages.

Note: Although Word Pro allows you to set every document margin to 0", most printers cannot print to every edge of the page. Many laser printers can only print to within 1/2" of every edge; many dot-matrix printers can print all the way over to the left and right edges, but can only print to within 1" of the top and bottom edges. Before attempting to set document margins to less than 1", check your printer's documentation.

CHANGING DOCUMENT MARGINS THROUGH THE PAGE LAYOUT INFOBOX

To change document margins using the Page Layout infobox:

- Choose *File, Document Properties, Page* (or click on the ruler with the *right mouse button* and choose *Set Margins*), to open the Page Layout infobox.
- Verify that the Size & Margins tab is displayed.
- Verify that the Settings For box is set to *All Pages*. (Word Pro allows you to set different document margins for left and right pages. To change document margins equally for *every* page, All Pages must be selected.)
- Use the Margins box's Left, Right, Top, and/or Bottom text boxes to specify the desired margin widths.
- Close the Page Layout infobox.

Let's use the Page Layout infobox to change your document's left margin:

1. Move to the top of the document (if necessary), and observe the document's left and right margins on the ruler. The left margin is set at 1"; the right margin is set at 7 1/2" (one inch from the right edge of the 8 1/2-by-11-inch page).
2. Click the **right mouse button** on the ruler to display the ruler's shortcut menu.
3. Choose **Set Margins** to open the Page Layout infobox to the Size & Margins tab (see Figure 6.7). This tab of the infobox allows you to control a number of page layout settings, including margins.
4. Observe the four Margins boxes: Left, Right, Top, and Bottom. They are each set to *1* (1").
5. Double-click in the **Margins Left** box to select it, and then type **1.25** and press **Enter** to increase the left margin by 1/4".
6. Observe your document and the ruler. The left margin has increased to 1 1/4" (see Figure 6.8).
7. Click on the **Cancel** button to close the Page Layout infobox.

Figure 6.7 The Size & Margins tab of the Page Layout infobox

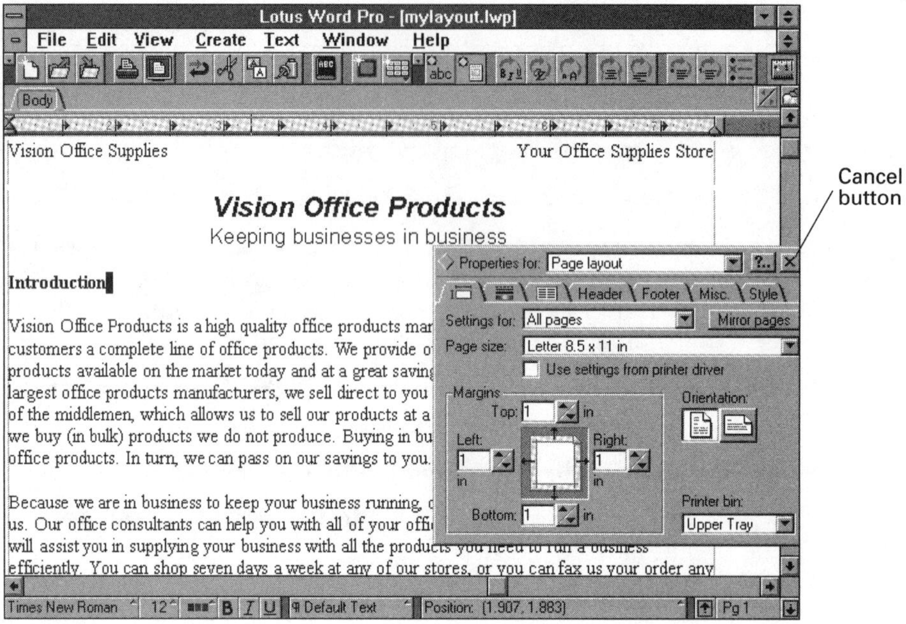

PRACTICE YOUR SKILLS

Let's change the right margin to match the left margin.

1. Use the **Size & Margins** tab in the Page Layout infobox to change the right margin to **1.25"**.
2. Close the Page Layout infobox.
3. Save the document.

PAGINATING A DOCUMENT

Pagination is the process of separating a document's text into separate pages. The separations between pages are called *page breaks*.

Word Pro provides two types of page breaks:

- *Automatic page breaks* are page breaks that Word Pro inserts automatically whenever a page runs out of room for text.

Figure 6.8 **MYLAYOUT.LWP, with a 1 1/4" left margin**

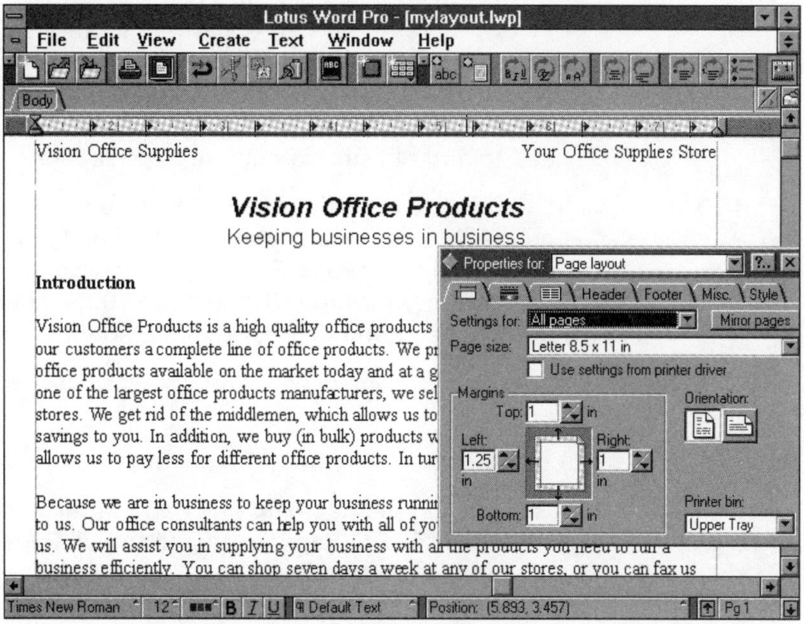

Whenever you add or delete text, increase or decrease the size of text, change margins or indents, or perform any action that creates more or less room for text on a page, Word Pro automatically repaginates your document, inserting or removing automatic page breaks as necessary.

- *Manual* (or *hard*) *page breaks* are page breaks that you insert wherever you want them. If you perform any action that creates more or less room for text on a page, you might need to manually add or remove these page breaks yourself.

Generally, you should use manual page breaks only when Word Pro's automatic page breaks do not produce the desired result. Otherwise, let Word Pro do the work of paginating your documents. Also, it's best to avoid inserting manual page breaks until you finish editing the document. If you don't, you might have to manually repaginate the document later.

VIEWING PAGE LAYOUTS IN FULL PAGE VIEW

As you saw in Chapter 2, you can use Word Pro's Full Page view to view entire pages of a document at a time. Full Page view can be very useful for examining each page's overall appearance on screen. For instance, you can use Full Page view to see if your margins should be wider or narrower, or to find out where you need to add or remove manual page breaks.

In addition to choosing View, Zoom To Full Page (as we showed you in Chapter 1), you can switch to Full Page view by clicking on the *Zoom To Full Page SmartIcon*. This SmartIcon displays a page in a computer monitor. To return to 100% view, just click on the Zoom To Full Page View SmartIcon again.

Let's use Full Page view to view your document's current pagination:

1. Return to the top of the document, if necessary.
2. Click on the **Zoom To Full Page SmartIcon** (or choose **View, Zoom To Full Page**) to switch to Full Page view. Word Pro displays a miniature of page 1 (see Figure 6.9).

Figure 6.9 Page 1 of MYLAYOUT.LWP, in Full Page view

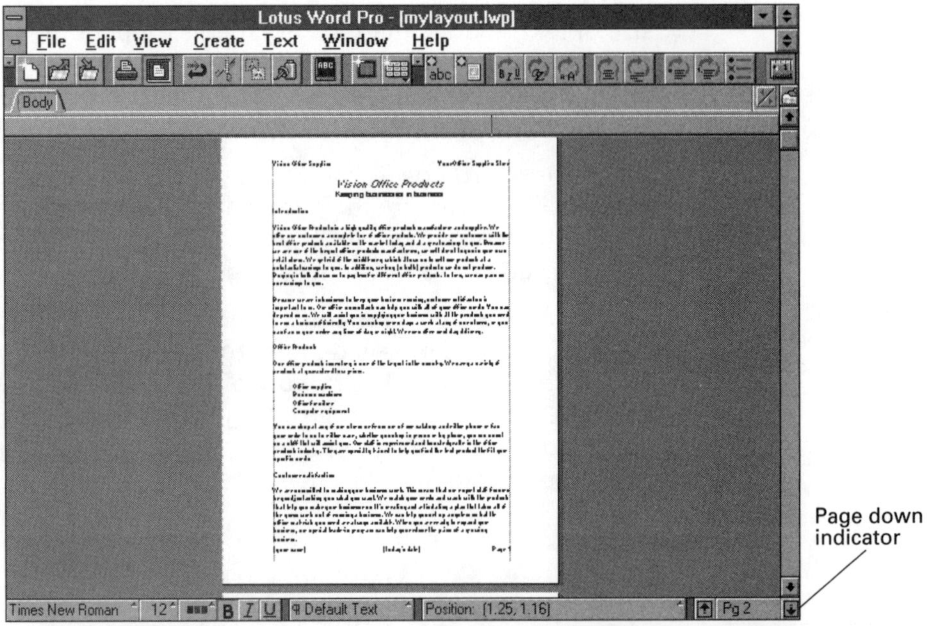

3. Click on the **Page Down indicator** to display page 2. Notice that the text on page 2 fills only a little more than half the page. We'll fix this problem shortly.
4. Scroll down to page 3.
5. Scroll down to page 4. Notice that there is some text on page 4, too.

INSERTING MANUAL PAGE BREAKS

To insert a manual page break:

- Place the insertion point immediately to the left of the first character that you want to appear on the new page.
- Choose *Text, Insert Page Break.*

You cannot view automatic page breaks on screen, but you *can* view the symbols for manual page breaks. By default, Word Pro displays page break symbols. If, however, page break symbols do not display on your screen, you can display them through the View Preferences dialog box. To display manual page breaks:

- Choose *View, Set View Preferences* to open the View Preferences dialog box.
- From the Show Marks checklist, select *Page Breaks.*
- Click on *OK.*

Let's observe automatic page breaks in action, and then insert a manual page break:

1. Click on the **Zoom To Full Page SmartIcon** (or choose **View, Zoom To 100%**) to return to 100% view.
2. Move to the bottom of page 1, and then select the entire paragraph beginning *We are committed* (under the heading *Customer Satisfaction*).
3. Observe the text on the bottom of page 1 as you press **Del**. Because deleting the paragraph creates empty space on page 1, Word Pro automatically moves some text from page 2 up to page 1.
4. Click on the **Undo Last Command Or Action SmartIcon** (or choose **Edit, Undo**) to restore the deleted paragraph. Word Pro automatically pushes some text back down to page 2.

5. Scroll down to the top of page 2, and look at the first sentence on the page. It is a paragraph that goes with the heading on page 1.
6. Scroll back up to the bottom of page 1, and place the insertion point before the *P* in the heading *Printing and Copying Services.*
7. Choose **Text, Insert Page Break** to insert a manual page break. *Printing and Copying Services* on page 1 moves to the top of page 2.
8. Scroll up to the bottom of page 1. Notice that Word Pro displays a symbol where you inserted the manual page break (see Figure 6.10). Like the symbols for tabs and returns, manual page break symbols only appear on screen; they do not print.

Figure 6.10 **Viewing a manual page break symbol**

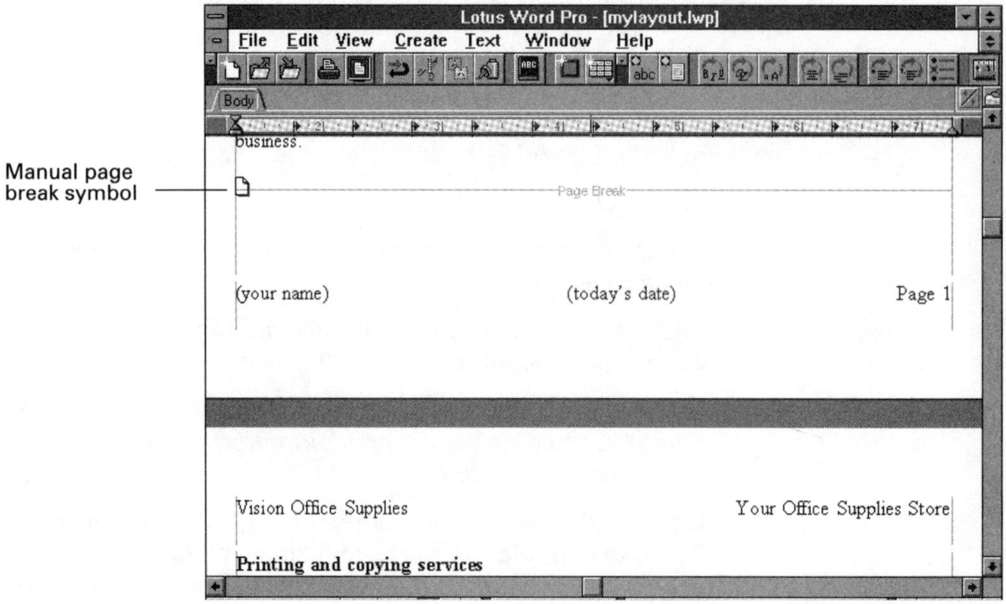

REMOVING A MANUAL PAGE BREAK

As we said earlier, one drawback of manual page breaks is that you sometimes have to remove them and insert new ones as you work in a document. To remove a manual page break:

- Place the insertion point to the left of the page break.
- Press *Del*.

Let's remove a manual page break now:

1. Switch to Full Page view (click on the **Zoom To Full Page SmartIcon**), and then observe page 2. Notice that the text extends only about halfway down the page.
2. Scroll to page 3. You can see that some of the text on this page could easily fit on page 2.
3. Return to 100% view (click on the **Zoom To Full Page SmartIcon**), and then move up to the end of the document text on page 2. The text on page 2 ends prematurely because of the manual page break here.
4. Place the insertion point to the left of the Page Break symbol and press **Del**. The text on page 3 moves up onto page 2.

PRACTICE YOUR SKILLS

1. Move to the bottom of page 2.
2. Insert a manual page break before the *F* in the heading *Fax Service Prices.*
3. Save the document.

CONTROLLING THE PRINTING OF YOUR DOCUMENTS

Several times in this book, you've used the Print dialog box to print your entire active document. Let's revisit this dialog box and learn how to use it to more specifically control your document printing. As we said way back in Chapter 1, in addition to printing a single copy of your entire document, options in the Print dialog box enable you to print multiple copies, the current page only, a specific range of pages, even-numbered pages only, and/or odd-numbered pages only.

Tip: Because it is often faster and cheaper to make large numbers of multiple copies with a photocopy machine, we suggest that you avoid using Word Pro to print multiple copies of a document.

As with many other commands, Word Pro provides a SmartIcon for opening the Print dialog box: the *Print SmartIcon*. The Print SmartIcon displays a printer.

Let's work with both the Print SmartIcon and the Print dialog box to print different pages of the current document:

1. Move to the top of the document.
2. Click on the **Print SmartIcon** to open the Print dialog box.
3. Observe the settings under Print Range. The current selection is All Pages, the Pages From box is set to *1*, and the Page To box is set to *3*. With these settings, Word Pro will print one copy of the entire document.
4. Select **Print Range Current Page,** and then observe the Pages From and Pages To boxes. As shown in Figure 6.11, each has changed to *1*, indicating that Word Pro will now only print page 1—the current page. (**Note:** Because Word Pro uses the Windows default printer, your dialog box might not exactly match Figure 6.11.)
5. Click on **OK** to print page 1.
6. After page 1 has finished printing, reopen the Print dialog box (click on the **Print SmartIcon** or choose **File, Print**). Notice that Current Page is still selected. Until you close this document, Word Pro will remember your most recent Print Range setting.
7. Select **Pages From** (double-click in the From box), and type **2**. Press **Tab** to move to the To box, and type **3**. You've now set Word Pro to print pages 2 and 3.
8. Click on **OK** to print pages 2 and 3 of MYLAYOUT.LWP.
9. Save and close your document.

SUMMARY

In this chapter, you learned the basics of page layouts, including how to create and edit headers and footers, add today's date, add page numbers, change margins, and control document printing.

Figure 6.11 **Setting Word Pro to print the document's current page**

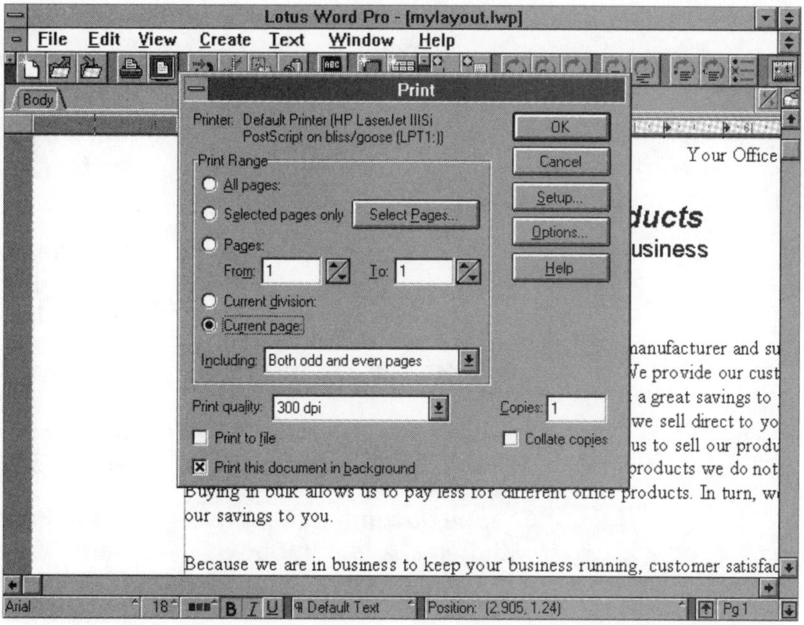

Congratulations on completing your foundation of skills for controlling document appearances! You now know how to format your documents at the character, paragraph, and page levels, using text formatting, text enhancements, and page layouts. These skills will enable you to create professional-looking documents.

Here's a quick reference guide to the Word Pro features introduced in this chapter:

Desired Result	**How to Do It**
Create fixed header or footer	Click in top or bottom margin; type header or footer text
Edit header or footer	Use any text-editing techniques

Desired Result	**How to Do It**
Delete fixed header or footer	Select header or footer text; press **Del**
Add today's date	Choose **Text, Insert Other, Date/Time**; select **Insert Today's Date** (if necessary); click on **OK**
Add page numbers	Choose **Text, Insert Page Number**; choose number style and type leading text (if desired); click on **OK**
Open Page Layout infobox	Choose **File, Document Properties, Page**; or click in typing area with right mouse button and choose **Page Properties**
Change document margins with Page Layout infobox	Open Page Layout infobox; verify that Size & Margins tab is displayed and **All Pages** is selected in Settings For box; set new values in Margins boxes; close Page Layout infobox
Switch to/from Full Page view with SmartIcon	Click on **Zoom To Full Page SmartIcon**
Insert manual page break	Place insertion point at desired location; choose **Text, Insert Page Break**
Remove manual page break	Place insertion point to left of page break symbol; press **Del**
Display manual page break symbols	Choose **View, View Preferences;** check **Page Breaks** in the Show Marks list; then click on **OK**

Desired Result	How to Do It
Hide manual page break symbols	Choose **View, View Preferences**; uncheck **Page Breaks**; then click on **OK**
Open Print dialog box with SmartIcon	Click on **Print SmartIcon**
Print current page	Open Print dialog box; select **Print Range Current Page**; then click on **OK**
Print range of pages	Open Print dialog box; select **Print Range From**; type first page number in range in **Print Range From** box and last page number in range in **Page Range To** box; then click on **OK**

In the next chapter, we'll explore ways in which Word Pro can help you improve your writing. You'll learn how to check your spelling; how to use Word Pro's on-line thesaurus to find alternative words; and how to check the grammar, style, mechanics, and readability of your documents.

IF YOU'RE STOPPING HERE

If you need to take a break here, please exit Word Pro. If you want to proceed to the next chapter, please do so now.

CHAPTER 7: PROOFING YOUR DOCUMENTS

Checking Spelling

Finding and Placing Synonyms with Thesaurus

Checking Grammar, Style, and Mechanics

Misspellings and grammatical errors can severely undermine the credibility of your documents. In this chapter, we'll introduce you to tools that help you to *proof* (check) your documents for repeated words and for potential spelling, grammar, style, and mechanical errors (such as incorrect punctuation). Wording is also a critical factor in determining the effectiveness of a document; using inappropriate words can alienate or confuse your readers. We'll explore Word Pro's online thesaurus to see how easy it is to find and use synonyms for existing words in your documents.

When you're done working through this chapter, you will know how to

- Check for spelling errors and repeated words
- Use the online thesaurus to find and place synonyms
- Check for grammar, style, and mechanical errors

CHECKING SPELLING

Word Pro provides a spelling checker, called *Spell Check,* that you can use to check the spelling in your documents. Word Pro compares each word in a document against the words in Word Pro's own 115,000-word dictionary and highlights the words it does not recognize, including words with irregular capitalization (such as *tHe*). Word Pro also checks for repeated words (such as *the the*).

Note: Do not depend solely on Spell Check or any of Word Pro's proofing tools for document correctness. Although spell-checkers, online thesauruses, and grammar-checkers are valuable tools, they are no substitute for a human proofreader. For best results, use Word Pro to proof your documents on line to catch obvious errors, and then have someone proofread the document for you.

USING SPELL CHECK

Word Pro provides these two methods for starting Spell Check:

- Choose *Edit, Check Spelling.*
- Click on the *Check Spelling* SmartIcon, which displays a book with the letters *ABC.*

You can select text before starting, and Word Pro will check only the selected text. Or you can just place the insertion point in the document, and Word Pro will check every word in the document.

To use Spell Check:

- Select the text you want to spell-check, or if you want to spell-check your entire document, place the insertion point anywhere in the main document text.
- Choose *Edit, Check Spelling* or click on the *Check Spelling SmartIcon.* Word Pro opens the Spell Check bar and highlights misspelled or unrecognized words in the document.

When it finds an unrecognized word, Word Pro places that word in the Spell Check bar's Word In Question text box. Word Pro often provides in the Alternatives list box a list of words with spellings that are similar to your unrecognized word. For example, if you typed *ther,* Word Pro might suggest *the, there,* and *their* as alternatives.

To correct a word if it is an error, or to skip past the word if it is correct, use one of the following methods:

- If the word is correct, click on *Skip* to leave the current word unchanged and have Word Pro continue checking. To skip every occurrence of that unrecognized word throughout the document, click on *Skip All.* To add the word to Word Pro's dictionary so that Word Pro will always recognize the word when you check spelling, click on *Add To User Dictionary.*

  Note: For Word Pro to use the words that you add to the dictionary for later spelling checks of all your documents, you must check *Include User Dictionary Alternatives* in the Spell Check Options dialog box. (To open the Spell Check Options dialog box, open the Spell Check bar and then click on *Options.*)

- If the word is incorrect and Word Pro has listed the correct word in the Alternatives list box, select the alternative word and then click on *Replace,* or simply double-click on the alternative word. To replace every occurrence of the unrecognized word throughout the document with the alternative word, select the alternative word and then click on *Replace All.*

- If the word is incorrect and Word Pro does *not* list a correct alternative, type the correct word in the Word In Question text box, and then click on *Replace.* To replace every occurrence of the incorrect word with the word you type, click on *Replace All.*

Once Word Pro finishes spell-checking all designated text, it opens a message box asking if you want to close Spell Check. Click on *Yes* to close Spell Check or *No* to return to your document and leave the Spell Check bar open.

If you are not running Word Pro, please start it now. Let's begin our work in this chapter by opening a document and spell-checking some selected text:

1. Open **proof.lwp**.

2. Select the two-line heading at the top of page 1 (from *Vision* through *Business*).
3. Choose **Edit, Check Spelling** to start spell-checking the selected text.
4. Examine the document. Word Pro has selected the first word it doesn't recognize, *busineses* (see Figure 7.1).

Figure 7.1 **Spell-checking selected text**

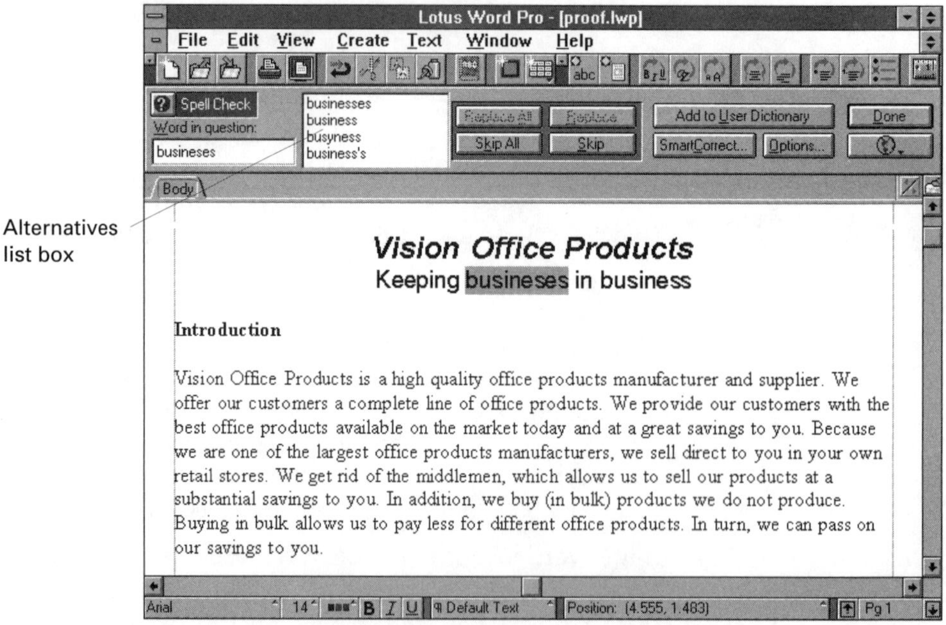

5. Observe the Spell Check bar. Word Pro has placed *busineses* in the Word In Question text box. In the Alternatives list box, Word Pro lists some correctly spelled alternatives (*businesses, business,* and so on).
6. Observe the Replace All and Replace buttons. They are dimmed because you haven't yet selected an alternative word.
7. In the Alternatives list box, select **businesses.** The Replace All and Replace buttons are now available.

8. Click on **Replace** to replace *busineses* with *businesses*, and to instruct Word Pro to continue spell-checking. Because it recognizes all the rest of the selected words, Word Pro opens a message box (see Figure 7.2).

Figure 7.2 **The no misspelled words message box**

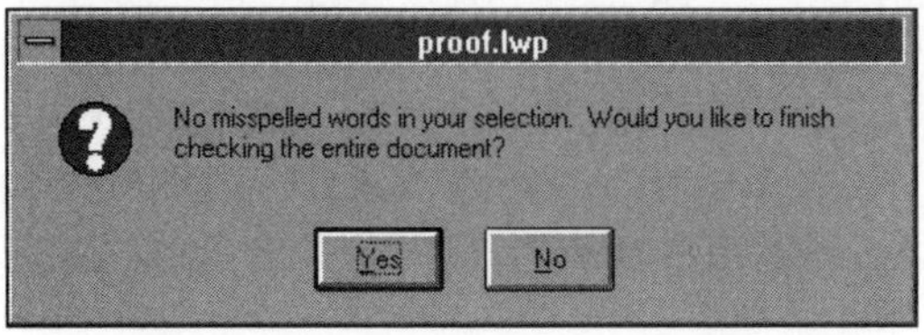

9. Click on **No** to close the Spell Check bar.

Now let's spell-check the entire document:

1. Click on the **Check Spelling SmartIcon** to open the Spell Check bar and begin checking the document.
2. Word Pro places the first word it doesn't recognize, *Arial*, in the Word In Question text box.
3. Click on **Skip** to leave *Arial* unchanged. Word Pro continues checking the document, finds *customters*, and lists *customers* as an alternative.
4. In the Alternatives list box, double-click on **customers** (or select **customers** and click on **Replace**) to replace *customters*. Word Pro continues checking and finds *purdhases*, but this time lists no alternative words.
5. In the Word In Question text box, type **purchases** and click on **Replace** to replace *purdhases* in the document. Word Pro continues checking and finds a place name that it doesn't recognize. Word Pro frequently doesn't recognize proper names.
6. Click on **Skip** to leave *Churchville* unchanged. Word Pro continues checking and finds a doubled word.
7. Click on **Yes** to close the message box and the Spell Check bar. (Or click on **Done** to close the Spell Check bar.)
8. Save the document as **myproof**.

USING SMARTCORRECT

In addition to the Spell Check bar, Word Pro offers a SmartCorrect feature. You can use SmartCorrect to automatically correct text as you type. For example, if you type *teh*, SmartCorrect replaces it with *the* as soon as you press the Spacebar. Word Pro supplies a number of default SmartCorrect entries. And, you can add your own entries. In addition to automatically correcting certain misspelled words, SmartCorrect includes options for correcting two consecutive initial caps and changing straight quotes to smart quotes. To select or edit SmartCorrect options:

- Choose *Edit, SmartCorrect* to open the SmartCorrect dialog box (see Figure 7.3).

Figure 7.3 **The SmartCorrect dialog box**

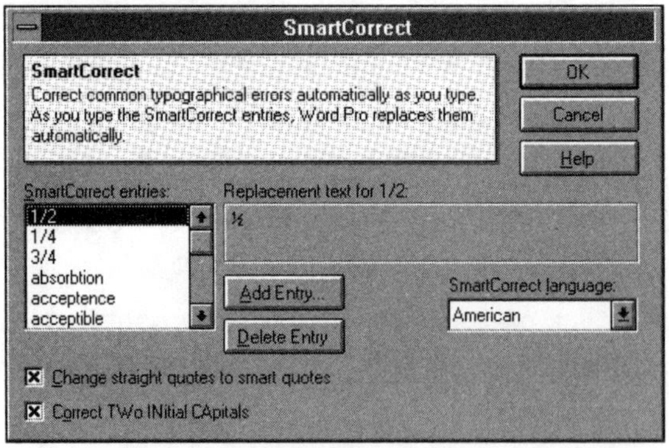

- Notice the following:
  - The *SmartCorrect Entries* list box contains the default SmartCorrect entries.
  - The *Replacement Text For* box displays the change SmartCorrect will make to the selected entry.
  - The *Add Entry* button allows you to add an entry to the SmartCorrect Entries list box.
  - The *Delete Entry* button allows you to delete the entry selected in the SmartCorrect Entries list box.
  - The *SmartCorrect Language* option is set by default to American.

  - By default, SmartCorrect will change straight quotes to smart quotes and correct two initial caps.

- Select or change any options you want.
- Click on *OK* to close the SmartCorrect dialog box.

If you frequently misspell a certain word, you might want to add it to the SmartCorrect Entries list box. Then, each time you mistype the word, Word Pro will automatically correct it. To add an entry to the SmartCorrect Entries list box:

- Click on *Add Entry* to open the Add SmartCorrect Entry dialog box.
- In the SmartCorrect Entry text box, type the text you want to create a smart entry for.
- In the Replacement Text text box, type the text as you want it to appear.
- Click on *OK*. Word Pro adds the entry to the SmartCorrect Entries list box.

It's possible that you might want to disable the SmartCorrect feature. For example, you might be sending a letter to Samuel *Teh*. If SmartCorrect is working, you would send your letter to Samuel *The*. To disable SmartCorrect:

- Choose *File, User Setup, Word Pro Preferences* to open the Word Pro Preferences dialog box.
- Click on the *Disable* check mark to display the Disable check list.
- Select *SmartCorrect*. Word Pro places a check mark to the left of the entry.
- Click on the *Disable* check mark again, to close the check list.
- Click on *OK*.

To enable SmartCorrect again:

- Choose *File, User Setup, Word Pro Preferences*.
- From the Disable check list, select *SmartCorrect* (to remove the check mark).
- Close the Disable check list.
- Click on *OK*.

FINDING AND PLACING SYNONYMS WITH THESAURUS

Thesaurus—Word Pro's 1,400,000-word, online thesaurus—helps you to look up *synonyms* for words that you've typed in your document. Synonyms are words with similar meanings. For example, if you typed the word *created*, Thesaurus would suggest alternatives such as *founded, constituted,* and *established.*

Although you should never use a word from a thesaurus—online or otherwise—that you don't recognize, Word Pro's Thesaurus feature can greatly enhance the quality of the writing in your documents by providing you with just the right word when you have trouble thinking of it by yourself. Using Thesaurus, Word Pro not only can look up synonyms, but can help you replace your original word with a synonym.

To use Thesaurus to look up a synonym and replace your original word:

- Select or place the insertion point in the word you wish to replace.
- Choose *Edit, Check Thesaurus* to open the Thesaurus dialog box.
- If the Synonyms For list box does not list the exact word you want, click on any of the words in the Meanings For list box, or click on a word in the Synonyms For list box and then click on *Lookup*. Word Pro will list the synonyms for the word you just selected. (To return to the previous list of synonyms after clicking on Lookup, select the original word from the Looked Up Word drop-down list.)
- Once you find the synonym you want, select it, and then click on *Replace*. In the document window behind the dialog box, Word Pro replaces your original word with the selected synonym.
- Click on *Cancel* to close the Thesaurus dialog box.

Let's practice using Thesaurus to find and place a synonym:

1. Scroll to the top of the document, if necessary, and place the insertion point anywhere in the word *created* (located in the paragraph beginning *Vision Office Products is a high-quality*).
2. Choose **Edit, Check Thesaurus** to open the Thesaurus dialog box and display a list of synonyms for *created* (see Figure 7.4).

Figure 7.4 **Finding synonyms with Thesaurus**

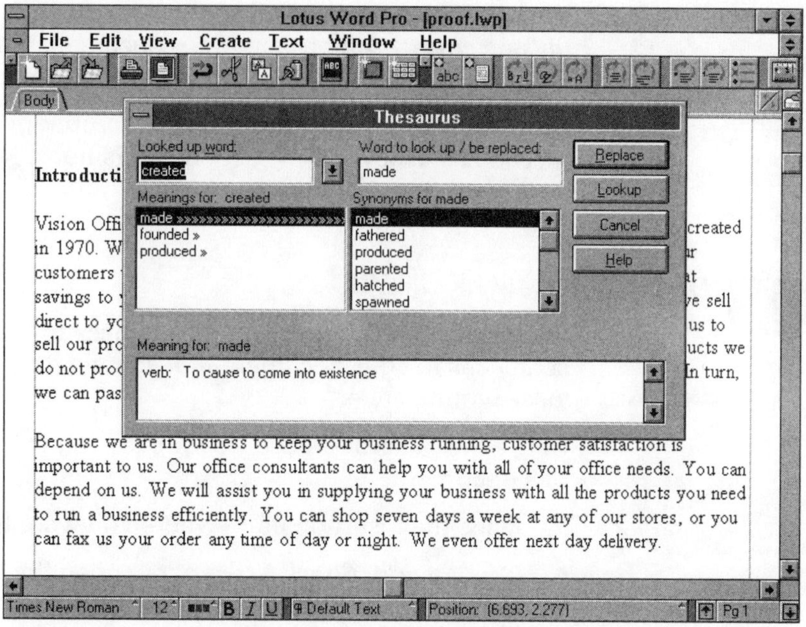

3. Observe the dialog box's Meanings For list box. It displays the definitions for the word in the Looked Up Word text box: *created.*
4. Observe the Synonyms For list box. It displays synonyms for the selected definition: *made.*
5. In the Meanings For list box, select **founded** to display a list of synonyms for *founded.*
6. In the Synonyms For list box, verify that **founded** is selected, and click on **Replace**.
7. Click on **Cancel** to close the Thesaurus dialog box, and then observe the document window. Word Pro has replaced *created* with *founded.*
8. Save and close the document

CHECKING GRAMMAR, STYLE, AND MECHANICS

Word Pro's grammar-checker, *Grammar Check*, helps you to identify and correct sentences in your document that contain grammatical and mechanical errors, and that exhibit a weak writing style.

Note: Explaining the ins and outs of proper grammar, style, and mechanics is beyond the scope of this book. For books on writing well, consult your local librarian.

USING GRAMMAR CHECK

You can use Word Pro's Grammar Check to identify and correct sentences in your document that contain grammatical errors and weak writing style.

Here's the general procedure for checking the grammar and style of a document:

- Place the insertion point where you want to begin.
- Choose *Edit, Check Grammar* to open the Grammar Check bar (see Figure 7.5).

When a potential grammar or style error is found, the Grammar Check bar displays the problem in the Questionable Item box and highlights it in the document. Word Pro might also provide one or more suggested corrections in the Suggestions list box. At this point, you can choose from the following options:

Option	**Action Required**
Accept suggested correction	Click on *Replace*.
Leave sentence as is and continue grammar check	Click on *Skip*.
Get more information about potential error	Click on *Explain*.
Change rules or style	Click on *Options*, select the options you want, click on *OK*.
Continue checking grammar after editing error in document	Click on *Continue*.
Stop grammar check	Click on *Done*.

Figure 7.5 **The Grammar Check bar**

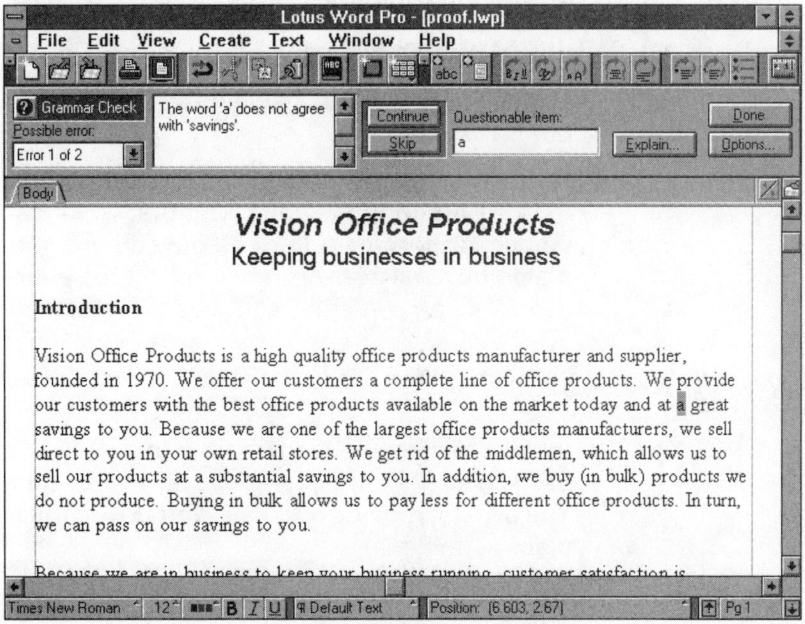

READABILITY STATISTICS

When you complete a grammar check, Word Pro will open a Readability Statistics dialog box (see Figure 7.6). This dialog box provides document statistics such as the total number of words, sentences, and paragraphs.

Figure 7.6 **The Readability Statistics dialog box**

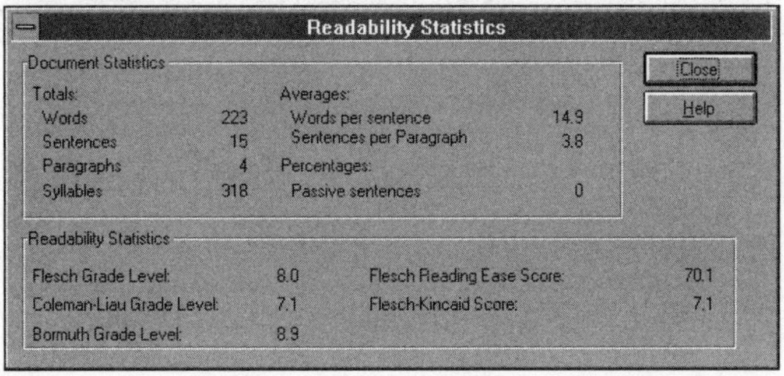

These document statistics are calculated into readability statistics which indicate the relative reading ease of your document. For more information on interpreting these readability statistics, see your Word Pro documentation.

Once you've finished viewing the Readability Statistics dialog box, click on *Close*.

Note: The Readability Statistics dialog box shows statistics only for the portion of the document that you most recently checked. If you used Grammar Check on only a portion of the document, this dialog box will not accurately reflect the entire document's totals, averages, percentages, and readability statistics.

SUMMARY

In this chapter, you learned how to proof your documents: You used Spell Check to check for spelling errors and repeated words. You also learned how to use Word Pro's Thesaurus to find and place synonyms.

Here's a quick reference guide to the Word Pro features introduced in this chapter:

Desired Result	**How to Do It**
Spell-check selected text	Select text; choose **Edit, Check Spelling** or click on **Check Spelling SmartIcon**; follow Spell Check prompts
Spell-check entire document	Place insertion point in main document text; choose **Edit, Check Spelling** or click on **Check Spelling SmartIcon**; follow Spell Check prompts
Use Thesaurus to find and place synonym	Select or place insertion point in existing word; choose **Edit, Check Thesaurus**; select desired synonym in Synonyms For list box; click on **Replace**
Grammar-check entire document	Place insertion point in main document text; choose **Edit, Check Grammar**; select grammar and style options (if desired); follow Grammar Check prompts

In the next chapter, you will explore some advanced editing and formatting techniques. You will learn how to copy and move text without using the Clipboard; copy text between documents; add bullets; and find and replace text attributes.

IF YOU'RE STOPPING HERE

If you need to take a break here, please exit Word Pro. If you want to proceed directly to the next chapter, please do so now.

CHAPTER 8: ADVANCED EDITING AND FORMATTING TECHNIQUES

Copying and Moving Text with Drag & Drop

Copying Text between Documents

Adding Bullets

Using Format Check

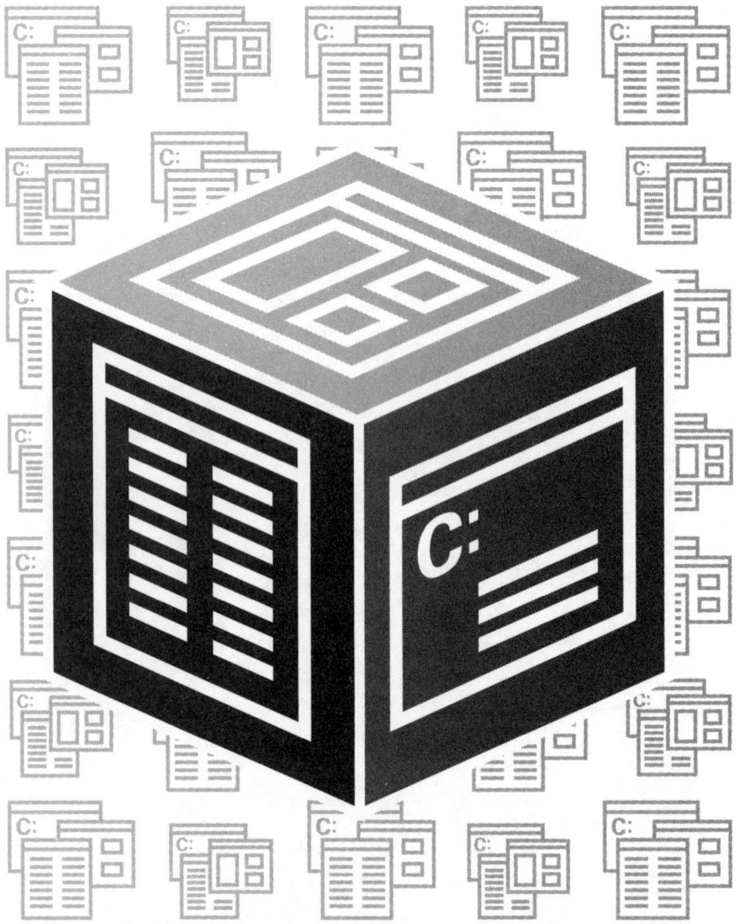

Back in Chapters 3 and 4, you learned basic techniques for moving and copying text, and for applying and removing text formats. In this chapter, you will build on these fundamental "survival skills" by learning some advanced methods for editing and formatting text.

When you're done working through this chapter, you will know how to

- Move and copy text by using Drag & Drop
- Copy text from one document to another
- Add bullets to your documents
- Use the Check Format bar

COPYING AND MOVING TEXT WITH DRAG & DROP

In Chapter 3, you saw how to copy and move text by using Edit commands and SmartIcons to cut, copy, and paste to and from the Windows Clipboard. You learned to follow these four steps when you want to move or copy text:

- Select the text.
- Cut or copy the text (using an Edit command or a SmartIcon).
- Position the insertion point.
- Paste the text (using an Edit command or a SmartIcon).

Word Pro also provides an even more convenient and shorter three-step method for moving and copying text, called *Drag & Drop*. With Drag & Drop, you simply drag the selected text to a new location without using any Edit commands or SmartIcons.

Follow these three steps when you want to move text with Drag & Drop:

- Select the text you want to move.
- Position the I-beam over the selected text, press and hold the mouse button, and then start dragging. When you do, Word Pro changes the mouse pointer to a hand. When you move off the selected text, the hand changes to a fist clutching the text, and Word Pro displays a colored insertion point near the hand.
- Drag the hand until the colored insertion point is where you want to move the text, and then release the mouse button. Word Pro moves your selected text to the new location.

The procedure to copy text with Drag & Drop is almost identical to moving; you only need to add the Ctrl key. Follow these three steps when you want to copy text with Drag & Drop:

- Select the text you want to copy.
- Position the I-beam over the selected text, press and hold Ctrl, press and hold the mouse button, start dragging, and then release Ctrl. When you start dragging, Word Pro changes the mouse pointer to a hand with a plus sign and displays a colored insertion point near the hand.
- Drag the hand until the colored insertion point is where you want to copy the text, and then release the mouse button. Word Pro copies your selected text to the new location, leaving your original in place.

When you use Drag & Drop, Word Pro does not use the Windows Clipboard. This can be an advantage when you have text on the Clipboard that you want to preserve. However, this means that if you want to copy some text to multiple locations, you cannot simply copy once and then paste repeatedly (as you did with the three-line page heading in Chapter 3). In such cases, you should use Edit commands and/or SmartIcons, rather than Drag & Drop, to copy and paste the text.

Note: If you find that you inadvertently move text with Drag & Drop, you can disable the feature through the File, User Setup, Word Pro Preferences command (check Drag & Drop in the Disable check list). For the remainder of this chapter, however, please leave Drag & Drop enabled.

If you are not running Word Pro, please start it now. Now let's practice moving text using Drag & Drop:

1. Open **advanced.lwp**.
2. Scroll down a few lines until you can see the headings *Customer Service, Introduction*, and *Office Products*.
3. Let's say *Introduction* and the five paragraphs below it should be above *Customer Service*. Select the six paragraphs from *Introduction* through to the blank line just above *Office Products*.
4. Position the I-beam over the selected text, press and hold the mouse button, and then start dragging up. As you drag, notice that the mouse pointer becomes a hand holding text, with a colored insertion point nearby (see Figure 8.1).

Figure 8.1 **Moving text with Drag & Drop**

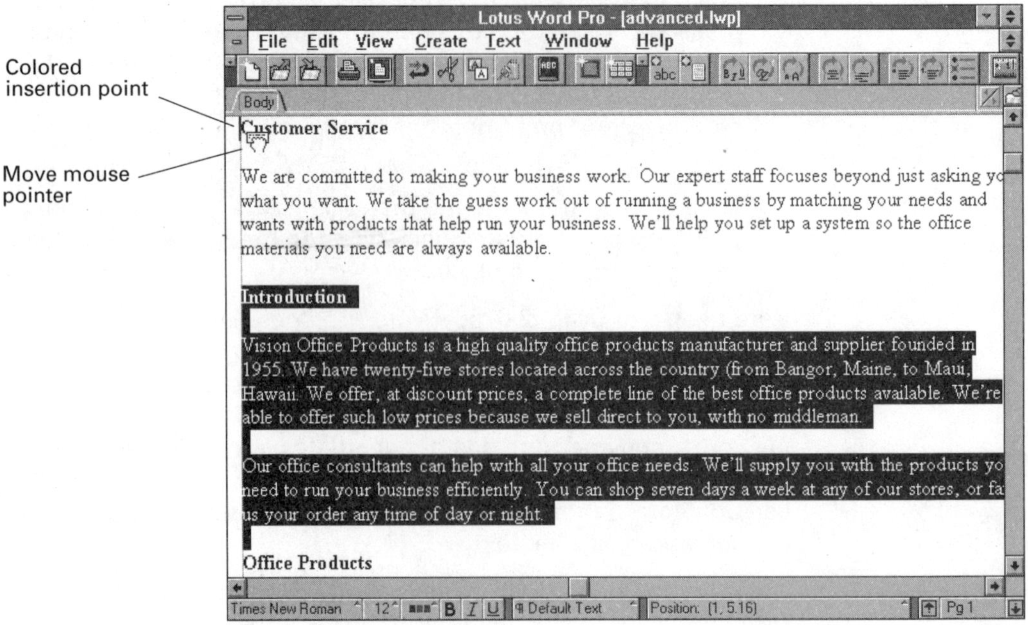

5. Drag the colored insertion point up, to the position immediately before the *C* in *Customer Service*, and then release the mouse button. Word Pro moves the selected text up and places it above *Customer Service*.

Now let's copy some text with Drag & Drop:

1. Scroll up (if necessary), and then select the two-line heading and the following blank line at the top of page 1.
2. Position the I-beam over the selected text, press and hold **Ctrl**, and then start dragging. This time, the mouse pointer changes to a hand with a plus sign in it (see Figure 8.2).
3. Release **Ctrl**, and then drag down to the top of page 2 until the colored insertion point is immediately before the *P* in the heading *Printing and Copy Services*.
4. Release the mouse button. Word Pro places a copy of the selected text at the top of page 2.
5. Return to and observe the top of page 1. Word Pro has left the original text in place.

Figure 8.2 **Copying text with Drag & Drop**

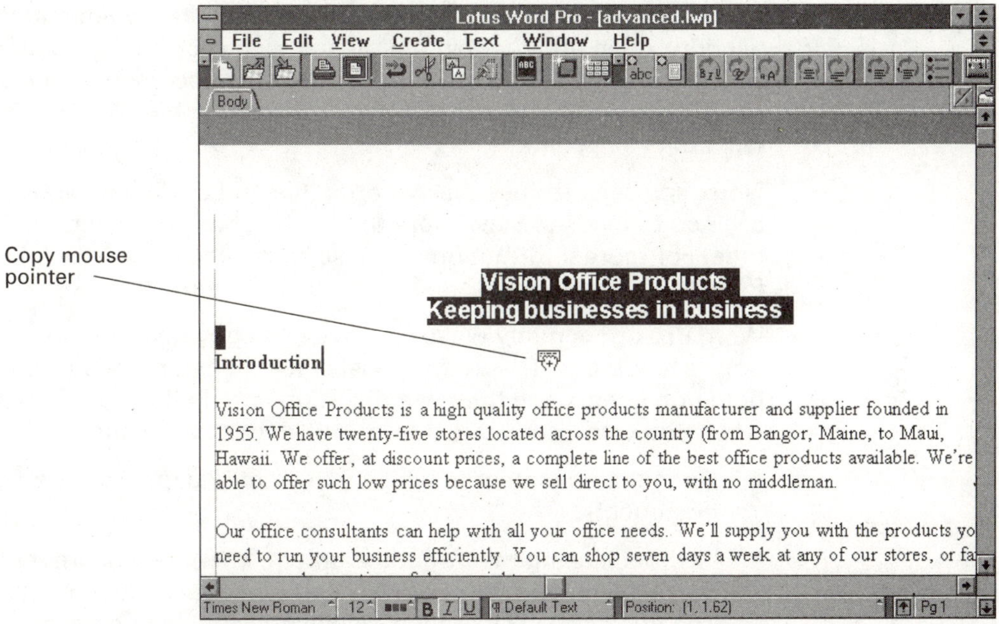

6. Save the document as **myadvanc**.

COPYING TEXT BETWEEN DOCUMENTS

Whenever you open a document, Word Pro places the document in its own document window. Throughout this book so far, you have opened and worked with only one document and document window at a time. In Word Pro, you can also create or open a second document, without closing the first one. Word Pro will open a second document window on top of the first document window so that both documents are open at the same time. The second document window then becomes the active document window; any document-specific commands you issue (such as saving and printing) will affect only the active window. You can open up as many document windows as your system can handle, but only one document window can be active at a time.

Opening multiple documents is useful for copying or moving text from one document to another, or for comparing the contents of two documents.

To help you manage multiple document windows, Word Pro lists the names of the first nine document windows (preceded by a number) in the Window menu. To activate an inactive document window, open the Window menu, and then click on the document window's name. If you have more than nine document windows open, choose More Windows, select the document window you want to activate, and click on OK.

Note: You can also use the Window, Tile and the Window, Cascade commands to view more than one document window at a time. For more information on these commands, see your Word Pro documentation.

Word Pro offers many ways to move and copy text from one document to another. One of the most convenient methods is to open both documents and then use the Clipboard. Follow these steps when you want to copy text from one document to another:

- Open the document to which you want to copy text (the *target* document).
- Without closing the target document, open the document that contains the text you want to copy (the *source* document). The title bar will change to display the source document's name.
- In the source document, select the text you want to copy; then choose Edit, Copy, or click on the Copy To The Clipboard SmartIcon.
- Open the Window menu, and then click on the name of your first document (the target document). Word Pro activates the target document window, moving it in front of the source document window, and changes the title bar to display the target document's name.
- In the target document, place the insertion point where you want to paste the copied text.
- Choose Edit, Paste or click on the Paste The Clipboard Contents SmartIcon.

When you finish working with the source document, you can close it by first activating its document window, and then choosing File, Close or double-clicking on the document window's Control menu box. Or, if you need to, you can leave the document open as long as you are in Word Pro. When you exit Word Pro, the document window will close along with any other open document windows.

Note: Although you can open many documents at a time, you might find that this makes your computer run more slowly. If this is a problem, close some document windows.

Let's open a second document, XTRATEXT.LWP, without closing MYADVANC.LWP, and then copy text between the two documents:

1. Choose **File, Open** or click on the **Open An Existing File SmartIcon** to display the Open dialog box.
2. Scroll to the bottom of the File Name list box, and then double-click on **xtratext.lwp**. Word Pro opens a document window for XTRATEXT.LWP on top of the MYADVANC.LWP document window.
3. Examine XTRATEXT.LWP. It consists of a multiple-line paragraph and a blank line.
4. Select the entire document (press **Shift+Ctrl+End**), and then choose **Edit, Copy** or click on the **Copy To The Clipboard SmartIcon**.
5. Open and examine the **Window** menu. It lists both open documents, MYADVANC.LWP and XTRATEXT.LWP. Because XTRATEXT.LWP is the active document window, Word Pro has checked 2 XTRATEXT.LWP (see Figure 8.3).
6. Select **1 MYADVANC.LWP** to activate the MYADVANC.LWP document window.
7. In the MYADVANC.LWP document window, move to page 2 and scroll down to view the headings *Business Forms* and *Custom Stamps and Stationery* (near the middle of page 2). Place the insertion point immediately to the left of the *C* in the heading *Custom Stamps and Stationery.*
8. Choose **Edit, Paste** or click on the **Paste The Clipboard Contents SmartIcon**. Word Pro inserts the selected paragraph and blank line from XTRATEXT.LWP at the insertion point.
9. Save MYADVANC.LWP.
10. Choose **Window, 2 XTRATEXT.LWP** to activate the XTRATEXT.LWP document window.

Figure 8.3 **The Windows menu, listing two open document windows**

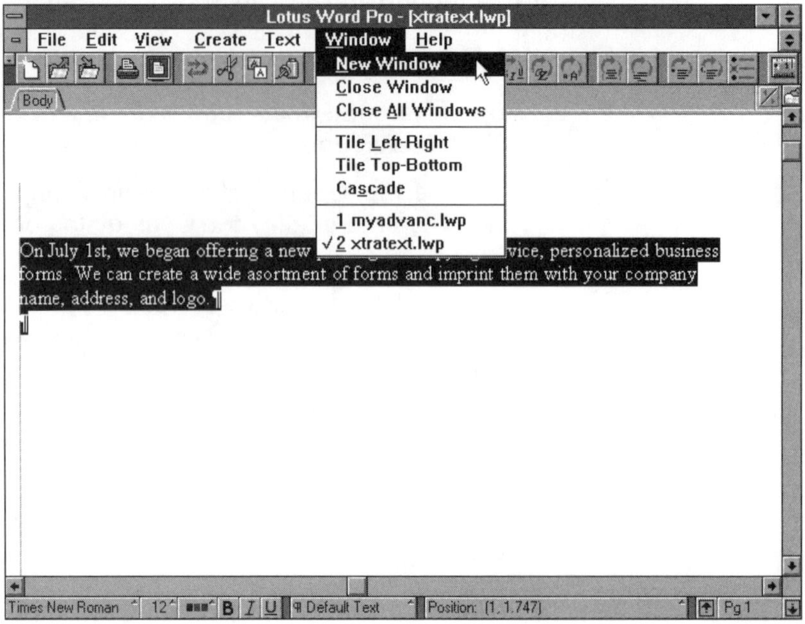

11. Choose **File, Close** or double-click on the XTRATEXT.LWP document window's **Control menu box** to close XTRA-TEXT.LWP. MYADVANC.LWP again becomes the active document window.

ADDING BULLETS

If you've used a typewriter before moving to Word Pro, you might have noticed that your computer keyboard is very similar to a typewriter keyboard. The computer keyboard probably has many more buttons, but both keyboards contain many of the same types of keys: letters, numbers, punctuation marks, and some symbols (such as @, #, and $). One of the limitations of both typewriter and computer keyboards, however, is that neither contains any good symbols for *bullets* (for example, •). Bullets are useful for organizing and drawing attention to certain text, as we have done in the *bulleted lists* throughout this book.

Word Pro provides many different *bullet styles*, from solid dots (•) to check boxes (❑) to arrows (➢). When you insert a bullet, Word Pro places the bullet at the beginning of the paragraph's first line, and then sets a hanging indent for the rest of the paragraph.

To insert a bullet:

- Place the insertion point in the paragraph where you want to insert the bullet. Word Pro automatically places the bullet at the beginning of the paragraph.
- Choose *Text, Bullets And Numbers* to open the Text Bullet tab of the Text infobox. This tab contains all the commands you need to create bulleted and numbered lists.
- Select a bullet style (click on the button of your choice). If you don't like any of the bullet choices, you can choose another bullet by clicking on Other.
- Close the Text infobox.

Note: Once they're inserted, you can delete bullets by selecting the paragraph and clicking on *None* in the Bullet Style list in the Text infobox.

Let's insert some bullets in a bulleted list:

1. Move to page 3 and scroll down until the heading *Catalogs* appears near the top of the document window.
2. Place the insertion point in the paragraph beginning *Special deals* (located beneath the *Catalogs* heading).
3. Choose **Text, Bullets & Numbers**, and then observe the Text Bullets tab. Note the following (see Figure 8.4):

Figure 8.4 **The Text Bullets tab of the Text infobox**

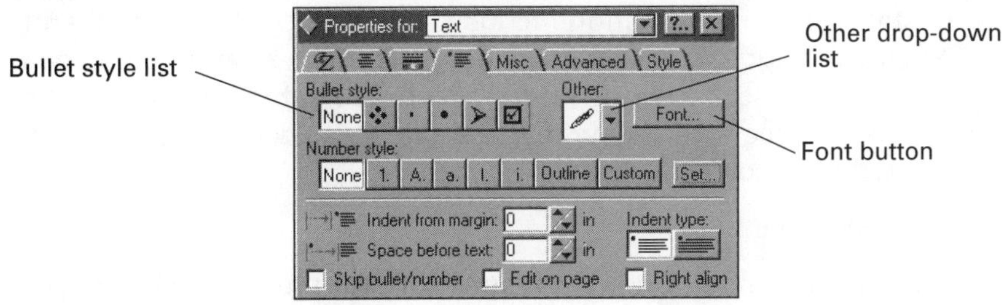

- The Bullet Style list contains five basic bullet options.
- The Other drop-down list contains additional bullet options.
- The Font button opens the Bullet Font dialog box. Here you can choose another font for additional bullet options.
- The Indent Type is set to create a hanging indent.
- Currently the Indent From Margin and Space Before Text boxes are set to 0 in.

4. In the Bullet Style list, click on the third bullet button (the large, solid dot). Word Pro inserts the bullet at the beginning of the paragraph.
5. Observe the Text infobox and the paragraph. Note that the Space Before text is set to .25 inch. There is a quarter-inch of space between the bullet and the first word of the paragraph. The rest of the lines of the paragraph are set as a hanging indent and align under the first word of the paragraph.
6. Close the Text infobox.

PRACTICE YOUR SKILLS

1. Insert a large, solid-dot bullet for the two paragraphs beginning *Office supplies* and *Office furniture*.
2. Close the Text infobox.
3. Compare your screen to Figure 8.5.
4. Save the document.

USING FORMAT CHECK

Format Check finds and highlights basic errors, common typing mistakes, and presentation inconsistencies you tell it to find, and gives you suggestions for correcting them. For example, you can tell Format Check to remove double spaces between words or sentences, replace asterisks with bullets, and replace characters such as *r* with the correct symbol, ®.

To use Format Check:

- Place the insertion point where you want to begin checking.

Figure 8.5 **Bulleted paragraphs**

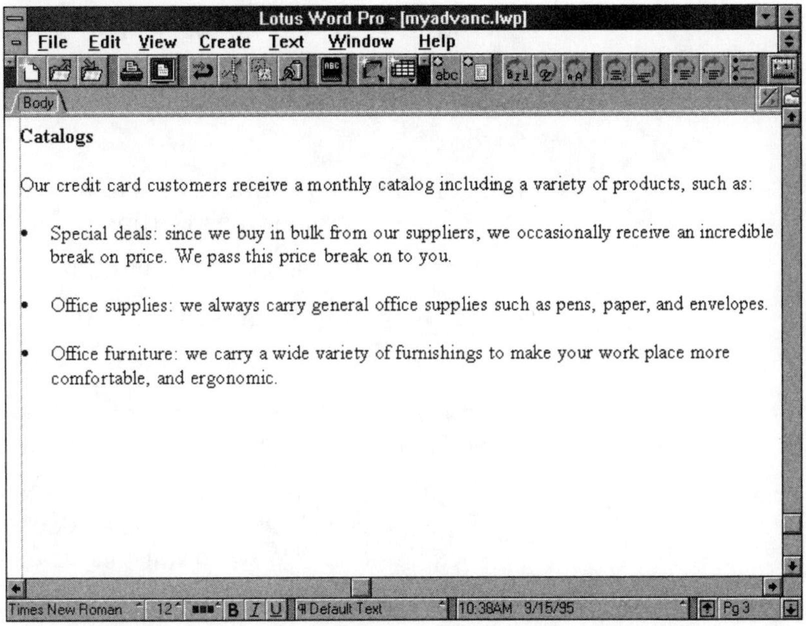

- Choose *Edit, Check Format* to open the Format Check bar.
- Click on *Options* to open the Format Check Options dialog box.
- Select the options you want to check for.
- Click on *OK* to close the Format Check Options dialog box.

Word Pro highlights each potential format error; it lists the rule that determines the first error in the Rule box, and the suggested correction for the error in the Suggestion box. To accept or reject Word Pro's suggested correction, choose one of the following:

- Click on *Replace* to replace the selected text with the suggested correction and move on to the next error.
- Click on *Replace All Of Rule* to replace all formatting errors related to the rule with the suggested correction. For example, if you are editing a document in which there are two spaces at the end of each sentence instead of one, you could choose Replace All Of Rule and Word Pro would run through the entire

document and replace every occurrence of two spaces with one space.

- Click on *Skip* to move to the next error without accepting the suggested correction.
- Click on *Skip All Of Rule* to skip all occurrences of the potential error.
- Click on *Continue Format Check* to resume the format check at the next error after the insertion point.
- Click on *Done* to close the Format Check bar.

Let's check the format of MYADVANC.LWP:

1. Move the insertion point to the top of the document.
2. Choose **Edit, Check Format** to open the Format Check bar (see Figure 8.6). Observe that Format Check
   - Highlights the potential errors in the document. The first highlighted selection is the asterisk beneath the heading *Office Products*. Word Pro will change an asterisk to a bullet.
   - Lists the rule for the first potential error in the Rule box. In this case, the rule is Bullets.
   - Gives a suggestion for fixing the error in the Suggestion box. Word Pro suggests improving the appearance of the bullet.
3. Click on **Replace** to replace the asterisk with a solid dot bullet. Word Pro automatically replaces all of the asterisks in the bulleted list and moves to the next error. There are two spaces after *and* in the paragraph beginning with *Office furniture*.
4. Click on **Replace** to replace the two spaces with one space. Word Pro displays a message box stating that Format Check is finished.
5. Click on **OK** to close the message box.
6. Click on **Done** to close the Format Check bar.
7. Save and close the document.

Figure 8.6 **The Format Check bar**

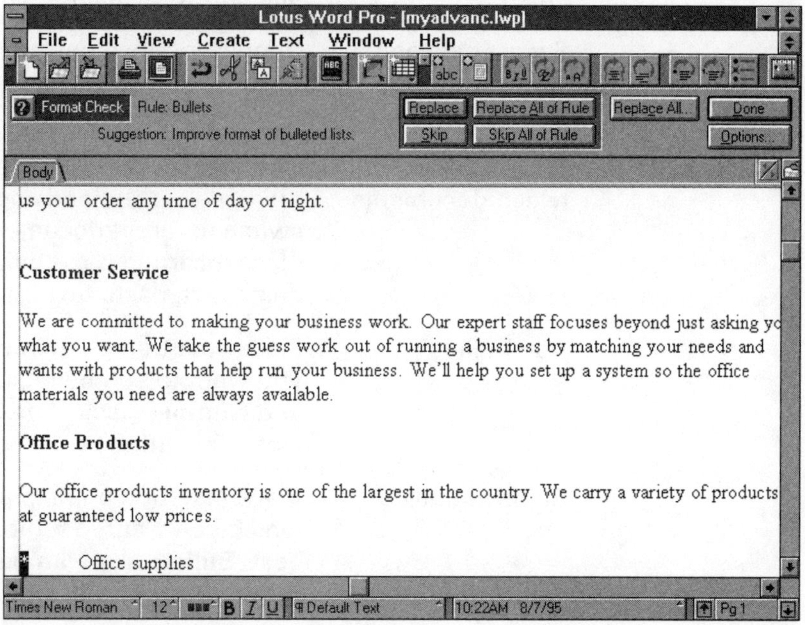

SUMMARY

In this chapter, you learned a number of advanced editing and formatting techniques. You learned how to move and copy text with Drag & Drop, copy text between documents, add bullets, and use the Format Check bar.

Here is a quick reference guide to the Word Pro features introduced in this chapter:

Desired Result	**How to Do It**
Move text with Drag & Drop	Select text you want to move; position I-beam over selected text; drag colored insertion point to new location
Copy text with Drag & Drop	Select text you want to copy; position I-beam over selected text; press **Ctrl** and drag colored insertion point to new location; release Ctrl

Open multiple document windows	Open document window without closing one currently open
Switch between open document windows	Open Window menu; select name of desired document window
Copy text between documents	Open target document; open source document; select text and copy it to Clipboard; switch to target document window and place insertion point where you want to paste text; paste text from Clipboard
Add bullets	Place insertion point in paragraph where you want to add bullet; choose **Text, Bullets and Numbers**; select desired bullet style; close Text infobox
Remove bullets	Place insertion point in paragraph from which you want to remove bullet; choose **Text, Bullets and Numbers**; select **None** from Bullet Style list; close Text infobox
Use Format Check	Place insertion point where you want to begin checking format; choose **Edit, Check Format**; set options you want to check for; click on **Skip** or **Replace** to skip or replace errors; click on **Done** to close Format Check bar

In the next chapter, you will learn how to use paragraph styles to format and reformat your documents quickly and easily.

IF YOU'RE STOPPING HERE

If you need to take a break here, please exit Word Pro. If you want to proceed directly to the next chapter, please do so now.

CHAPTER 9: PARAGRAPH STYLES AND STYLE SHEETS

Understanding Paragraph Styles

Assigning Styles

Redefining Styles

Creating Styles

Copying Styles

Understanding SmartMasters

By applying and modifying text formatting, text enhancements, and page layouts, you've been able to control many aspects of your document's appearance. In this chapter, you'll learn how to use paragraph styles and SmartMasters to very quickly and easily create, format, and reformat a wide variety of documents to the desired appearance. You'll also see how paragraph styles and SmartMasters promote consistency among similar types of documents.

When you're done working through this chapter, you'll know

- About paragraph styles
- How to assign paragraph styles
- How to modify paragraph styles
- How to create paragraph styles
- How to copy paragraph styles
- About StyleMasters
- How to select and use a SmartMaster

UNDERSTANDING PARAGRAPH STYLES

Paragraph styles are named sets of paragraph-appearance instructions that help you to format paragraphs quickly and easily. (**Note:** To make this book easier to read, from now on we'll generally refer to paragraph styles as simply *styles*.)

Whenever you create a document, Word Pro provides a number of built-in styles for your use. Styles are helpful because most paragraphs within a document fall into a particular category; for example, many paragraphs are either headings, subheadings, body text, headers, or footers. With styles, you don't have to select and modify the appearance of paragraphs on a paragraph-by-paragraph basis; instead, you can assign an appropriate style to each paragraph. For instance, rather than individually formatting every heading paragraph as Arial 12-point, italic and centered, you can just tell Word Pro that certain paragraphs are heading paragraphs. Then, by controlling the heading style itself, you can directly control the appearance of every paragraph in your document that you have assigned that style.

Styles incorporate a number of the following *style elements* (including many of the appearance elements you've already learned about):

- Fonts, text attributes, capitalization, and special effects
- Tabs and indents
- Paragraph alignment

- *Spacing* (the amount of vertical space between lines and paragraphs) and *kerning* (the amount of horizontal space between letters)
- Page breaks
- Leading bullets, numbers, and text
- Horizontal lines above and below paragraphs
- Numeric formatting
- Hyphenation

Because there are so many style elements, we can't cover all of them in a single chapter, but we'll show you all the necessary basics of using styles. In later chapters, we'll show you some additional style elements when appropriate. For information on style elements not covered in this book, see your Word Pro documentation.

ASSIGNING STYLES

Paragraph styles, as the term suggests, work at the paragraph level—you can assign styles only to entire paragraphs at a time, not just to selected text. For this reason, you can use the paragraph selection shortcuts you learned for applying text enhancements (in Chapter 5) to select paragraphs for assigning styles. Here's a recap of the shortcuts:

- To select a single paragraph for assigning a style, place the insertion point anywhere within that paragraph.
- To select multiple paragraphs for assigning a style, select at least part of each paragraph.

If you prefer, you can instead select entire paragraphs before assigning styles; the methods above are just convenient shortcuts.

Once you've selected a paragraph or paragraphs, you can use either the *Style Status button* (the button in the middle of the status bar), or *Fast Format* to assign a style.

In this chapter, you'll learn how to use the Style Status button to assign styles. For more information on assigning styles with Fast Format, see your Word Pro documentation.

ASSIGNING STYLES WITH THE STYLE STATUS BUTTON

To assign a style using the Style Status button:

- Select the appropriate paragraph or paragraphs.
- Click on the *Style Status button* to display a list of available styles.
- From the list, select the desired style.

Like many of the status bar's other buttons, the Style Status button works as a status indicator: It displays the name of the style currently assigned to the paragraph that contains the insertion point or current selection. (Throughout this book, you might have noticed that the Style Status button has always read *Default Text*, the style that Word Pro by default assigns to all paragraphs.)

If you are not running Word Pro, please start it now. Let's use the Style Status button to assign some styles:

1. Open **styles.lwp**.
2. Place the insertion point in the heading *Introduction* (near the top of page 1).
3. Observe the Style Status button. Word Pro by default assigns the Default Text style to all paragraphs.
4. Click on the **Style Status button** to open a list of available styles (see Figure 9.1).
5. Select **Bullet 1** from the styles list, and then look at *Introduction*. Word Pro adds a small bullet to the beginning of the paragraph, and indents the rest of the paragraph .25".
6. Observe the Style Status button. It confirms that you've successfully assigned the Bullet 1 style.
7. Click on the **Style Status button**, and then select **Number List** to assign the Number List style to *Introduction*. Word Pro replaces the bullet with the number *1*.
8. Assign the **Heading 2** style to *Introduction* (click on the **Style Status button**, and then select **Heading 2**). Word Pro removes the number *1*, removes the indent, applies the Bold text attribute, and changes the font to Arial.
9. Select the two-line heading at the top of the document, **Vision Office Products** and **Your Office Supplies Store**, and

Figure 9.1 **Viewing the Style Status button's styles list**

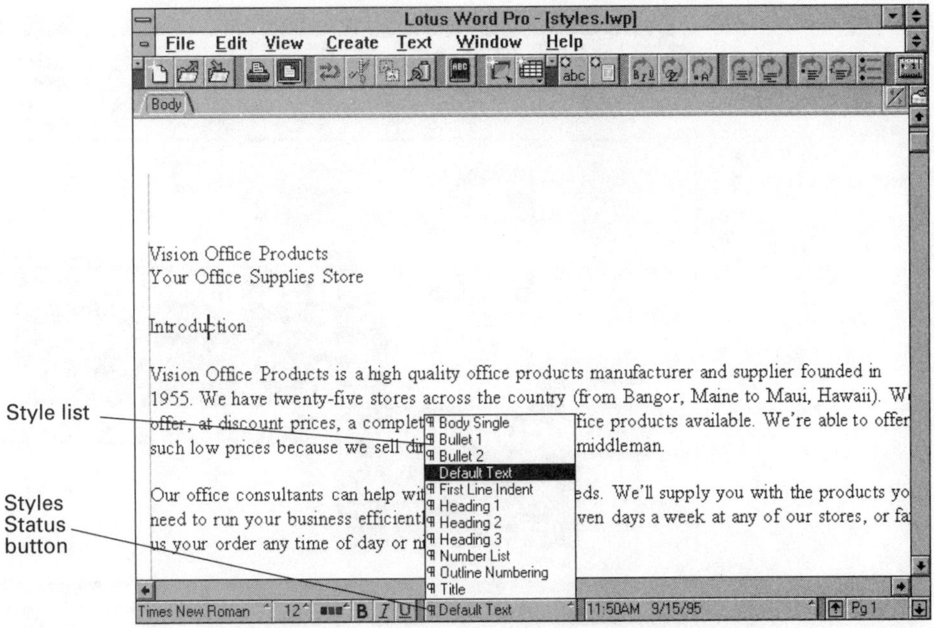

then assign the **Title** style. Word Pro changes the characters in both paragraphs from Times New Roman 12-point to Arial 24-point boldface, and centers the paragraphs (see Figure 9.2).

PRACTICE YOUR SKILLS

In the following steps, use the Style Status button to assign styles:

1. Assign the **Heading 2** style to the remaining headings:

```
Customer Service
Office Products
Ordering
Catalogs
Printing and Copying Services
```

2. Assign the **Title** style to the two-line heading on the top of page 3.

Figure 9.2 **STYLES.LWP, with styles assigned**

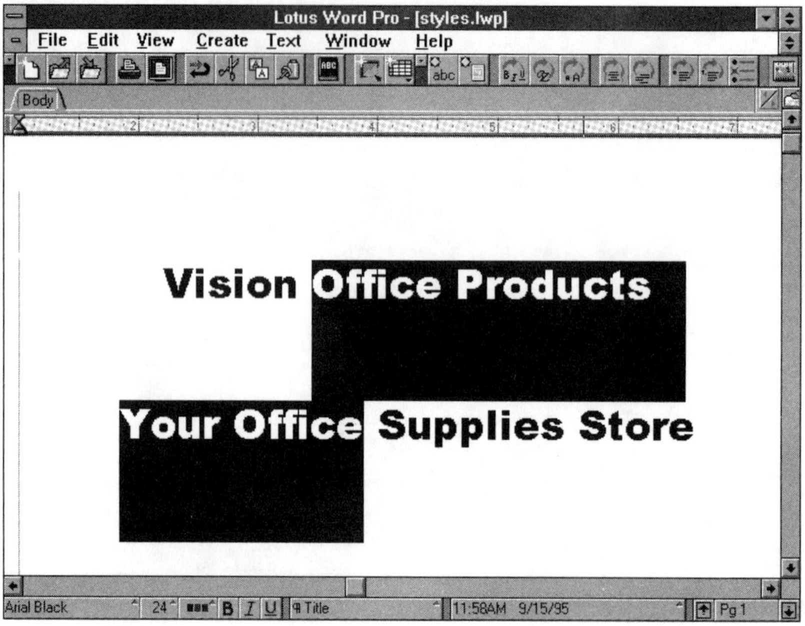

3. Under the heading *Catalogs*, assign the **Number List** style to the three paragraphs that begin with *Special deals, Office supplies,* and *Office furniture*.
4. Save the document as **mystyles**.
5. Compare your screen to Figure 9.3.

REDEFINING STYLES

Although Word Pro provides an assortment of styles for various paragraph types, there's no guarantee that those styles will contain exactly the style elements that you want. For example, Word Pro defines the Heading 2 style as Arial 12-point bold, but you might want your headings to appear as Arial 14-point boldface. For this reason, Word Pro allows you to redefine styles.

When you redefine a style, you start to see more of the potential power of Word Pro's styles capability. By redefining a single style, you can automatically change the appearance of every one of a

Figure 9.3 **MYSTYLES.LWP, after assigning the Number List style**

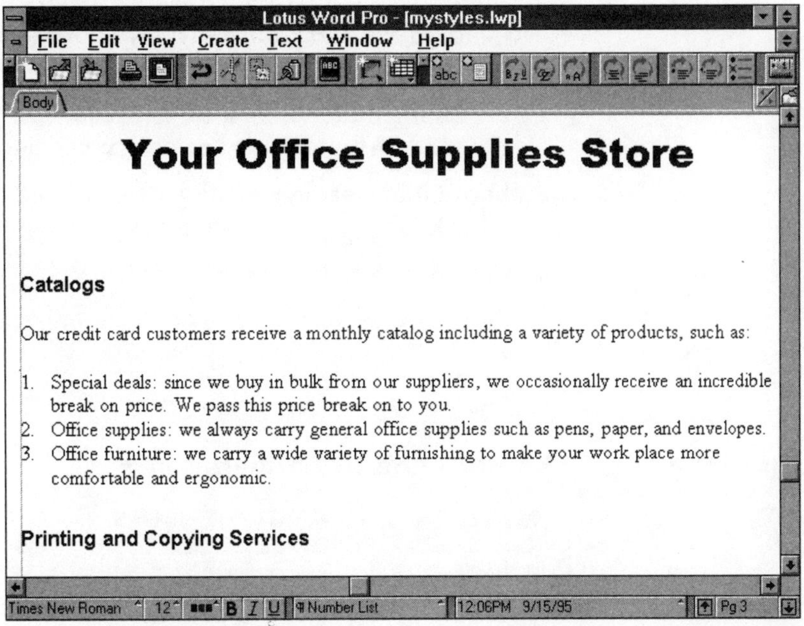

document's paragraphs that has that style assigned. Without styles, you would have to reformat each of those paragraphs manually.

To redefine a style:

- Select a paragraph formatted with the style you want to change.
- Change any text formatting you want. For example, you can change the font, text attributes, the alignment, and/or the line spacing.
- With the paragraph still selected, choose *Text, Named Styles, Redefine* to open the Redefine Styles dialog box.
- Click on *OK* to redefine the style based on the selected paragraph.

Note: By default, style modifications affect only the current document.

Let's redefine the Heading 2 style, and see how it affects paragraphs with that style assigned:

1. Return to the top of the document, and then examine the heading *Introduction*. It displays both the Bold and Italic text attributes.
2. Select **Introduction**. (**Note**: Because we are going to change the text attributes, it is easier if you select the entire word.)
3. Verify that **Heading 2** is the style applied to *Introduction* (check the Style Status button).
4. Change the font's point size to 14 pt.
5. Choose **Text, Named Styles, Redefine** to open the Redefine Style dialog box (see Figure 9.4).

Figure 9.4 **The Redefine Style dialog box**

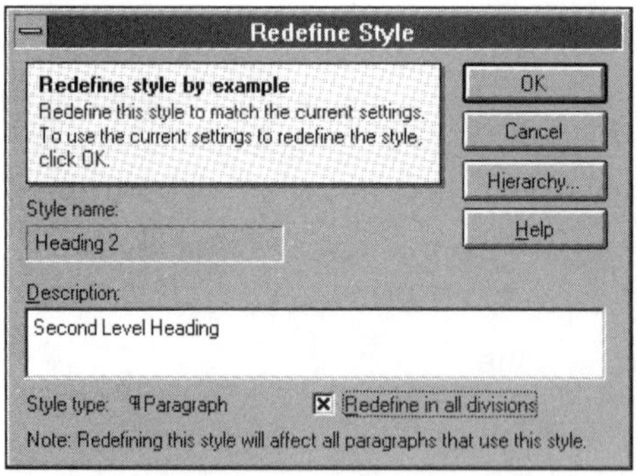

6. Observe the Redefine Style dialog box. Note that:
   - The Style Name box says *Heading 2*. Because you have selected a paragraph with the *Heading 2* style applied to it, Word Pro assumes you want to redefine that style.
   - The Style Type is *Paragraph*. Word Pro allows you to create many types of styles. For more information about other types of styles, see your Word Pro documentation.
   - There is a warning at the bottom of the dialog box, letting you know that if you choose to redefine this style, Word

Pro will reformat, with the new attributes, all paragraphs that use this style.

7. Click on **OK** to redefine the style based on the new attributes for *Introduction*.
8. Scroll down through the document and observe all the other headings with the Heading 2 style. By redefining the Heading 2 style, you have automatically changed the point size of every heading assigned that style.
9. Save MYSTYLES.LWP.

REDEFINING A STYLE'S SPACING

In addition to changing the appearance of text for a style, you can change the appearance of the paragraph. You might decide to change the *paragraph spacing* (the space above and/or below paragraphs). For example, you might use paragraph spacing to add some space before every heading in a document; that way you wouldn't have to keep pressing the Enter key to insert blank lines manually.

Note: Be careful not to confuse *line spacing* with *paragraph spacing*. As you learned in Chapter 5, line spacing determines the vertical distance between lines of text *within* a paragraph. Paragraph spacing, on the other hand, determines the *additional* amount of vertical space *between* paragraphs.

To add or remove space above or below paragraphs that are assigned a particular style:

- Select the paragraph.
- Choose *Text, Text Properties*.
- Click on the *Alignment* tab.
- From the Paragraph Spacing Above and Below boxes, select the desired amount of space.
- Click on the *Styles* tab.
- Click on *Redefine Style*.
- Click on *OK*.

Because Word Pro's title style incorporates paragraph spacing that is not appropriate for MYSTYLES.LWP, let's modify the style and change the paragraph spacing to None.

1. Move to the top of page 1 (press **Ctrl+Home**), and observe the page's two-line heading. There is too much space between the heading's two lines.
2. Choose **Text, Text Properties** to open the Text infobox.
3. Click on the **Alignment** tab to display it (Alignment is the second tab).
4. Observe Paragraph Spacing in the lower-right corner of the tab. Notice that the Above box is set to none, while the Below box is set to two lines. Word Pro defines the Title style as having two lines below each paragraph. This is the style element that is causing the wide gap between the page heading's two lines.
5. From the Paragraph Spacing Below drop-down list, select **None** to remove the extra spacing after the paragraph. Notice that the second line of the heading moves closer to the first line of the heading.
6. Click to display the Style tab (see Figure 9.5). You can use this tab in the Text infobox to control styles.
7. Click on **Redefine Style** to open the Redefine Style dialog box, and click on **OK** to redefine the Title style with no space between paragraphs.
8. Close the Text infobox and observe the two-line heading on page 1. The lines are now closer together and closer to the *Introduction* paragraph (see Figure 9.6).
9. Go to the top of page 3 to verify that the two-line heading there has also changed.

PRACTICE YOUR SKILLS

1. Change the Heading 2 style's Paragraph Spacing Above and Below to *None*.
2. Scroll through the document and verify that you successfully changed the spacing above and below for every paragraph with the Heading 2 style.
3. Save the document.

Figure 9.5 **The Styles tab in the Text infobox**

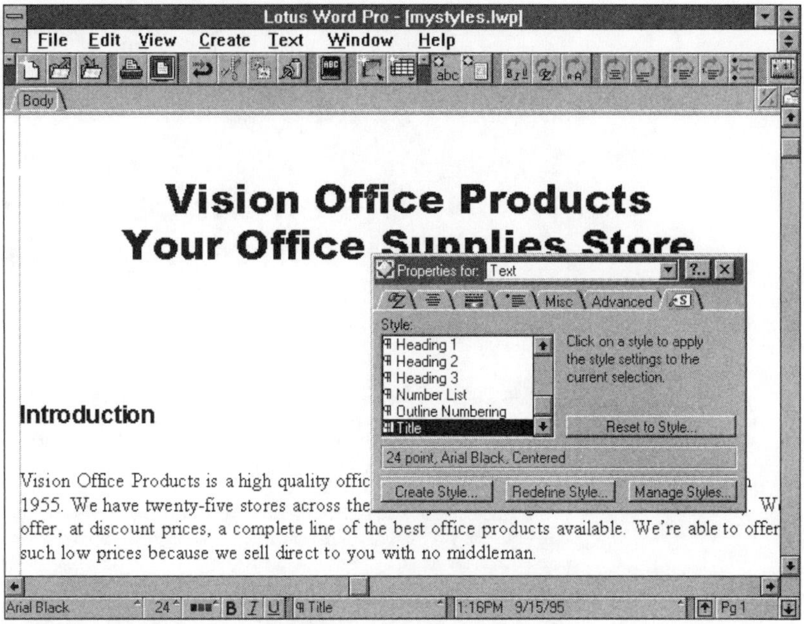

OVERRIDING STYLES

As you've learned, styles affect entire paragraphs at a time. However, you may want (for example) to apply text formatting to only a single word within a paragraph. In this case, you need to *override* the style assigned to that paragraph. You might also decide to override a style when you want to change text enhancements for only one or a few paragraphs within a document, *without* modifying or creating any styles. (You'll learn how to create your own styles later in this chapter.)

Don't think of overriding styles as something new; you've been overriding styles since Chapter 4. Whenever you applied text formatting or enhancements using the Text menu or SmartIcons, you overrode the Default Text style. Think of overriding styles as applying an extra layer of appearance options on top of an existing style. For example, though the Default Text style is set by default to Times New Roman, you can change the font for any paragraph with that style by selecting the entire paragraph and then using the Text, Font & Color command to change the font for

Figure 9.6 **MYSTYLES.LWP, after redefining the Title style**

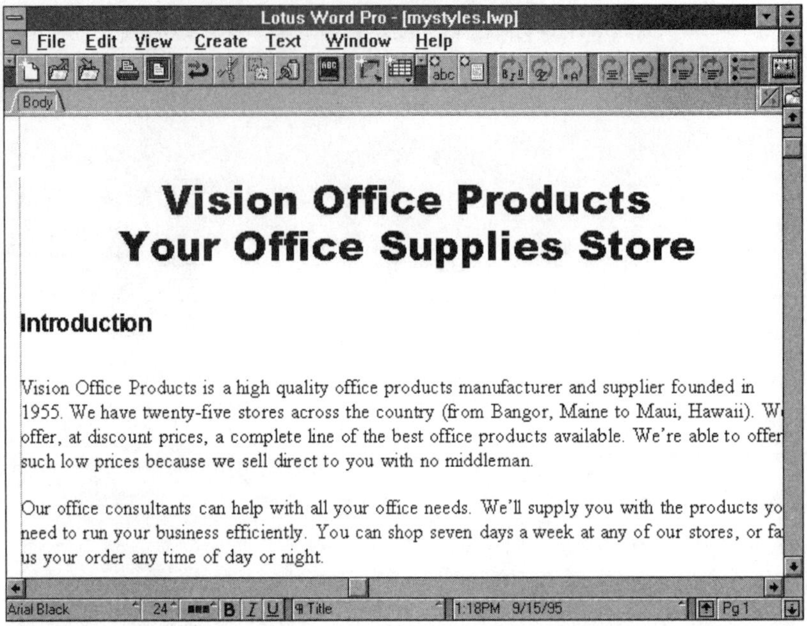

just that paragraph. Overriding a style in one paragraph does not affect any other paragraph with that same style.

Caution: Because text formatting and enhancements act as an extra layer of appearance options on top of a style, they can interfere with paragraph reformatting when you modify a style. For example, if you use the Text, Attributes, Bold command or the Bold Text Status button to apply the Bold text attribute to a paragraph, and then later assign a style that does not incorporate boldface formatting, the paragraph might still display in boldface. To remove the extra layer of boldface formatting, select the entire paragraph and then choose Text, Normal.

Let's override some styles:

1. Scroll to the three numbered paragraphs on page 2, below the heading *Catalogs*.
2. Select **Special deals**, and then click on the **Bold Text Status button** (or choose **Text, Attributes, Bold**). Word Pro applies the Bold text attribute to the selected text, but leaves the rest of the paragraph unchanged.

3. Use the same technique to apply the Bold text attribute to **Office supplies** and **Office furniture** (located in the next two paragraphs).
4. Save your document.

CREATING STYLES

If Word Pro does not provide the styles to meet your exact formatting needs, you can create your own styles. You can design a new style based on the elements of an existing style, or based on the formatting and enhancements of selected text.

CREATING A NEW STYLE BASED ON SELECTED TEXT

Designing a new style based on selected text is called creating a style "by example." For example, if you've underlined, italicized, and centered a heading paragraph, you can create a style based on that paragraph, and then use the style to underline, italicize, and center other headings.

Follow these steps when you want to create a new style based on selected text:

- Select text that displays the appearance elements you want to include in your new style. Regardless of how much text you select, Word Pro will base your style on the appearance elements of the first word in your selection.
- Choose *Text, Named Styles, Create Style* to open the Create Style dialog box.
- In the *Style Name* text box, type a name for your new style. Be sure not to use the name of an existing style.
- Type a description for the style.
- Verify that Style Type is set to *Paragraph*.
- Click on *OK* to create your new style, close the Create Style dialog box, and apply the new style.

To add other style elements that are not included in your selected text,

- Choose *Text, Text Properties*.

- Select the desired elements.
- Click on the *Style* tab.
- Click on *Redefine Style* and click on *OK*.

Let's create a new style now based on selected text:

1. Observe the three headings under *Printing and Copying Services* on page 2: *Copying, Business Forms,* and *Custom Stamps and Stationery* (scroll down, if necessary).
2. Select the entire heading *Copying*.
3. Apply the **Bold** text attribute, and then change the heading's font name to **Arial**.
4. Choose **Text, Named Styles, Create**, and then type **Subhead** in the Style Name text box (see Figure 9.7).
5. Press **Tab** and type **Style for second level headings in this document.** to add a description to the new style.

Figure 9.7 **Creating a style by example**

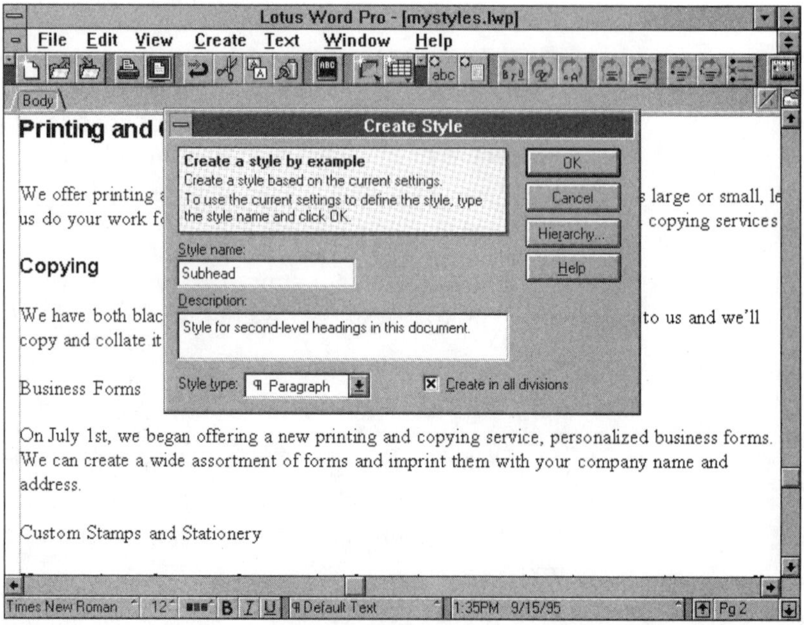

6. Click on **OK** to create the Subhead style, close the Create Style dialog box, and apply Subhead to the *Copying* paragraph.
7. Open and examine the styles list. Notice that Word Pro has added your new style to the list.
8. Assign **Subhead** style to the headings *Business Forms,* and *Custom Stamps and Stationery.*

USING THE STYLE HIERARCHY DEFINITION DIALOG BOX TO INHERIT PROPERTIES

Say you want to create three different heading styles: heading, subheading 1, and subheading 2. You probably want all three heading styles to use the same font; to alleviate boredom, you sometimes want to change the font you use. What a drag it would be to redefine all three heading styles. Fortunately, you don't have to. If you create the Heading style and then base the Subheading 1 and Subheading 2 styles on the Heading style, then you can simply change the font of the Heading style, and Word Pro changes the font for all three styles.

To inherit properties using the Style Hierarchy Definition dialog box:

- Create a base style.
- Select and modify the base style.
- Choose *Text, Named Styles, Create.*
- Type a name and definition for your style.
- Click on *Hierarchy* to open the Style Hierarchy Definition dialog box.
- Check any properties that you do not want to inherit from the base style.
- Click on *OK* twice to close the Style Hierarchy Definition dialog box and the Create Style dialog box.
- Repeat the preceding second through sixth steps as necessary until you've created all the styles you want.

Let's create a new style based on the existing Title style:

1. Move to the top of page 1, and look at the page's two-line heading. This heading might look better if the font size of the second line were smaller.

2. Select the second line of the heading and change the font size to **18** (use the **Size Status button** or the **Text** infobox to change the font size).
3. Choose **Text, Named Styles, Create**, and then type **Title 2** in the Style Name text box.
4. Press **Tab** and type **Style for second line of title.** to add a description to the style.
5. Click on **Hierarchy** to open the Style Hierarchy Definition dialog box (see Figure 9.8).

Figure 9.8 **The Style Hierarchy Definition dialog box**

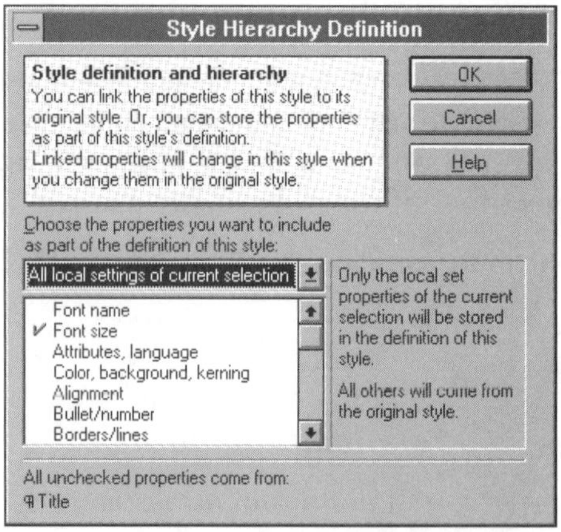

6. In the Properties list, uncheck **Font Name** if necessary and observe the bottom of the dialog box. When you uncheck a property in the list box, Word Pro pulls it from the style upon which the new style is based. In this case, the new style *Title 2* is based on *Title*. Since Font Name is unchecked, Word Pro will always determine the font for *Title 2* style by looking at the font for *Title* style. This makes your life a little easier if you decide to change the font for your two-line heading. We'll change the font for the Title style a little later.
7. Click on **OK** to close the Style Hierarchy Definition dialog box.
8. Click on **OK** to close the Create Style dialog box and apply the new style *Title 2* to the second line of the heading (see Figure 9.9).

9. Assign your Title 2 style to the second line of the two-line heading on the top of page 2.
10. Save MYSTYLES.LWP.
11. Print the document, and then compare it to Figure 9.10.

Figure 9.9 **MYSTLES.LWP, after assigning the Title 2 style**

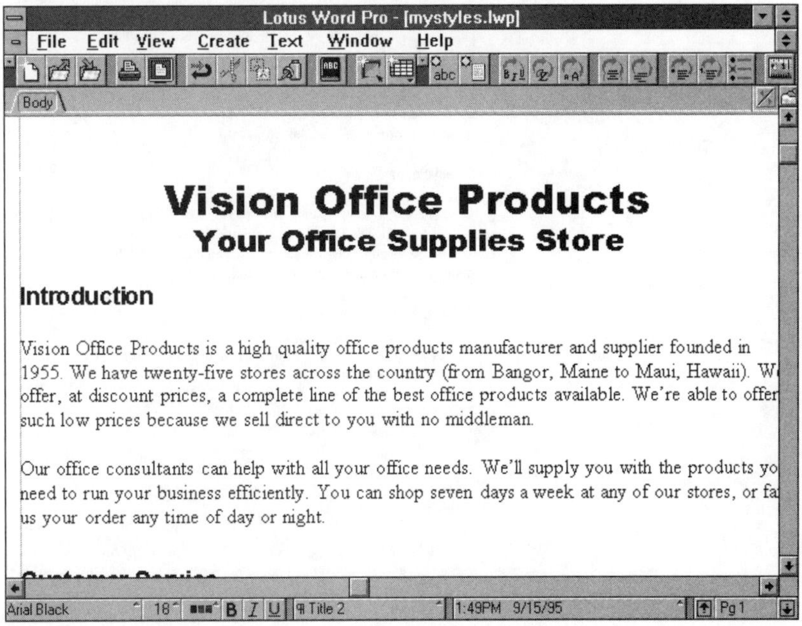

PRACTICE YOUR SKILLS

1. Change the Title styles font to **Times New Roman**. (**Note**: you must redefine the style.)
2. Observe the second line of the heading. The second line of the heading is also Times New Roman. Because you told Word Pro to inherit Title 2 style's font from Title style, Word Pro automatically changed the font of Title 2 style when you changed the font of Title style.
3. Close MYSTYLES.LWP without saving changes.

Figure 9.10 Completed MYSTYLES.LWP

Vision Office Products
Your Office Supplies Store

Introduction

Vision Office Products is a high-quality office products manufacturer and supplier founded in 1955. We have twenty-five stores across the country (from Bangor, Maine to Maui, Hawaii). We offer, at discount prices, a complete line of the best office products available. We're able to offer such low prices because we sell direct to you.

Our office consultants can help with all your office needs. We'll supply you with the products you need to run your business efficiently. You can shop seven days a week at any of our stores, or fax us your order any time of day or night.

Customer Service

We are committed to making your business work. Our expert staff focuses beyond just asking you what you want. We take the guess work our of running a business, by matching your needs and wants with products that help run your business. We'll help you set up a system so the office materials you need are always available.

Office Products

Our office inventory is one of the largest in the country. We carry a variety of products at guaranteed low prices.

* Office supplies
* Business machines
* Furniture
* Computer equipment

Ordering

You can shop at any of our stores or order from one of our three catalogs. Whether you shop in person or by catalog, you can count on experienced and knowledgeable staff to assist you.

If you shop from one of our catalogs, you can phone or fax us your order and we promise to ship it within twenty-four hours.

Figure 9.10 Completed MYSTYLES.LWP (continued)

Vision Office Products
Your Office Supplies Store

Introduction

Vision Office Products is a high-quality office products manufacturer and supplier founded in 1955. We have twenty-five stores across the country (from Bangor, Maine to Maui, Hawaii). We offer, at discount prices, a complete line of the best office products available. We're able to offer such low prices because we sell direct to you.

Our office consultants can help with all your office needs. We'll supply you with the products you need to run your business efficiently. You can shop seven days a week at any of our stores, or fax us your order any time of day or night.

Customer Service

We are committed to making your business work. Our expert staff focuses beyond just asking you what you want. We take the guess work our of running a business, by matching your needs and wants with products that help run your business. We'll help you set up a system so the office materials you need are always available.

Office Products

Our office inventory is one of the largest in the country. We carry a variety of products at guaranteed low prices.

* Office supplies
* Business machines
* Furniture
* Computer equipment

Ordering

You can shop at any of our stores or order from one of our three catalogs. Whether you shop in person or by catalog, you can count on experienced and knowledgeable staff to assist you.

If you shop from one of our catalogs, you can phone or fax us your order and we promise to ship it within twenty-four hours.

COPYING STYLES

When you create a style, it is only available in the document in which you created it. However, you can copy styles from one document to another. To copy a style:

- Open the document to which you want to copy the style.
- Choose *Text, Named Styles, Manage* to open the Manage Styles dialog box. It contains a list of all the styles in the document.
- Click on *Copy From* to open the Copy Styles From dialog box.
- Check *Another File*, if necessary, and click on *Browse*.
- From the List Files of Type box, select *Lotus Word Pro*.
- Select the file that contains the style you want to copy (you might need to change the directory) and click on *OK*.
- Select the Style(s) you want to copy.
- Click on *Copy*. Word Pro closes the Copy Styles From dialog box. The style(s) you copied appear in the Style Name list.
- Click on *Close* to close the Manage Styles dialog box.

Let's open a document and copy the Title 2 style:

1. Open COPYSTYL.LWP and observe the Styles list. Title 2 is not listed in the Styles list because it was not created in this document.
2. Choose **Text, Named Styles, Manage** to open the Manage Styles dialog box (see Figure 9.11). This dialog box lists all of the styles contained in the COPYSTYL.LWP document.
3. Click on **Copy From** to open the Copy Styles From dialog box (see Figure 9.12).
4. Verify that **Another File** is selected, and click on **Browse** to open the Browse dialog box (see Figure 9.13).
5. From the List Files of Type drop-down list, select *Lotus Word Pro*.
6. In the Directories list box, double-click on **Wordpro** and then double-click on **wprowork** to display the files in the WPROWORK directory.

Figure 9.11 The Manage Styles dialog box

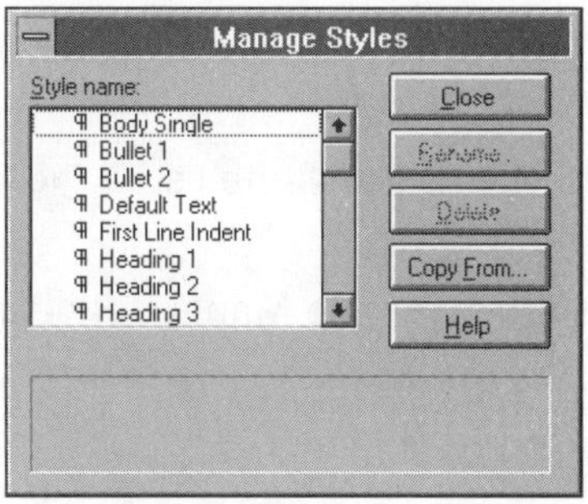

Figure 9.12 The Copy Styles From dialog box

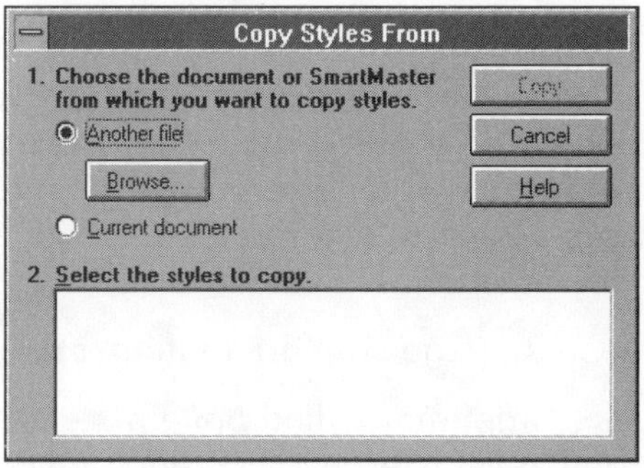

Figure 9.13 The Browse dialog box with MYSTYLES.LWP selected

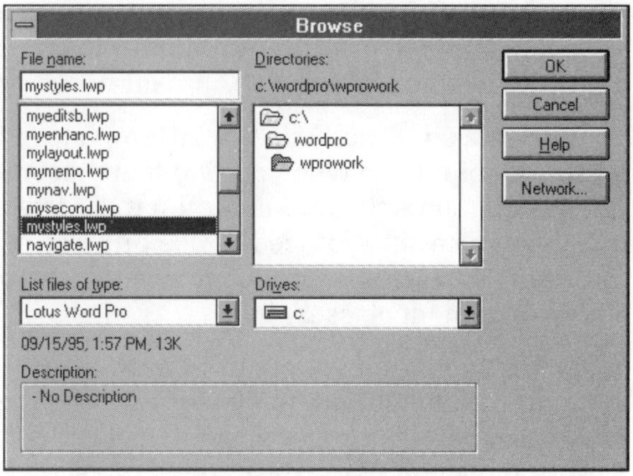

7. Select **mystyles.lwp** and click on **OK** to display a list of the styles stored in MYSTYLES.LWP.
8. In the Select Styles To Copy list, select **Body: Title 2** (you might need to scroll to find it) and click on **Copy**.
9. Scroll through the Style Name list in the Manage Styles dialog box. Title 2 is there.
10. Click on **Close** to close the Manage Styles dialog box.
11. Open the Styles list and note that Title 2 is there.
12. Close the Styles list.
13. Save the file as **mycopy** and close the file.

UNDERSTANDING SMARTMASTERS

You've now learned how to assign, modify, override, and create styles. But where do styles come from? The answer is style sheets called SmartMasters. Each time you create a new document, Word Pro uses a SmartMaster as a source for styles and other document characteristics, including

- *Page layouts*—Page size, orientation, margins, and so on
- *Contents* (sometimes called *boilerplate text*)—Text or other elements, such as letterhead text and/or a company logo, that you want to include in every document that is based on that SmartMaster
- *Macros* (also called *scripts*)—Recorded sets of steps (like small computer programs within Word Pro) that you can run whenever you create a document based on that SmartMaster

You can think of SmartMasters as templates, much like the patterns you might use when cutting fabric or wood. SmartMasters provide elements that are common to a certain class of documents—such as interoffice memos or press releases—and therefore can increase your productivity and promote consistency within document classes.

Word Pro supplies a variety of SmartMasters to help you meet your various document needs, for example, basic letters, appointment calendars, fax cover sheets, mailing labels, memos, press releases, and so on. For a description of each of these SmartMasters, see your Word Pro documentation.

USING SMARTMASTERS

When you create a new document by using the File, New command (you last used this command in Chapter 1), Word Pro requires you to base the new document on a SmartMaster. By default, Word Pro bases new documents on the Default - Most Frequently Used Paragraph Styles SmartMaster; however, you can instruct Word Pro to use any available SmartMaster when creating a new document.

To create a new document and specify a particular SmartMaster:

- Choose *File, New Document* to open the New dialog box.
- Click on *Create From Any SmartMaster* to display other available SmartMasters.
- In the "1. Select A Type Of SmartMaster" box, select a SmartMaster type (for example, fax, memo, or business letter).
- Select a SmartMaster file from the "2. Select A Look" box. Word Pro displays an example of the SmartMaster on the right-hand side of the dialog box.
- Click on OK.

Once you click on OK in the New dialog box, Word Pro creates a new document based on the style sheet you selected. It copies the SmartMaster's page layout, and creates a link between your new document and the SmartMaster to provide access to that SmartMaster's styles.

USING A SMARTMASTER TO CREATE A CALENDAR

Because SmartMasters can incorporate so many elements, they may seem somewhat confusing—that is, until you start to use them. In this next task, we'll create a new document based on one of Word Pro's built-in SmartMasters—Calendar - Monthly, Automated—to create a one-month calendar. This SmartMaster is fairly complex; it has a nonstandard page layout, specialized styles, contents, and a macro. Practicing with it will show you how easy and convenient even the most complex SmartMasters can be. Let's start:

1. Choose **File, New**, and observe the New dialog box. As you saw in Chapter 1, Word Pro normally creates new documents based on the Default SmartMaster.

2. Click on the **Create From Any SmartMaster** to display the tab.
3. Scroll down through the 1. Select A Type Of SmartMaster list box. Word Pro provides SmartMasters for a variety of documents, from calendars and fax cover sheets to forms and letters.
4. Scroll back to the top of the 1. Select A Type Of SmartMaster list box, and then select **Calendar** (see Figure 9.14).

Figure 9.14 **Using the Calendar SmartMaster**

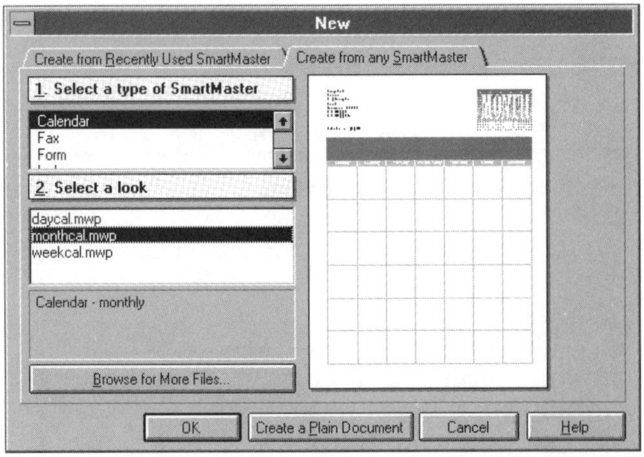

5. Observe the 2. Select A Look list box. Word Pro has SmartMasters to create a daily calendar, a weekly calendar, and a monthly calendar.
6. In the 2. Select A Look list box, select **monthcal.mwp**. Word Pro displays a preview of the SmartMaster on the right side of the dialog box.
7. Click on **OK** to open the new document.
8. After a few moments, Word Pro displays a calendar template in Full Page view and opens a Monthly Calendar dialog box asking you to specify the month and year for your calendar. (If your computer's internal clock is correct, Word Pro automatically selects the current month and year.)

9. In the Month drop-down list box, select **November**.
10. In the Year drop-down list box, select **1996**.
11. Click on **OK**, and you'll see Word Pro build a calendar for November 1996 right on your screen, as shown in Figure 9.15. (If you wanted to, you could now switch to 100% view and fill in appointments on this calendar.)
12. Save the document as **mycalen**, then close MYCALEN.MWP.

Figure 9.15 **The completed calendar**

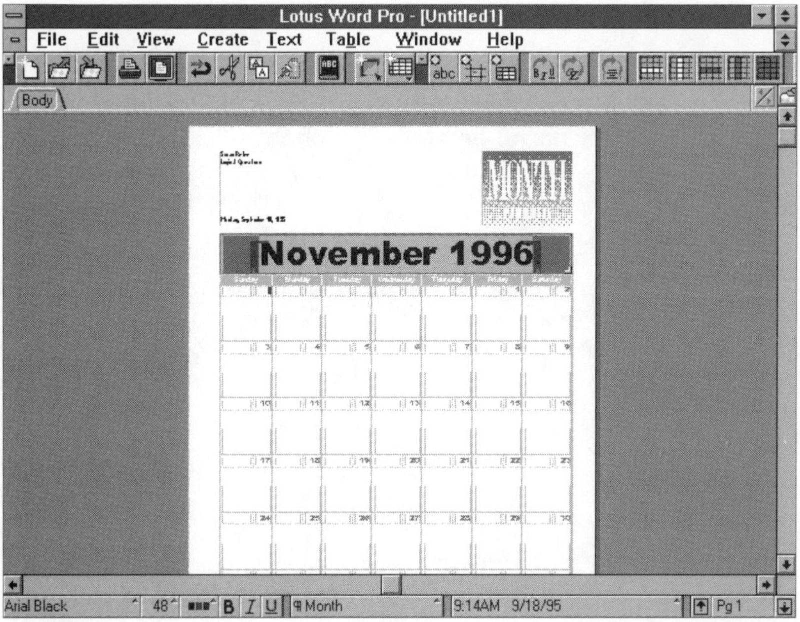

SUMMARY

In this chapter, you learned how to assign styles with the Style Status button and function keys, modify a style's text-formatting and paragraph-spacing elements, create new styles based on selected text and on other styles, and use Word Pro's built-in style sheets.

Here is a quick reference guide to the Word Pro features introduced in this chapter:

Desired Result	How to Do It
Assign style	Select paragraph(s); click on **Style Status button**; select style
Redefine style	Applied desired text formatting and/or enhancements to paragraph with style applied; choose **Text,Named Styles, Redefine**; click on **OK**
Override style	Apply desired text formatting and/or enhancements to selected text
Create new style based on selected text	Select text displaying desired appearance; choose **Text, Named Styles, Create**; type new style name in Style Name text box; type style description in Description text box; click on **Create**
Create new style based on another style	Select base style; choose **Text, Named Styles, Create**; type new style name in Style Name text box; type style description in Description text box; click on **Hierarchy**; change any settings; click on **OK**; click on **Create**
Inherit properties from base style	Create base style; select and modify base style; choose **Text, Named Styles, Create**; type name for new style; type description for new style; click on **Hierarchy**; uncheck any properties you want new style to inherit from base style
Create new document based on nondefault SmartMaster	Choose **File, New**; click on **Create From Any SmartMaster**; select type of SmartMaster; select SmartMaster file from Select A Look box; click on **OK**

In the next chapter, you'll learn how to use tables to arrange text and numbers into rows and columns, and to perform calculations on numbers within tables.

IF YOU'RE STOPPING HERE

If you need to take a break here, please exit Word Pro. If you want to proceed directly to the next chapter, do so now.

CHAPTER 10: WORKING WITH TABLES

Creating Tables

Modifying Tables

Enhancing Tables

Converting Tabbed Text to a Table

A table can be useful for enhancing the presentation of data in your document, for creating side-by-side paragraphs, and for organizing information used in form letters. If you wanted to arrange information in a table, you could do so by setting tabs. However, creating tabbed tables is a slow and tricky process; you must figure out exactly how the table should look, measure the width of each column, and then set tabs that correspond to each measurement. (Recall the tabbed tables in Chapter 5, Figures 5.6 and 5.8). Word Pro's Table feature allows you to create rows and columns of information without having to set tabs. You can even convert tabbed text to a table.

When you're done working through this chapter, you will know

- How to create a table
- How to modify a table
- How to enhance a table
- How to convert tabbed text to a table

CREATING TABLES

To insert a table in your document:

- Place the insertion point where you want to insert the table.
- Choose *Create, Table*, or click on the *Create A Table Grid SmartIcon*.

When you create tables by using the menu command, you specify the number of columns and rows in the Create Table dialog box. You can also specify the size and location of the table. When you use the Create A Table Grid SmartIcon to create tables, you drag on the Create A Table Grid SmartIcon grid to specify the number of columns and rows.

Word Pro creates a table that fills the area inside the margins. The width of the columns adjusts automatically according to the amount of space available between the left and right margins.

A table consists of vertical *columns* and horizontal *rows* (see Figure 10.1). The intersection of a column and a row is called a *cell*. By default, Word Pro places border lines around each cell in the table. If you remove these border lines, you can see light gray lines called *table guides* displayed between the columns. Table guides are for visual reference only; they do not appear when you print the document. (**Note:** You'll learn how to remove border lines later in this chapter.)

You can use the *column guides* to adjust the width of the columns by dragging them left or right. When you place the insertion point in a column, indent markers for that column are displayed in the ruler, enabling you to indent selected text as you desire. (**Note:** You need to display the ruler, first.)

Let's create and examine a table:

1. Open **table.lwp**.

Figure 10.1 Table components

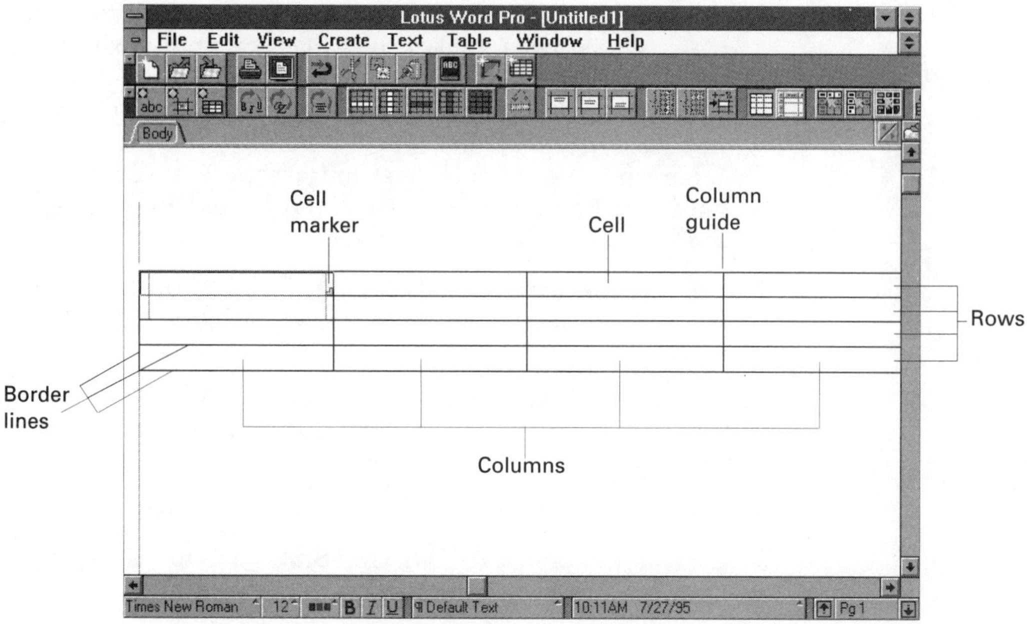

2. Go to page 2 and scroll to place the paragraph that begins *Vision Office Products guarantees* under the heading *Discounts* near the top of the document window. Place the insertion point in the blank line directly above the paragraph that begins *Our quality-control*.

3. Choose **Create, Table** to open the Create Table dialog box, shown in Figure 10.2.

Figure 10.2 The Create Table dialog box

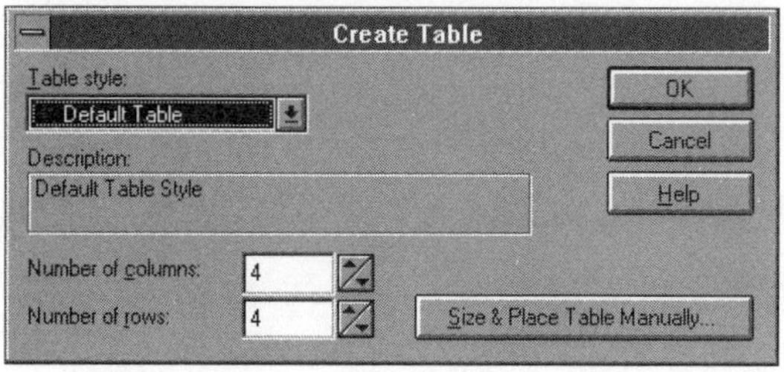

4. Observe the *Table Style* drop-down list box (see Figure 10.2). The default table style creates a table with four rows and four columns that reaches from the left to the right margin. If there is a particular table you always create (for example, a table with five columns and 14 rows), you can create the table once and save it as a table style. Then, anytime you want to create that table, you have simply to choose **Create, Table**, and select that table style from the Table Style drop-down list. For more information about creating table styles, see your Word Pro documentation.
5. Observe the *Number Of Columns* text box. You can change the number of columns by typing a number in the text box or by clicking on the increment indicators.
6. Observe the *Number Of Rows* text box. You can change the number of rows by typing a number in the text box or by clicking on the increment indicators.
7. Click on **Cancel**.
8. Click on the **Create A Table Grid SmartIcon** to display the Create A Table Grid SmartIcon grid.

9. Point to the upper-left corner of the Create A Table Grid SmartIcon grid.
10. Press and hold the mouse button and drag down to select four rows of the grid. Then drag to the right to select two columns of the grid. The bottom of the grid displays *Table: 2 × 4* (see Figure 10.3).
11. Release the mouse button to display the table at the insertion point.
12. Observe the *columns*, which are displayed vertically on the page (see Figure 10.1).
13. Observe the *rows,* which are displayed horizontally on the page.
14. Observe the *cells*, which are the intersections of columns and rows.

Figure 10.3 **Specifying table size in the Create A Table Grid SmartIcon grid**

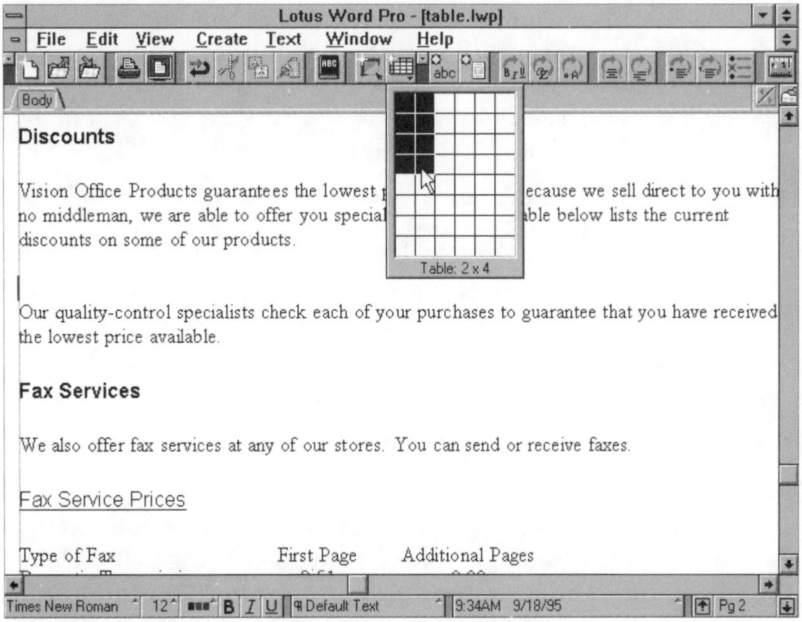

15. Observe the *border lines*, which are the lines around the cells.

16. Observe the *cell marker* in the bottom right corner of the first cell of the table.

DISPLAYING ROW AND COLUMN HEADINGS

When you're working with tables, you might want to display *row and column headings*. Row and column headings act as a road map to Word Pro's row and column identification system: Columns are referred to by letters (A, B, C) with the leftmost column always being A; rows are referenced by numbers (1, 2, 3) with the topmost row always being 1. By combining a specific cell's row and column label, Word Pro provides each cell with a unique *cell address*. For example, the cell at the intersection of column B and row 4 is called "cell B4." (Think of cell addresses as street intersections: "Meet me at the corner of Avenue B and 4th Street.") To keep cell references consistent, Word Pro always refers to a cell first by its column letter, and then by its row number. Thus, the cell address for a cell in column B and row 4 is B4 and never 4B.

When you display row and column headings, Word Pro clearly labels each row and column for you on screen. Word Pro displays row and column headings only when the insertion point or current selection is inside a table. Row and column headings never print; Word Pro displays them on screen for your visual reference only.

To display or hide row and column headings:

- Click on the *Show/Hide Table Headings SmartIcon.*
- Or, choose *View, Set View Preferences*; check or uncheck *Show Table Row/Column Headings*, as appropriate; and click on *OK*.

MOVING A SMARTICONS BAR

As you've probably noticed, some of the SmartIcons change depending upon what you are doing. The Universal SmartIcons bar is always displayed; however, Word Pro has several SmartIcons bars that are context sensitive. (When you work with text, the Text SmartIcons bar is displayed. When you work with Headers, the Headers SmartIcons bar is displayed, and so on.) Because these context-sensitive SmartIcons bars display to the right of the Universal SmartIcons bar, the entire context-sensitive SmartIcons bar may not always fit on your screen. To see all the SmartIcons in a SmartIcons bar, you may need to move the bar. You can move any SmartIcons bar anywhere on the screen.

To move a SmartIcons bar:

- Place the mouse pointer on the lower half of the divider for the SmartIcons bar you want to move. The mouse pointer should display a hand.
- Drag the bar to its new location.

Note: Selecting exactly the right spot on the SmartIcons bar divider is tricky, so don't get discouraged if it takes several tries to get the mouse pointer in the right position.

You can also customize SmartIcons bars so only the SmartIcons you use are displayed. For more information about customizing SmartIcons bars, see your Word Pro documentation.

Let's move the Text In A Table Cell SmartIcons bar and display the row and column headings for the table:

1. Observe the SmartIcons bar. The left half is the Universal SmartIcons bar. This bar contains the universal commands such as New, Open, and Save, and is always displayed (see Figure 10.4).

Figure 10.4 **The SmartIcons bars**

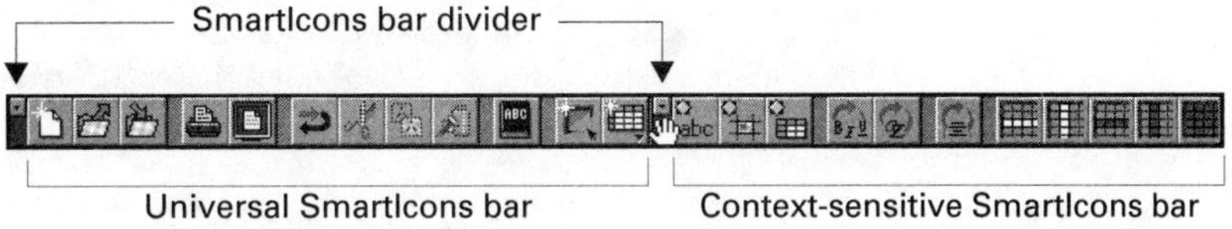

2. Observe the two SmartIcons bars dividers (see Figure 10.4). The one to the left of the Universal SmartIcons bar allows you to move the Universal SmartIcons bar. The divider to the left of the context-sensitive SmartIcons bar (in this case the Text In A Table Cell SmartIcons bar) controls the context-sensitive SmartIcons bar. (**Note:** If the insertion point is not in your table, Word Pro displays a different context-sensitive SmartIcons bar.)
3. Place the tip of the mouse pointer in the space immediately below the divider's down-arrow for the Text In A Table Cell SmartIcons bar. The mouse pointer changes to a hand (see Figure 10.4).
4. Press and hold the mouse button. A dashed line surrounds the SmartIcons bar, indicating that it is selected.
5. Drag down until the dashed outline of the SmartIcons bar expands to fill the width of the screen.

6. Release the mouse button. The Text In A Table Cell SmartIcons bar is displayed below the Universal SmartIcons bar. As you can see from Figure 10.5, there are several more icons that weren't visible when the SmartIcons bars were displayed side-by-side.

Figure 10.5 **Showing row and column headings**

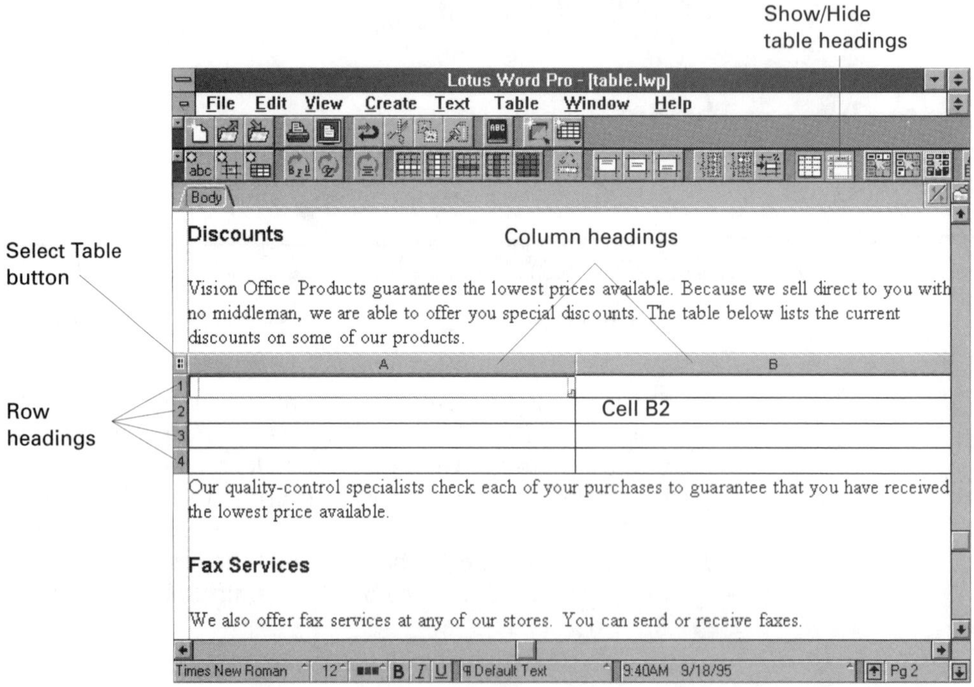

7. Click on the **Show/Hide Table Headings SmartIcon** (near the right end of the SmartIcon bar). Word Pro places letters across the top of the table and puts numbers along the table's left side (see Figure 10.5).

8. Observe the letters at the top of the table (*A* and *B*). These are the column headings; each letter identifies an individual column.

9. Observe the numbers to the left of the table (*1, 2, 3, 4*). These are the row headings; each number identifies an individual row.
10. Observe the intersections of the columns and rows. Each intersection of a column and row is a cell. For example, cell B2 is at the intersection of column B and row 2.
11. Click outside the table. Word Pro displays column and row headings only when the insertion point or the current selection is inside the table. Note that when you click outside the table, Word Pro changes the context-sensitive SmartIcons bar.
12. Click in the table. Word Pro once again displays row and column headings.

MOVING IN A TABLE

You can use the mouse to move to a table cell, or you can use the keyboard. To move to a specific cell using the mouse, simply place the I-beam on the desired cell, and click. Table 10.1 lists the keystrokes used for moving within a table.

Table 10.1 Moving in a Table Using the Keyboard

Desired Result	**How to Do It**
Move one cell to right	Press *Tab*
Move one cell to left	Press *Shift+Tab*
Move up one row	Press *Up Arrow*
Move down one row	Press *Down Arrow*

If the insertion point is in the last cell of a row when you press Tab, the insertion point will move to the first cell in the next row. Likewise, if the insertion point is in the first cell of a row when you press Shift+Tab, it will move to the last cell in the previous row.

Note: If you use the arrow keys on the numeric keypad, Num Lock must be turned off.

Let's practice moving in the table we've created:

1. Click in cell **A1** (the cell at the intersection of column A and row 1) to place the insertion point in that cell.
2. Press **Tab** to move the insertion point to cell B1 (the second column of the first row).
3. Press **Tab** to move the insertion point to cell A2 (the first column in the second row).
4. Press **Shift+Tab** to move back to cell B1.
5. Press **Down Arrow** to move down one row to cell B2.
6. Press **Up Arrow** to move up one row to cell B1.
7. Place the I-beam in cell B4 and click the mouse button to place the insertion point in the last cell.

PRACTICE YOUR SKILLS

Place the insertion point in the first cell of the table.

SELECTING TABLE COMPONENTS

You can select a cell, a row, a column, or the entire table. Table 10.2 lists the methods used for making these selections.

Table 10.2 **Selecting in a Table**

Desired Selection	**How to Do It**
Cell	Place insertion point anywhere within desired cell and choose *Table, Select, Cells* or *Table, Select, Cell Contents*. Or, click on cell's cell marker.

Table 10.2 Selecting in a Table (Continued)

Desired Selection	How to Do It
Row	Place insertion point anywhere within desired row and choose *Table, Select, Row Contents*. Or, click on row heading. (You can also double-click on row heading to select entire row.)
Column	Place insertion point anywhere within desired column and choose *Table, Select, Column Contents*. Or, click on column heading. (You can also double-click on column heading to select entire column.)
Entire table	Place insertion point anywhere within table and choose *Table, Select, Entire Table* or *Table, Select, Entire Table Contents*. Or, double-click on Select Table button (see Figure 10.5).

Let's try various selection techniques within our table:

1. Click on the **cell marker** in the bottom right corner of the first cell in the table to select the cell. Compare your screen to Figure 10.6.
2. Point to the row heading for the first row. The mouse pointer becomes a horizontal arrow.
3. Double-click the mouse button to select the entire row (see Figure 10.7).
4. Point to the column heading for the second column (B), until the mouse pointer becomes a down-arrow. Then double-click to select the entire column (see Figure 10.8).
5. Choose **Table, Select, Entire Table** to select the entire table. Compare your screen to Figure 10.9.
6. Deselect the table (click above or below the table). Notice that when the insertion point is not in the table, the Table menu disappears from the menu bar.

Figure 10.6 **The selected cell**

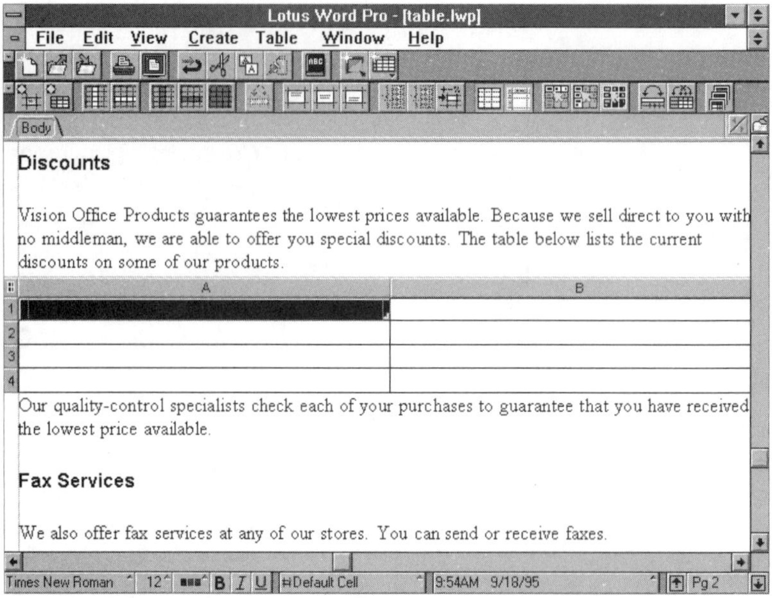

Figure 10.7 **The selected row**

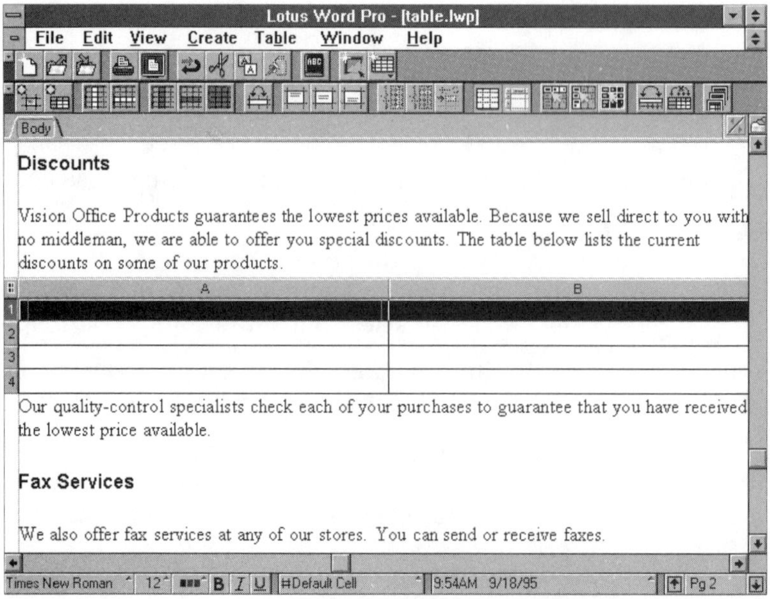

Figure 10.8 **The selected column**

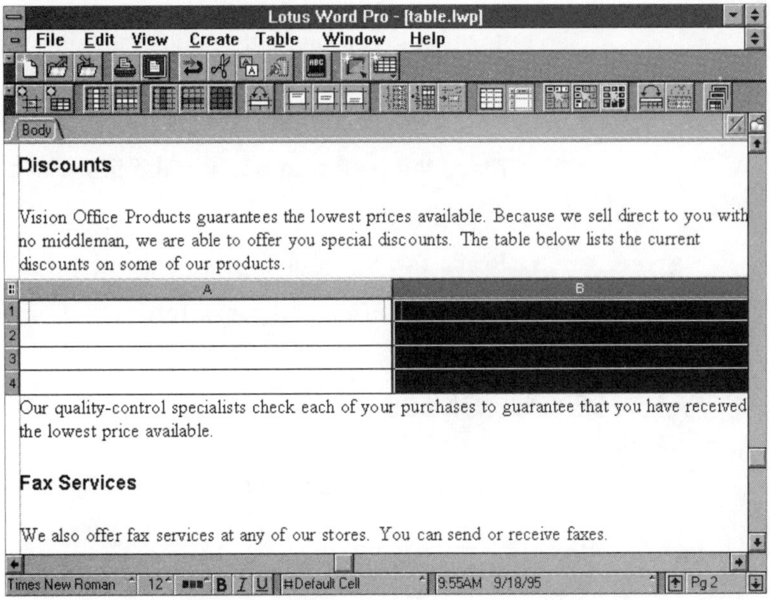

Figure 10.9 **The selected table**

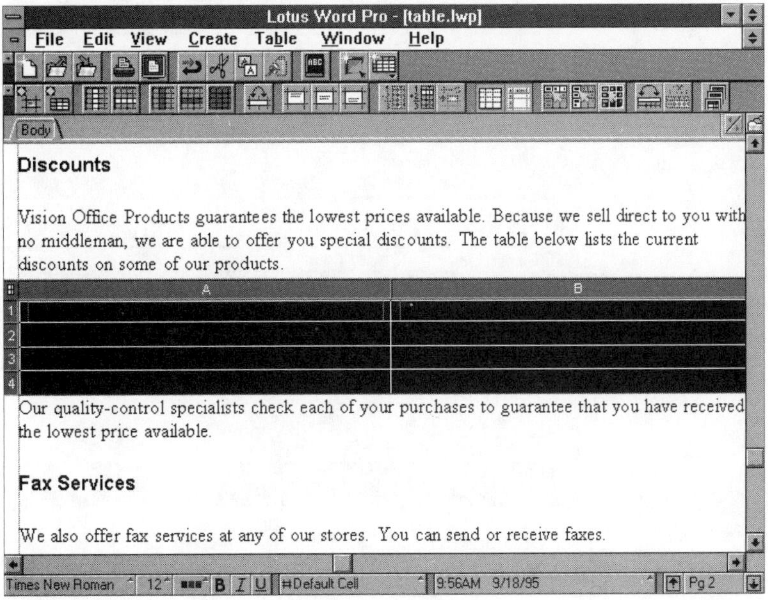

ENTERING TEXT IN A TABLE

To enter text in a table, either select a cell or place the insertion point in the cell; then begin typing.

Let's enter text in our table:

1. Place the insertion point in the first cell of the table (cell A1).
2. Type **Product**.
3. Press **Tab** to move to the next cell.
4. Type **Our Price** and press **Tab**.

PRACTICE YOUR SKILLS

1. Complete the table as shown in Figure 10.10.

Figure 10.10 The completed table

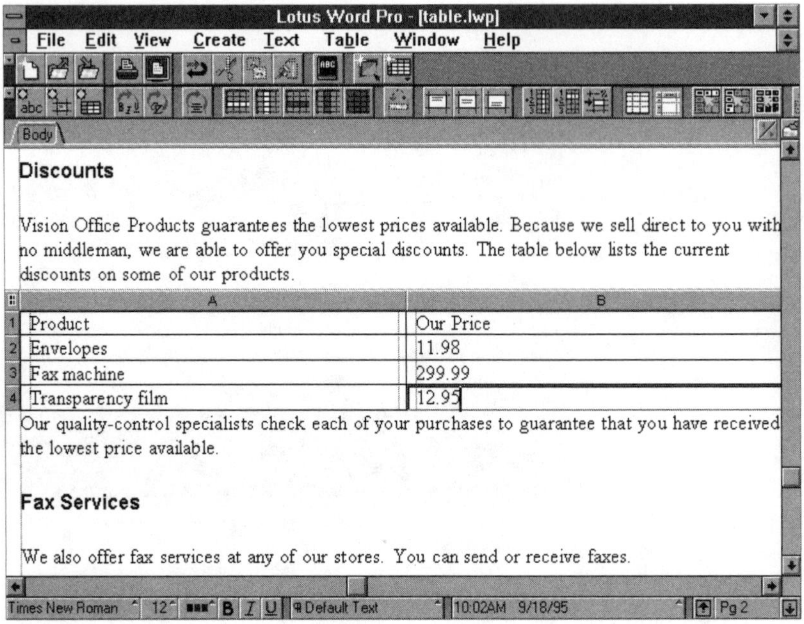

2. Save the file as **mytable**.

MODIFYING TABLES

After you have created your table—even after you have entered all the desired data—you can still change its structure. You can insert rows and columns within the table, add rows to the bottom or columns to the right side of the table, change the width of the columns, and delete rows and columns.

INSERTING ROWS AND COLUMNS

To insert a row at the end of a table, place the insertion point in the last cell of the table and press the Tab key. To insert a row *within* a table, select the row where you want to insert the new row (the new row will be inserted below the selected row) and choose *Table, Insert, Row,* or click on the *Insert Row In A Table* SmartIcon. To insert more than one row in a table, select the row where you want to insert the new rows (by default, the new rows will be inserted after the selected row) and choose *Table, Insert, Row/Column*. Then, set the number of rows you want to insert and click on OK.

To insert a column within a table, select the column where you want to insert a new column (the new column will be inserted to the right of the selected column); then choose *Table, Insert, Column* or click on the *Insert Column In A Table* SmartIcon. To insert more than one column, select a column and use the *Table, Insert, Row/Column* command to set the number of columns you want to insert.

Let's insert rows and columns in our table:

1. Verify that the insertion point is in the last cell of the table.
2. Press the **Tab** key. Voilà! A new row is inserted at the end of the table.
3. Type **Copier paper** and press **Tab**.
4. Type **33.01**.
5. Select the first row of the table, and choose **Table, Insert, Row/Column** to open the Row/Column dialog box.
6. Select the text in the Number To Insert text box, type **2**, and click on **OK** to insert two rows below the selected row. Compare your screen to Figure 10.11.

Figure 10.11 **The inserted rows**

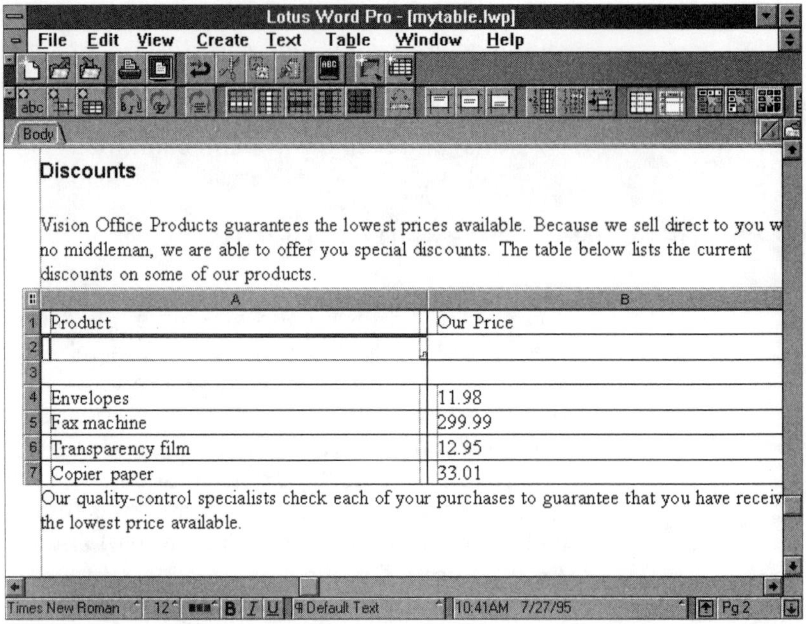

7. Select the entire first column (click on the column heading).
8. Click on the **Insert Column In A Table SmartIcon**, and then compare your screen to Figure 10.12.

PRACTICE YOUR SKILLS

1. Insert a column after the third column in the table.
2. In the first row of the second column, enter the heading **Standard Price.**
3. Complete the second column as shown in Figure 10.13.
4. In the first row of the fourth column, enter the heading **Savings.**
5. Complete the fourth column as shown in Figure 10.13.
6. Save the file.

Figure 10.12 The inserted column

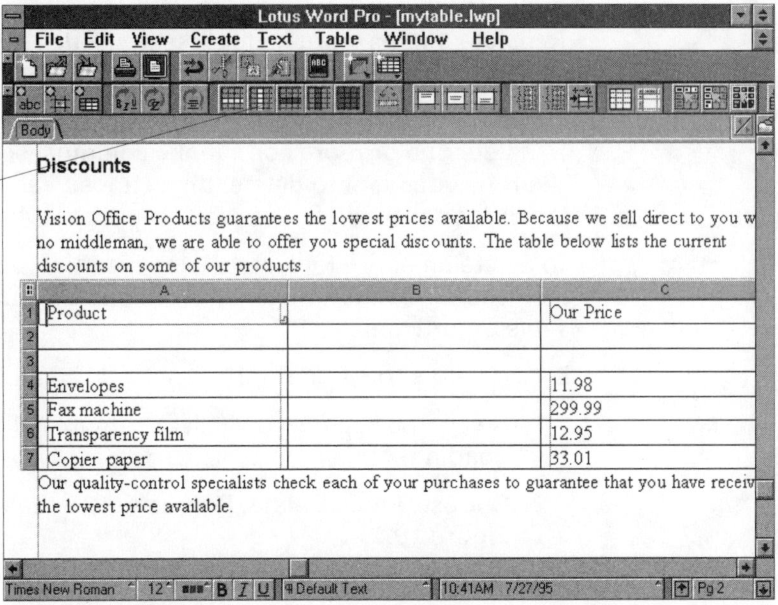

Figure 10.13 The data entered in the second column

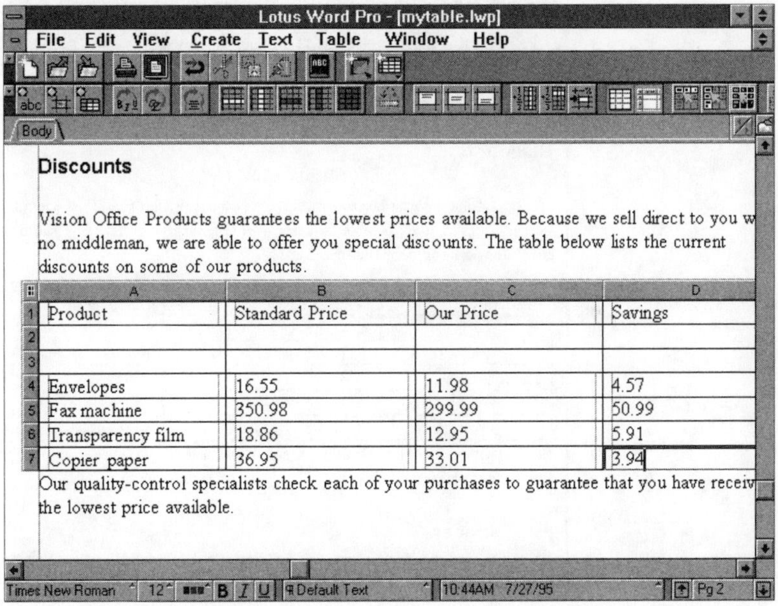

DELETING ROWS, COLUMNS, AND ENTIRE TABLES

To delete one or more contiguous rows in a table, select the row or rows that you want to delete; then choose *Table, Delete, Row*. Or, click on the *Delete Selected Rows In A Table* SmartIcon.

To delete one or more contiguous columns, select the column or columns you want to delete; then choose *Table, Delete, Column*. Or, click on the *Delete Selected Columns In A Table* SmartIcon.

To delete an entire table, place the insertion point in the table; then choose *Table, Delete, Entire Table*. Or, click on the *Delete Table* SmartIcon.

Let's delete a row in our table:

1. Select the second row (click or double-click on the row heading).
2. Choose **Table, Delete, Row** to delete the selected row (see Figure 10.14).

Figure 10.14 The table after deleting a row

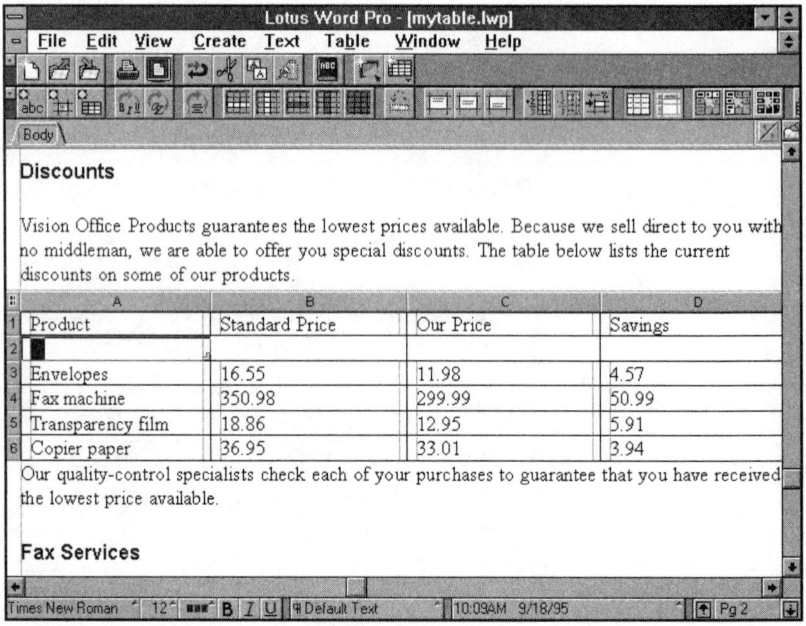

CHANGING COLUMN WIDTH

To change column width by dragging column guides:

- Point to the column guide (the border lines display over the guide lines) you want to move; the mouse pointer will become a horizontal, double-headed arrow.
- Press and hold the mouse button.
- Drag the column guide to the desired location.
- Release the mouse button.

To change column width by using the menu:

- Select the desired column (or the entire table).
- Choose *Table, Size Row/Column*.
- Set the appropriate width in the Column Dimensions Width text box.
- Press Enter.
- Close the Table Cell infobox.

Let's try changing the width of columns in our table:

1. Point to the column border between the *Product* and *Standard Price* headings. The mouse becomes a double-headed arrow.
2. Press and hold the mouse button, and drag the column border to the left until it is just to the right of *Transparency film*. This decreases the width of the first column. Release the mouse button. The second column is now wider.
3. Select the second column and choose **Table, Size Row/Column** to open the Table Cell infobox to the Size Row/Column tab (see Figure 10.15).
4. Select the Column Dimensions Width text box, type **1.25**, and press **Enter** to change the width of the second column to 1.25 inches.
5. Select the third column and change the width to **1.25**. (**Note**: You might need to move the Table Cell infobox out of the way.)

Figure 10.15 **The Size Row/Column tab of the Table Cell infobox**

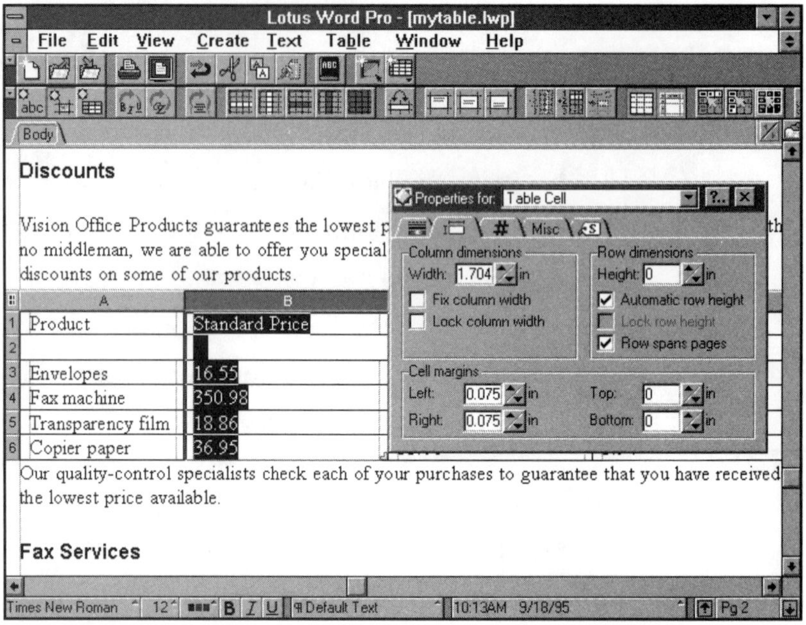

PRACTICE YOUR SKILLS

1. Change the width of the fourth column to **1.25**. (**Note**: don't panic if it appears the width of the fourth column doesn't change. As you'll see later, it really does change.)
2. Close the Table Cell infobox.

ENHANCING TABLES

You already know how to enhance text in your document; doing so can improve its appearance and often its readability. By accentuating important text, you help the reader to locate these reference points. The same text enhancements that are available in standard document text are also available when working in tables, including, for example, bold and italic text attributes, changes in font and font size, and text alignment within a cell. In addition, you can alter the alignment of the entire table relative to the margins you're using. You can apply any font formats to text within a table. You can also enhance a table by adding a border around the table or changing or removing the cell border lines.

ALIGNING A TABLE

To align a table between the left and right margins:

- Select the entire table.
- Choose *Table, Alignment* and select the desired alignment.

Let's format and align text in our table, and then center the table between the left and right margins:

1. Select the first row, which contains the column headings.
2. Make all of the text in the first row bold.
3. Select the entire second column, and then drag (within the table) to select the third and fourth columns. The second through fourth columns are now selected.
4. Choose **Text, Alignment, Right** to right-align the selected text.
5. Select the entire table. Then choose **Table, Alignment, Center Table** to center the table between the left and right margins. Click anywhere in the table and compare your table to that shown in Figure 10.16.
6. Save the file.

ADDING AND CHANGING BORDERS

To add a border around the outside of the table:

- Select the entire table.
- Choose *Table, Table Properties*.
- Click on the Lines Around Table button you want.
- Set any other line and color options you want. For more information about the options on the Lines & Fill Color tab, refer to your Word Pro documentation.
- Close the Table infobox.

Figure 10.16 **The centered table**

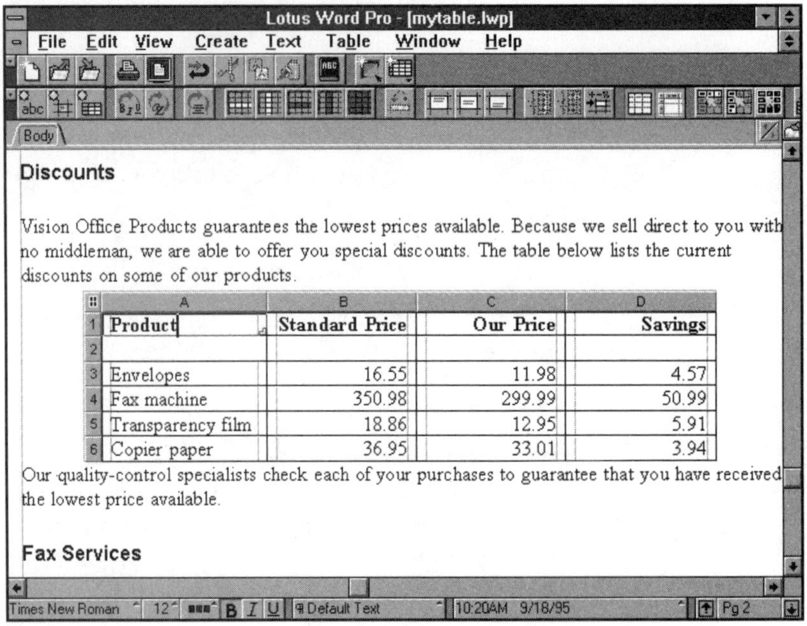

To change border lines around cells:

- Select the entire table.
- Choose *Table, Cell Properties*.
- Click on the Lines Around Cells option you want. (**Note:** To remove the border lines, click on the first Lines Around Cells button. Word Pro will remove the border lines and show grid lines that display on screen, but do not print.)
- Set any other line and color options.
- Close the Table Cell infobox.

Let's add a border around our table:

1. Select the entire table.
2. Choose **Table, Table Properties** to open the Table infobox to the Lines & Fill Color tab (see Figure 10.17).
3. In the Lines Around Table list, click on the last option (a shadowed rectangle with rounded corners).

Figure 10.17 **Selecting a table border**

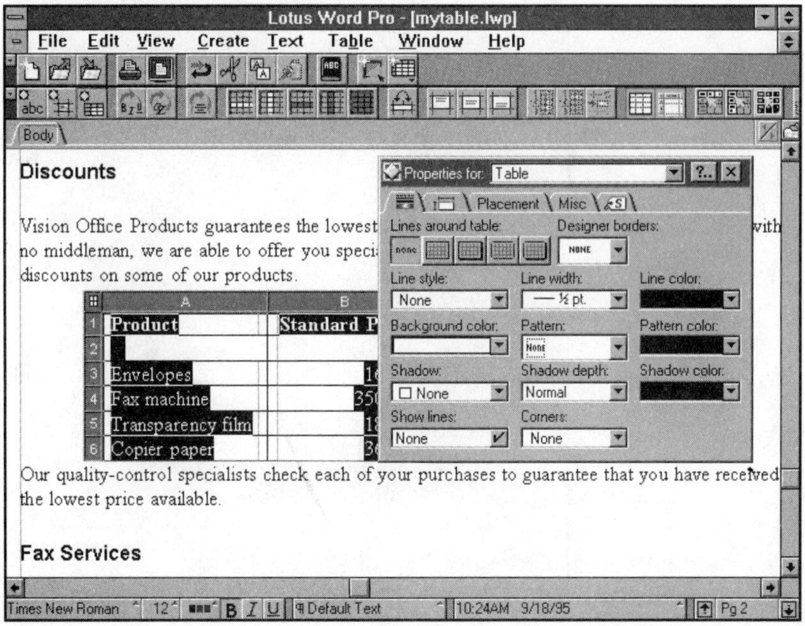

4. Observe the table. The drop-shadow rounded rectangle is displayed around the table.
5. Close the Table infobox. Deselect the table. Notice that the selected border is displayed around the table. However, the border lines around the cells make the table look cluttered.
6. Select the entire table.
7. Choose **Table, Cell Properties** to open the Lines & Color tab of the Table Cell infobox (see Figure 10.18).
8. Click on the first button in the Lines Around Cells list to remove the border lines from the cells in the table.
9. Close the Table Cell infobox. Deselect the table and notice that the solid border lines are gone and you can see dotted grid lines or *guides* around each cell in the table. These guides do not print. (**Note:** Where the guides and the table border overlap, you may see only the guides. Don't worry, the border will print. If you want to turn off the table guides, simply click on the **Show/Hide Table Grid Lines SmartIcon**.)

Figure 10.18 Removing border lines around cells

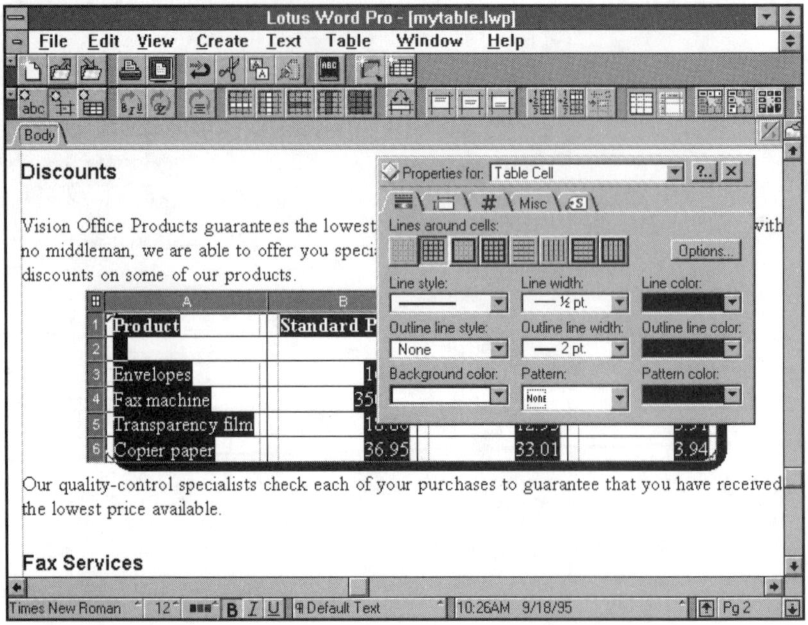

10. Click on the **Show/Hide Table Headings SmartIcon** to hide the row and column headings. (**Note:** If you clicked outside the table to deselect it, you will need to click in the table to display the Text In A Table Cell SmartIcons bar again.)

CONVERTING TABBED TEXT TO A TABLE

Word Pro enables you to convert a tabbed table created by inserting tabs between columns of text into an actual table consisting of cells, rows, and columns. To convert tabbed text to a table:

- Select the text that you want to convert to a table.
- Choose *Create, Table.*
- Click on *Yes.*

Let's convert tabbed text to a table:

1. Scroll to place the heading *Fax Service Prices* (at the bottom of page 2), at the top of the screen.

2. Observe the tabbed table.
3. Select all of the lines in the tabbed table from *Type of Fax* to *Receptions*, that will be placed in the table. (**Note:** You must select *all* of each line you want to convert.) Notice that our tabbed table consists of three columns of information in four rows. We'll retain this structure.
4. Choose **Create, Table**. A message box opens asking if you want to convert the selected text to a table (see Figure 10.19).

Figure 10.19 The message box

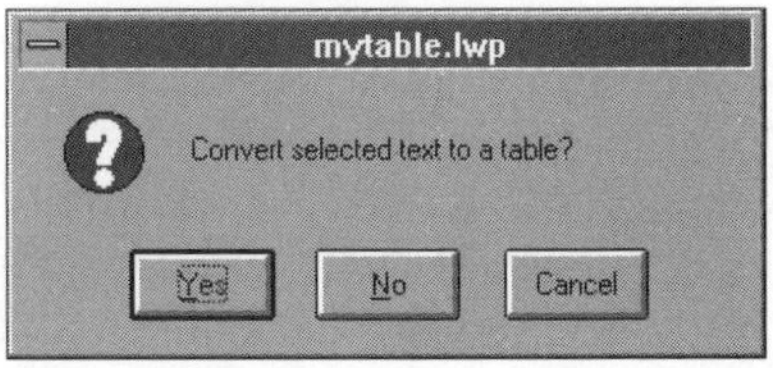

5. Click on **Yes**. The selected text appears in a table. Notice that the column widths need some adjustment.
6. Select the entire table. Then choose **Table, Size Row/Column** to open the Size Row/Column tab of the Table Cell infobox.
7. In the Column Dimensions Width text box, type **1.5** to set the width of all the columns to 1.5", and press **Enter**. The table now consists of three equally sized columns, although they may not yet appear to be equally sized.
8. Close the Table Cell infobox and deselect the table.

PRACTICE YOUR SKILLS

1. Right-align all the information in columns 2 and 3.
2. Center the table between the left and right margins.
3. Save the file and compare your screen to Figure 10.20.
4. Close the document.

Figure 10.20 **The converted table**

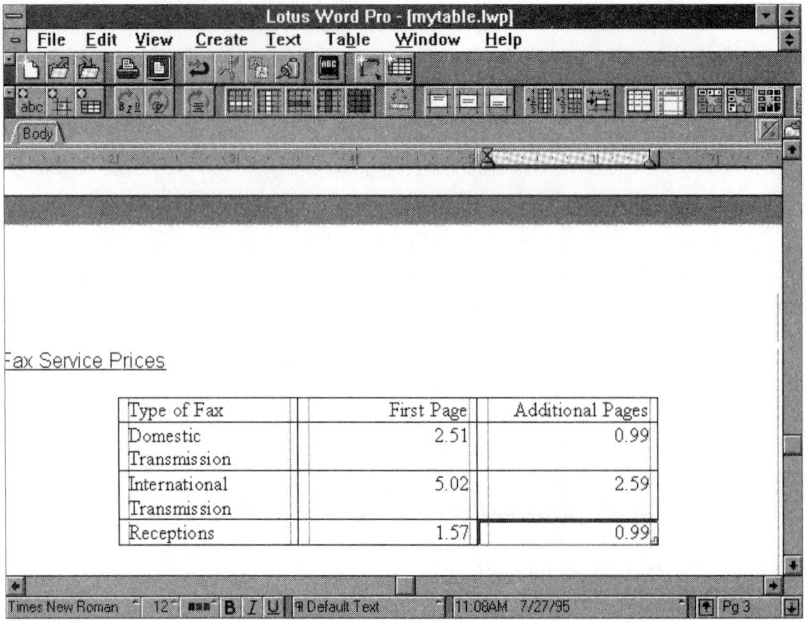

PRACTICE YOUR SKILLS

This exercise gives you the opportunity to practice the skills you just learned. The following instructions lead you through the steps necessary to edit the disk file PRAC10A.LWP to produce the document in Figure 10.21.

1. Open **prac10a.lwp** (Chapter 2).
2. Display table headings for the *Projected Quarterly Sales* table.
3. Type the following information into the table titled *Projected Quarterly Sales* :

Figure 10.21 The completed MYPRAC10A.LWP document

The Garden Patch
Product Line Announcement

Introduction

The Garden Patch is pleased to announce the unveiling of a new food line in the Garden Patch series: the Fruit Patch. The Fruit Patch product line was developed after two years of intense work through the cooperation and dedication of Dr. Faye Shad and her staff. The FDA recently approved the food and it will be released for public sale in three weeks.

The Fruit Patch includes a variety of organically grown fruit: berries (cherries, strawberries, raspberries, blackberries, and blueberries), apricots, peaches, grapes, and plums.

Projected Quarterly Sales

Our finance department has been hard at work, determining sales projections for the next quarter. The results are shown in the following table.

Projected Quarterly Sales

Vendors	Boxes Sold	Profit (per box)
Trader Tom's	2300	1.49
Aunt Emily's Market	4900	1.29
Hamlet Farms	6500	1.29
B and Js	10000	.79
Hout and Wallace Inc.	11500	.79

Row 3:	**Trader Tom's**	**2300**	**1.49**
Row 4:	**Aunt Emily's Market**	**4900**	**1.29**
Row 5:	**Hamlet Farms**	**6500**	**1.29**

4. Delete the row that contains information for *Price Farms*.
5. Right-align the text in the second and third columns.
6. Change the column width for the *Boxes Sold* column to **1"**.
7. Change the column width for *Profit (per box)* to **1.25"**.
8. Center the table on the page.
9. Save the file as **mypr10a** (Chapter 1).
10. Print the document and compare it to Figure 10.21 (Chapter 1).
11. Close the document (Chapter 1).

If you have finished the first activity, you might like to try a more challenging one requiring similar skills. In the next activity you will edit PRAC10B.LWP to create the document shown in Figure 10.22.

1. Open **prac10b.lwp** (Chapter 2).
2. Below the centered *Projected Quarterly Sales* heading, create a table that contains three columns and five rows.
3. Enter the data as shown in Figure 10.22.
4. Make the column headings in the first row bold.
5. Right-align the text in the second and third columns.
6. Decrease the column width for the second and third columns to **1.5"**.
7. Center the table on the page.
8. Remove the border lines from each cell in the table.
9. Add a border around the outside of the table.
10. Save the file as **mypr10b** (Chapter 2).
11. Print the document and compare it to Figure 10.22 (Chapter 1).
12. Close the document (Chapter 1).

Figure 10.22 The completed MYPR10B.LWP document

The Garden Patch
Product Line Announcement

Introduction

The Garden Patch is pleased to announce the unveiling of a new food line in the Garden Patch series: the Fruit Patch. The Fruit Patch product line was developed after two years of intense work through the cooperation and dedication of Dr. Faye Shad and her staff. The FDA recently approved the food and it will be released for public sale in three weeks.

The Fruit Patch includes a variety of organically grown fruit: berries (cherries, strawberries, raspberries, blackberries, and blueberries), apricots, peaches, grapes, and plums.

Projected Quarterly Sales

Our finance department has been hard at work, determining sales projections for the next quarter. The results are shown in the following table.

Projected Quarterly Sales

Vendors	**Boxes Sold**	**Total Profits**
Trader Tom's	2,300	3,427.37
Aunt Emily's Market	4,900	6,321.25
Hamlet Farms	6,500	7,085.98

SUMMARY

In this chapter, you learned how to create tables using the Create, Table command or the Create A Table Grid SmartIcon. You learned how to move within a table; how to select cells, rows, columns, and the entire table; and how to enter data in a table. You also learned how to insert and delete rows and columns, how to change column width, how to change the alignment of a table between the left and right margins, and how to enhance the appearance of a table by creating various types of borders. Finally, you learned how to convert tabbed text to a table.

Here is a quick reference guide to the Word Pro features introduced in this chapter:

Desired Result	How to Do It
Create table using menu	Choose **Create, Table**; type desired number of columns in Number Of Columns text box; type number of rows in Number Of Rows text box; click on **OK**
Create table using Universal SmartIcons bar	Click on **Create A Table Grid SmartIcon**; drag to select boxes of grid corresponding to desired number of rows and columns; release mouse button
Move SmartIcons bar	Place mouse pointer below down-arrow in divider of bar you want to move; drag to new location
Display row and column headings	Click on **Show/Hide Table Headings SmartIcon**; or choose **View, Set View Perferences**, check **Show Table/Col. Headings**, and click on **OK**.
Display or Hide table grid (guide) lines	Click on **Show/Hide Table Grid Lines SmartIcon**; or choose **View, Set View Perferences**, check **Show Table Guides**, and click on **OK**.
Move within table using mouse	Place I-beam on desired cell; click mouse button

Desired Result	How to Do It
Move within table using keyboard:	
Move one cell to right	Press **Tab**
Move one cell to left	Press **Shift+Tab**
Move up one row	Press **Up Arrow**
Move down one row	Press **Down Arrow**
Select cell	Click on cell's cell marker
Select row	Click the mouse button on the row heading. Or, place the insertion point in the row and choose **Table, Select, Row Contents**
Select column	Click mouse button on column heading. Or, place insertion point in column and choose **Table, Select, Column Contents**
Select entire table	Place insertion point in table; choose **Table, Select, Entire Table**
Add row end of table	Place insertion point in last cell of table; press **Tab**
Insert row within table	Select row after which you want to insert new row; choose **Table, Insert, Row**, or click on **Insert Row In A Table SmartIcon**
Insert more than one row in table	Select row after which you want to insert new rows; choose **Table, Insert Row/Column**; set number of rows; click on **OK**

Desired Result	**How to Do It**
Insert column within table	Select column to left of where you want to insert new column; choose **Table, Insert, Column** or click on **Insert Column In A Table SmartIcon**
Insert more than one column within table	Select column to left of where you want to insert new columns; choose **Table, Insert, Row/Column**; set number of columns; click on **OK**
Delete one or more rows	Select row or rows you want to delete; choose **Table, Delete, Row**
Delete one or more columns	Select column or columns you want to delete; choose **Table, Delete, Column**
Delete entire table	Place insertion point in table; choose **Table, Delete, Entire Table**
Change column width by dragging column guides	Point to column guide you want to move until the mouse pointer becomes horizontal, double-headed arrow; drag column guide to desired location; release mouse button
Change column width by using menu	Select desired column (or entire table); choose **Table, Size Row/Column**; type desired width in Width text box; close Table Cell infobox
Align table between left and right margins	Select entire table; choose **Table, Alignment** and select desired alignment
Create table border	Select table; choose **Table, Table Properties**; select options you want; close Table infobox
Change cell border lines	Select cell(s); choose **Table, Cell Properties**; select desired options; close Table Cell infobox

Desired Result	How to Do It
Convert tabbed text to table	Select tabbed text you want to convert to table; choose **Create, Table**; click on **Yes**

In the next chapter, you will learn how to use Word Pro to create form letters, labels, and envelopes.

IF YOU'RE STOPPING HERE

If you need to take a break here, please exit Word Pro. If you want to proceed directly to the next chapter, please do so now.

CHAPTER 11: FORM LETTERS, LABELS, AND ENVELOPES

The Components of a Merge Operation

Creating Form Letters

Creating Mailing Labels

Creating an Envelope

In Word Pro, *merging* (also known as *mail-merging*) is the process of combining information from two different documents to create customized printed documents. For example, you can merge a generic form letter together with a mailing list to produce a personalized form letter for each person on the list (just as the people who send you those $1,000,000 contest announcement letters do). Merging helps you avoid the tedium of manually generating many personalized letters. Other common uses for merging include creating mailing labels and personalizing interoffice memos and reports.

Word Pro's Text, Merge command helps to take you step by step through the merging process.

For simple addressing when you're sending out a single letter, Word Pro also enables you to print a single envelope based on the letter's inside address.

When you're done working through this chapter, you will know how to

- Create and edit the two component documents of a merge
- Use merging to generate form letters
- Sort merge data
- Create a single envelope

THE COMPONENTS OF A MERGE OPERATION

Before using Word Pro's Text, Merge command, you should be familiar with the three components of the merge process: the *merge data file*, the *merge document*, and the *merged documents*. Figure 11.1 illustrates how these three components work together.

THE MERGE DATA FILE

The *merge data file* contains the variable information (you can use the terms *information* and *data* interchangeably) with which you will personalize the merged documents. Very often, a merge data file contains a list of names and addresses. Every merge data file contains three vital elements:

- *Fields*, which are categories of data. For example, you might put everyone's first name in a first-name field and everyone's last name in a last-name field.
- *Field names*, which identify each field. For example, you might use the field name *First Name* to identify the first-name field.
- *Records*, each of which contains a complete set of fields for a person or other subject. For example, one record in a name-and-address merge data file might contain one person's first name, last name, company name, street address, city, state, and zip code.

If you use the Text, Merge command to create and edit your merge data files, Word Pro enables you to work with your merge data on electronic index cards, which look very much like the

Figure 11.1 The components of a merge

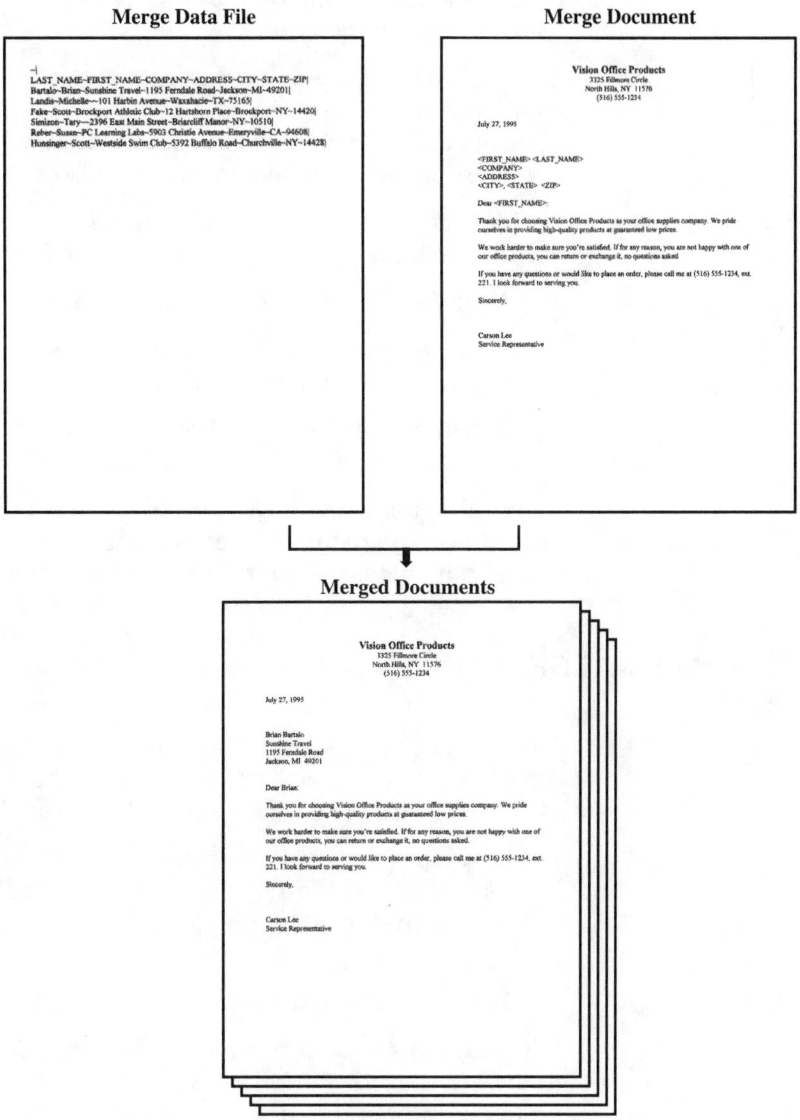

rotary card-files that many of us use to organize our name-and-address data. For each record in your merge data file, Word Pro displays a corresponding index card that contains the data for every field in that record.

Like their paper-based counterparts, these electronic index cards even come complete with *tab dividers* that stick up from the top of each card to help you identify it when it is behind other cards. For example, a tab divider for Igor Bonski's card might say *Bonski*.

Besides using merge data files created through Text, Merge, you can also use the following as merge data files:

- Word Pro documents that contain tables
- Files created by database and spreadsheet applications, such as 1-2-3 for Windows or dBase
- Documents created in other word processing applications, such as Word for Windows or WordPerfect

In this chapter, we'll show you how to use Text, Merge to create and edit merge data files. For information on using other types of merge data files, see your Word Pro documentation.

THE MERGE DOCUMENT

The *merge document* contains the *standardized* (nonvariable) data in a merge, as well as *merge fields* that serve as placeholders for the variable data stored in the merge data file.

Merge documents for form letters can look a lot like fill-in-the-blanks forms, and Word Pro essentially uses them that way. For example, a merge document for a form letter might start out like this:

```
Dear <FIRST_NAME>:
```

In this example, *Dear*, the space following *Dear*, and the colon following *<FIRST_NAME>* are all standardized text; they'll print on every merged document, regardless of the data contained in the merge data file. *<FIRST_NAME>*, on the other hand, is a merge field that Word Pro will see as a "blank" to be filled in; when merging, Word Pro will look in the merge data file to find the personalized data to replace this merge field. After merging, the above example might print as:

```
Dear Carol:
```

or

```
Dear Michael:
```

By default, Word Pro prints one personalized merged document for every record in a merge data file.

THE MERGED DOCUMENTS

When performing a merge, you can send the resulting merged documents directly to the printer, pause to view each merged document before printing, or save all the merged documents together on disk as a single Word Pro document.

Tip: Because you usually can re-create your merged documents by performing another merge, you should in most cases avoid saving your merged documents. By not saving merged documents on disk, you save disk space and help ensure that the data in your merged documents is as current as possible.

CREATING FORM LETTERS

Producing form letters is one of the most common uses for merging. In this next section, we'll use form letters to show you the three steps of a merge:

- Creating and/or editing the merge data file
- Creating and/or editing the merge document
- Performing the merge

The Text, Merge command opens the Merge Assistant dialog box, which serves as a control center for your merge operations. As we perform merges throughout this chapter, we'll return time and again to the Merge Assistant dialog box to determine and then carry out the next step in the merging process.

Note: The Text, Merge command is designed to take you through merging in one continuous procedure, but the aim of this section is to stop periodically and closely examine merge components and options along the way. As you work through the activities, it may seem that Word Pro is making some poor guesses on how to proceed. Once you've learned the merge process in its entirety, however, you will find that Text, Merge works very well in carrying you smoothly through the entire merge process.

CREATING A MERGE DATA FILE

To use Text, Merge to create a merge data file:

- Choose *Text, Merge* to open the Merge Assistant dialog box.
- Click on *New Data File* to create a new document and open the Create Data File dialog box.
- In the Field Name text box, type a field name, and then click on *Add*. Field names can contain letters, numbers, spaces, and many special characters. (Common field names include First Name, Last Name, Company, Address, City, State, and Zip.) Repeat this step as necessary, until you've named every field you think you'll need in your merge data file.
- Click on *OK*. Word Pro adds the field names you specified to the merge data file, and then opens the Edit Data File dialog box, which displays blank electronic index cards so that you can start entering records.
- On the first blank card, type all the data for one record, and then click on Add. Word Pro adds the data you typed to the merge data file.
- Click on *New Record*. Word Pro displays a new, blank card. Repeat this step as necessary until you have entered all of your records.
- Click on *Close File* to close the dialog box and the merge data file. Word Pro will prompt you to name and save the merge data file before closing it.
- Click on *Yes* to open the Save As dialog box. Then specify a name for the document and click on *OK*.
- Word Pro automatically returns you to the Merge Assistant dialog box.

As you work with the electronic index cards in the Data File dialog box, Word Pro translates your field names and records into a *de-limited* format, and places them in a document. "Delimited" is just a fancy way of saying that Word Pro uses special characters to mark the ends of field names, fields within records, and records. By default, Word Pro uses a *tilde* (~) as a *field delimiter* to mark the end of each field name and each field within a record, and a *vertical bar* (|) as a *record delimiter* to mark the end of each record.

For the most part, you don't have to worry about delimited formats and delimiters, because you can use Text, Merge to translate the delimited format into the easier-to-use electronic index cards. However, it's important sometimes to be able to recognize a merge data file when you see one.

Note: Because entering data for multiple records can be time-consuming, in this next activity we'll only ask you to name fields and then enter one record—just so you can see how it's done. In the activity following this one, we'll have you open a merge data file that we provided on this book's Data Disk; this merge data file will resemble the file you'll be creating here, but it will contain more records.

If you are not running Word Pro, please start it now. Let's create a merge data file:

1. Click on the **Create New Document SmartIcon**. Select **default.mwp**, and click on **OK** to create a new document based on the Default SmartMaster.
2. Choose **Text, Merge**, and then examine the Merge Assistant dialog box (see Figure 11.2). This dialog box will guide you through the three steps of merging. The Step 1:Data File tab should be displayed.
3. Click on **New Data File** to indicate that you want to create a new merge data file. Word Pro opens the Create Data File dialog box, where you will provide field names for your data file.
4. In the Field Name text box, type **Last Name**, and then click on **Add**. Word Pro adds *Last Name* to the Fields For New Data File list box, and leaves the insertion point in the Field Name text box, ready for you to type another field name.

Figure 11.2 **The Merge Assistant dialog box**

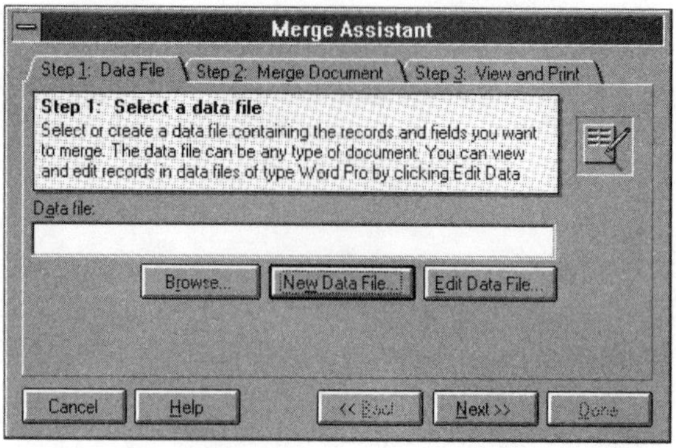

5. Type the following field names in the Field Name text box, clicking on **Add** after entering each name:

```
First Name
Company
Address
City
State
Zip
```

6. Observe the Fields For New Data File list box. It should now list the seven field names you added (see Figure 11.3).

Figure 11.3 **Naming fields**

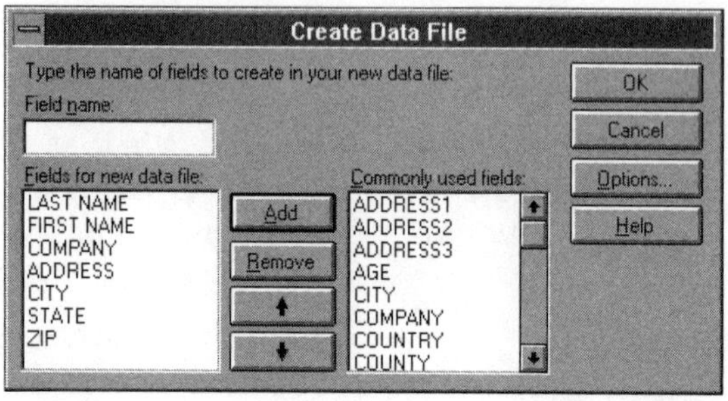

7. Click on **OK**. Word Pro opens the Edit Data File dialog box, which displays your field names along with corresponding

text boxes on an electronic index card. This card enables you to enter all the data for one data record (see Figure 11.4).

Figure 11.4 **Electronic index cards**

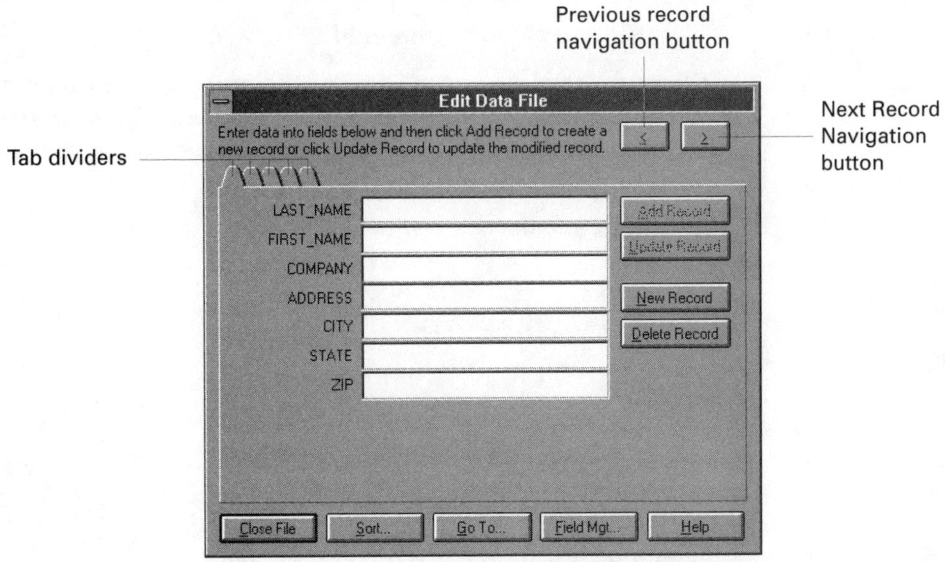

8. Verify that the insertion point is located in the Last Name text box. Then type **Hunsinger** and press **Tab** to enter the last name and move toothe next field on the index card. **Note**: Do not press Enter.
9. Enter the following data to fill in the index card fields:

```
Last Name: Hunsinger
First Name: Scott
Company: Westside Swim Club
Address: 3956 Buffalo Road
City: Churchville
State: NY
Zip: 14420
```

   Note: Press **Tab** to move to the next field.

10. Click on **Add Record** to add your typed data as a record in your data file.

11. Click on **New Record**. Word Pro moves the card back one in the "stack" (notice that *Hunsinger* appears on the tab divider sticking up from the second card), and displays a new, blank card.
12. Rather than type in a lot of records, let's stop here. Click on **Close File**. Word Pro prompts:

    `Untitled1 has changed. Save changes?`

13. Click on **Yes** to open the Save As dialog box, type **mydata1** in the File Name text box, and then click on **OK**. Word Pro returns to the Merge Assistant dialog box, assuming that you want to continue your merge operation.
14. Click on **Cancel** to close the Merge Assistant dialog box.

EDITING AN EXISTING MERGE DATA FILE

Once you've created a merge data file, you'll probably need to edit it at some point. You can open a delimited merge data file through Text, Merge, and Word Pro will automatically translate the delimited format into electronic index cards and display those cards in an Edit Data File dialog box. Or you can open a delimited merge data file through File, Open or by using the Open An Existing File SmartIcon; you will then need to use Text, Merge to instruct Word Pro to translate your data to index cards.

Note: If you prefer, you can also edit the merge data file's delimited text directly, though you might find it more difficult to keep track of your data.

To open and translate a delimited merge data file through Text, Merge:

- Choose *Text, Merge*.
- Make sure that *Step 1: Data File tab* is selected, and then click on *Browse*. Word Pro opens the Browse dialog box.
- Specify the appropriate drive and directory, if necessary.
- In the File Name list box, select the merge data file's name.
- Click on *OK*.
- Click on *Edit Data File*.

Once you've opened a delimited merge data file and translated the records into electronic index cards, you can use the Edit Data File dialog box to edit your records. Word Pro automatically displays the first record in your merge data file; to view other records, use one of these three methods:

- Use the *tab dividers* that stick up from the top of each card and are visible for the first five cards displayed. To move to a card whose tab divider is visible, click on the card's tab divider.
- Use the *Go To button*, which opens the Go To Record dialog box. You can use this dialog box much as you did the Find & Replace bar you learned about in Chapter 2, to move to a record that contains specific information. For example, you might want to move to the next record where the Last Name field is *Bonski*. You can also use the Go To Record dialog box to move to the merge data file's first or last record.
- Use the *navigation buttons*, which enable you to move to the previous or next record. The *Previous Record navigation button* displays a single left-pointing triangle, and the *Next Record navigation button* displays a single right-pointing triangle. (Refer back to Figure 11.4 for the locations of these buttons.)

Once you've displayed the record you want to edit, you can directly edit the data in any or all fields. Then click on the Update Record button to apply your changes to the merge data file, or the Add button to add your edited record as a new record to the merge data file.

If you want to delete the current record, click on the Delete Record button. Or, to enter a brand-new record, click on the New Record button to display a new, blank card; enter the appropriate data; and then click on Add Record.

Once you've finished adding and editing records, click on Close File to close the Edit Data File dialog box and the merge data file. Word Pro prompts you to save your changes; click on Yes to do so. Word Pro returns to the Merge Assistant dialog box.

As you'll see at the end of this next activity, after you edit records through the Edit Data File dialog box, Word Pro does not provide any opportunity for you to use File, Save As to save your edited merge data file with a new name. This is usually not a problem, because it usually makes little sense to maintain two copies of very similar merge data files. However, when you want to preserve your unedited merge data file and save your edited merge data file with a new name, follow these steps:

- Open the merge data file through *File, Open* or by using the *Open An Existing File SmartIcon*.
- Save the document with a new name.
- *Then* use *Text, Merge* to translate the records to electronic index cards.

We want you to preserve the merge data file we provided on this book's Data Disk, so we'll have you use this procedure in this next activity. Let's open and edit an existing merge data file:

1. Open and examine **datafile.lwp**. This is how the data file you created in the last activity might look after you entered more records. Because Word Pro does not automatically open an Edit Data File dialog box to let you view your records on electronic index cards, the data is somewhat difficult to read (see Figure 11.5).

Figure 11.5 **Delimited data**

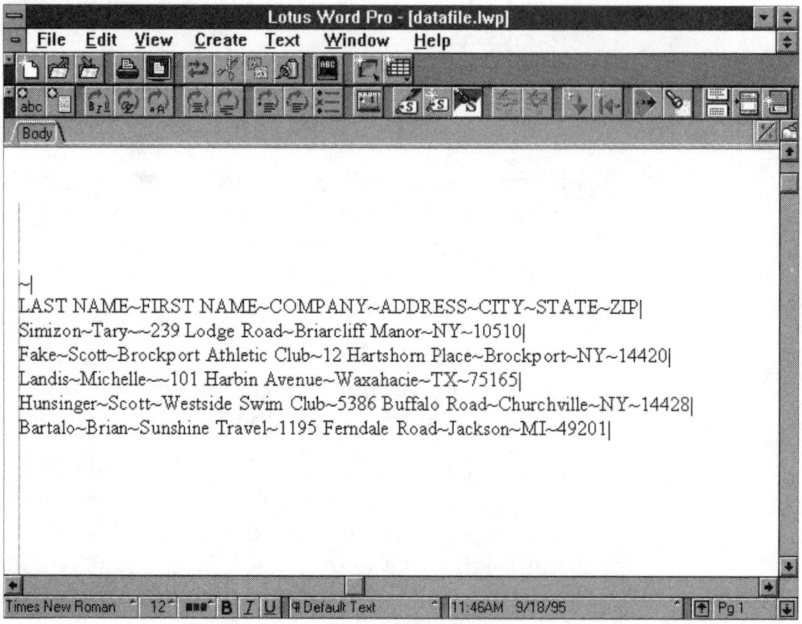

2. Save the document as **mydata2** and close the document.
3. Choose **Text, Merge** to open the Merge Assistant dialog box. You need to tell Word Pro which merge data file you want.
4. Click on **Browse** to open the Browse dialog box and select a data file.
5. Select **mydata2.lwp** and click on **OK**.
6. Click on **Edit Data File**. Word Pro reads the data in MYDATA2.LWP, and then opens the Edit Data File dialog box to display the file's records on electronic index cards.
7. Observe the navigation buttons in the dialog box's upper-right corner. You can use these to move to the previous or next record in your data file (these buttons are labeled in Figure 11.4).Observe Tary Simizon's record. Notice that Tary's Company field is blank. Later in this chapter, we'll see how Word Pro manages blank fields when merging files.
8. Click on the **Next Record navigation button** to display the next card.
9. Click on the **Next Record navigation button** three more times, pausing between each click to view each of the records in MYDATA2.LWP. Notice that some of the other records, too, have blank Company fields.
10. When you reach the last record (Brian Bartalo's record), click on **New Record** to display a new, blank card.
11. On the new card, type in your own data.
12. Click on **Add Record** to add your record to the merge data file.
13. Click on **Close File** to close the dialog box and the merge data file. Word Pro prompts:

    ```
    MYDATA2.LWP has changed. Save changes?
    ```

14. Click on **Yes**. Once again, Word Pro returns to the Merge Assistant dialog box.
15. Click on **Cancel** to close the dialog box.

EDITING A MERGE DOCUMENT

Step 2 of a merge operation is creating and editing the merge document. To create a merge document, you can take any normal Word Pro document, assign a merge data file to the document, and then insert merge fields from that merge data file.

When you work through Text, Merge to create or open your merge documents, you first assign a merge data file on the Step 1: Data File tab. Next, you use the Step 2: Merge Document tab to tell Word Pro which document to use. Then, click on Insert Merge fields. Word Pro automatically displays an Insert Merge Field bar, which lists all the available field names from the assigned merge data file.

Once the Insert Merge Field bar is open, you are ready to insert merge fields into your merge document. This bar stays on screen so that you can move freely between the document window and the bar.

Note: Regardless of how you typed field names in your merge data file, field names are displayed all in uppercase in the Insert Merge Field bar and in the merge document. In addition, spaces within field names are replaced with underscores. For example, if you have a field named First Name, Word Pro will display the field name as FIRST_NAME. When you merge, however, Word Pro inserts the variable data for each field exactly as you typed that data in your merge data file.

Follow these steps when you want to insert a merge field:

- Place the insertion point where you want to insert the merge field.
- Select the desired field name in the bar's Field Names list box, and then click on *Insert Field*. Or, simply double-click on the field name.
- Repeat the previous two steps as necessary to insert all of the desired merge fields.

Note: When Word Pro inserts a merge field into a merge document, the merge field looks just like the field name, surrounded by *angle brackets* (< and >). Don't be fooled, however, into thinking that you can type the brackets and field names as merge fields yourself; Word Pro only recognizes merge fields inserted through the Insert Merge Field bar.

If you want the fields in your merged document to be separated by spaces, commas, or other punctuation, type those characters *between* the merge fields. For example, if you want the last line of an address to read

```
Orchard Park, NY  14127
```

then the corresponding line in your merge document should look something like this:

```
<CITY>, <STATE>  <ZIP>
```

Now let's open a partially created merge document, assign your MYDATA2.LWP merge data file to it, and then insert some merge fields to complete the document:

1. Open and examine **mergedoc.lwp**. It is a one-page form letter. Notice the merge fields for the document's inside address: <FIRST_NAME>, <LAST_NAME>, and so on. We've already done a little of the work for you by inserting these merge fields to match the field names in MYDATA2.LWP.
2. Scroll down a few lines. We've also inserted a <FIRST_NAME> merge field in the letter's greeting (see Figure 11.6).
3. Choose **Text, Insert Other, Merge Field**, and then examine the Insert Merge Field bar. Because you just finished editing MYDATA2.LWP, Word Pro assumes you want to use that merge data file. It now lists all the field names from MYDATA2.LWP. Notice that Word Pro has capitalized all the field names; for field names that include spaces, Word Pro has replaced each space with an underscore.
4. Place the insertion point in the first blank line under <ADDRESS>. To complete the inside address, you need to add merge fields for the city, state, and zip code.
5. In the Insert Merge Field bar's Field Names list box, select **CITY**, and then click on **Insert Field**. (Or just double-click on **CITY**.) Word Pro inserts a merge field for CITY at the insertion point (see Figure 11.7).
6. Type a comma and then press **Spacebar** to insert a comma and a space after <CITY>.

Figure 11.6 **Merge fields in a merge document**

Figure 11.7 **Inserting merge fields**

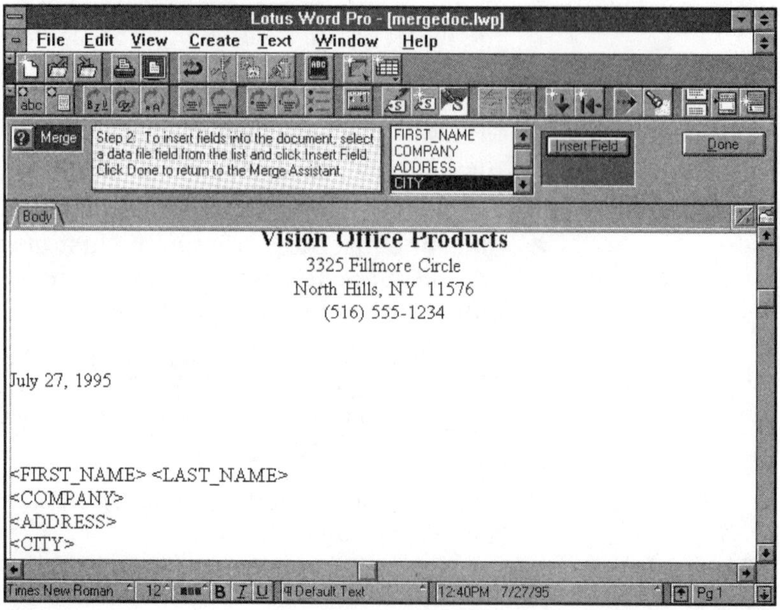

7. Insert a merge field for **STATE**, press **Spacebar** twice, and then insert a merge field for **ZIP**. Your new line should now read

    ```
    <CITY>, <STATE> <ZIP>
    ```

8. Click on **Done** to close the Insert Merge Field bar. (If necessary, click on **Cancel** to close the Merge Assistant dialog box.)
9. Save your merge document as **mymerge**.

MERGING THE FORM LETTERS

Once you've created and edited your merge data file and a merge document, the third and final step is the actual merging.

To start a merge from a merge document:

- Open the Merge document
- Choose *Text, Merge* to open the Merge Assistant dialog box.
- Select a data file, if necessary.
- Click on *Next* to move to the Step 2: Merge Document tab.
- Verify that the *Use The Current Document* option is selected.
- Click on *Insert Merge Fields*, if necessary.
- Insert any fields you want and click on *Done*.
- Click on *Next* to move to the Step 3: View And Print tab.
- To send your entire merge directly to the printer, select *Send Directly To Printer*. To view (and possibly edit) each merged document before printing, select *View On-Screen Before Printing*.
- Click on *Done* to open the Merge bar.

Note: The View And Print tab also provides options for *conditional merges* (which enable you to merge using only records that meet specific criteria) and changing your print options. For more information on these options, refer to your Word Pro documentation.

If you select View On-Screen Before Printing in the foregoing procedure, Word Pro will merge the merge data file's first record with the merge document, and display the resulting merged document in the document window. Word Pro will also display four command buttons in the Merge bar. Click on

- *Print And View Next* to print the current merged document and then merge and display the next merged document
- *Skip And View Next* to bypass the current merged document and then merge and display the next merged document
- *Print All* to print the current merged document and then merge and print all of the remaining merged documents, without displaying them first
- *Done* to stop merging

The Print And View Next and Skip And View Next options are good to use for running on-the-fly conditional merges. For example, if you want to print form letters for everyone in your merge data file except the one person who lives in Nebraska, you can view each document and choose *not* to print that merged document when it is displayed. These two options also enable you to edit merged documents before printing them. For instance, you might have only one or two merged documents to which you want to add some extra text; you can directly edit those documents when they are displayed, print them, and then continue with the rest of the merge.

MERGING RECORDS THAT CONTAIN BLANK FIELDS

It's not uncommon to have records with blank fields in your merge data file. For example, if you have a company name field, most records with a home address or for people who are not employed will probably have blank company name fields.

When Word Pro encounters a blank field during a merge, it looks to see if the corresponding merge field in the merge document is in a paragraph by itself. If it is, Word Pro deletes the empty paragraph.

Because some of your records contain blank Company fields, you'll see this feature in action during the merge.

Let's complete our merge now:

1. Verify that MYMERGE.LWP is still open, and then choose **Text, Merge**. Your merge document is already open, and you've already assigned MYDATA2.LWP as the merge data file and inserted the fields you want.

2. Click on **Step 3: View And Print**. Word Pro displays the Step 3: View And Print tab.

3. Select **View On-Screen Before Printing**, if necessary, and then click on **Done**. Word Pro merges the first form letter (for Tary Simizon), displays it in the document window, and opens the Merge bar. The Merge bar now enables you to print this form letter or skip to the next one (see Figure 11.8).

Figure 11.8 **Viewing a merged document**

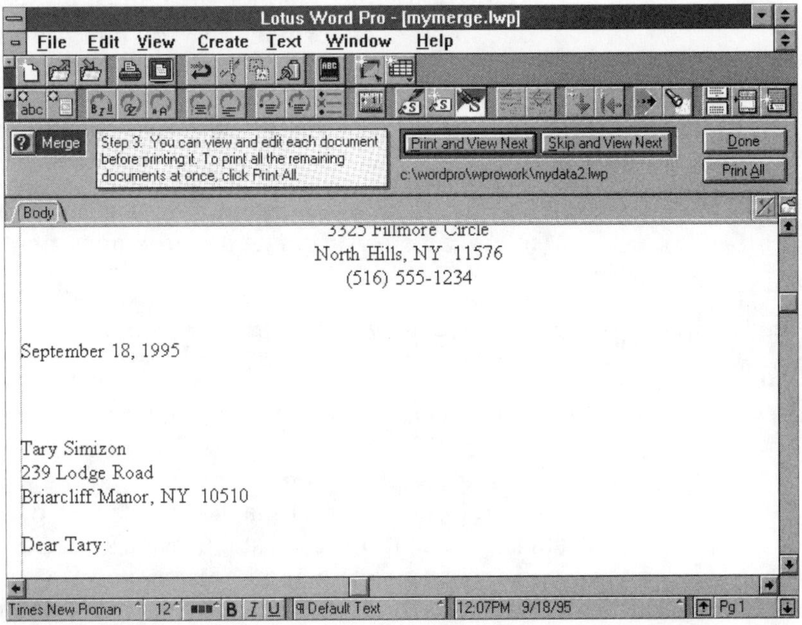

4. Examine the form letter. Into every merge field in the merge document, Word Pro has merged data from Tary Simizon's record. Remember from earlier in this chapter that Tary's Company field was blank. Notice how Word Pro has automatically compensated for this by deleting the paragraph containing the COMPANY merge field. In this way, the form letter does not contain a gap between Tary's name and her street address.

5. If you want to conserve your printer paper, click on **Skip And View Next**. If you'd prefer to print the merged document, click on **Print And View Next** instead.

PRACTICE YOUR SKILLS

1. View the rest of the form letters until Word Pro closes the Merge bar.
2. Save and then close MYMERGE.LWP.

CREATING MAILING LABELS

A merge operation to create mailing labels works much the same as one to produce form letters. You need a merge data file to supply the names and addresses, and a merge document to provide the proper layout for the labels. To create the mailing labels themselves, you simply merge these two documents.

In this section, you'll see how to sort a merge data file's records into zip code order, and then how to use one of Word Pro's SmartMasters to help you create a merge document for your labels.

SORTING RECORDS IN A MERGE DATA FILE

When you want to create mailing labels (or any kind of merged document, for that matter), it's often useful to sort the records in your merge data file before performing the merge. For example, you might want to sort mailing labels by zip code in order to take advantage of the U.S. Postal Service's special rates for presorted mail. Or, if you use a hand-delivery service, you could sort by company name to make it easier to bundle together letters for people who work at the same company.

By default, Word Pro stores records in the order they were entered, and creates merged documents in that same order.

If you use Text, Merge to create and edit delimited merge data files, Word Pro helps you to sort records easily from the Edit Data File dialog box (the dialog box that displays electronic index cards). To sort records in a delimited merge data file:

- Select the merge data file and open the Edit Data File dialog box. (For help with this, refer back to "Editing an Existing Merge Data File" earlier in this chapter.)
- Click on *Sort* to open the Sort Records dialog box.

- In the Sort By Field drop-down list, select the field by which you want to sort.
- To sort fields that contain all letters, or a mixture of letters and numbers (such as street addresses), select *Sort Type Alphanumeric*. To sort fields that contain only numbers (such as zip codes), select *Sort Type Numeric*.
- To sort fields in *ascending order* (for example, from A to Z or from 1 to 100), select Sort Order Ascending. To sort fields in *descending order* (for example, from Z to A or from 100 to 1), select Sort Order Descending.
- Click on *OK* to sort all of the records according to your specifications.

After sorting, Word Pro displays on the tab dividers for the first five electronic index cards.

Once you've finished sorting records, click on *Close File* and then on Yes to close the dialog box and to save and close the merge data file.

Let's sort the records in MYDATA2.LWP:

1. Open a new document based on the Default SmartMaster.
2. Choose **Text, Merge** and in the Data File text box, type **c:\wordpro\wprowork\mydata2.lwp** if necessary to select a data file.
3. Click on **Edit The Data File**. Word Pro opens the Edit Data File dialog box and displays the file's records on electronic index cards.
4. Click on **Sort**, and then examine the Sort Records dialog box (see Figure 11.9). You can sort records by any one field, alphanumerically or numerically, and in ascending or descending order.
5. Select **Last Name** in the Sort By Field drop-down list box.
6. Verify that *Sort Type Alphanumeric* and *Sort Order Ascending* are selected, and then click on **OK**.
7. Observe the five visible tab dividers. You can see by these dividers that Word Pro has sorted the records in ascending order by last name.

Figure 11.9 **The Sort Records dialog box**

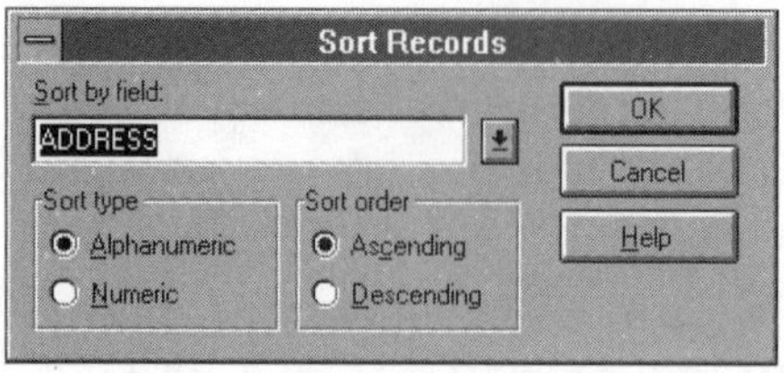

8. Click on **Close File**. Word Pro prompts:

    `MYDATA2.LWP has changed. Save changes?`

9. Click on **Yes**.
10. Click on **Cancel** to close the Merge Assistant dialog box.

CREATING AN ENVELOPE

If you're creating a single letter, you can use Word Pro's Create Envelope command to print a single envelope.

Note: If your printer has an envelope tray, Word Pro will attempt to use that tray. Otherwise, it will use your printer's *manual feed* option, if it has one. If you have trouble printing an envelope, check your printer's documentation.

Follow these steps when you want to print a single envelope:

- Open the letter for which you want to create an envelope.
- Choose *Create Envelope* to open the Envelope bar. In the document window, Word Pro will attempt to find and select your document's inside address. If Word Pro selects no address or the wrong address, click in the *Address blocks* and type or edit the address. Word Pro finds the return address on the Personal tab in the Word Pro Preferences dialog box. (**Note:** You can set this data by choosing *File, User Setup, Word Pro Preferences*, and clicking on *Personal*.)
- In the Size box, select the desired envelope size. (If the envelope size you want isn't listed in this box, select *Custom* and type the appropriate dimensions in the Width and Height boxes in the Custom Page Size dialog box and click on *OK*.)

- Click on *Print* to open the Print dialog box. Or, click on *Done* to close the Envelope bar and attach the envelope to the document.

Let's open a document that has an inside address, and then create an envelope for the document:

1. Open and examine **envltr.lwp**. It's a simple, one-page letter with an inside address.
2. Choose **Create, Envelope**. Word Pro automatically finds and selects the document's inside address, and then opens the Envelope bar (see Figure 11.10).

Figure 11.10 **The Envelope bar**

3. Select **Envelope Size Size 10** (the standard size for business envelopes), and then click on **Done**. Word Pro closes the Envelope bar and attaches the envelope to your document. (**Note:** To print the envelope click on **Print** and **OK** instead of Done.)
4. Compare your envelope to Figure 11.11. Your return address may be different from that shown in Figure 11.11.
5. Save the document as **myenvel** and close MYENVEL.LWP.
6. Exit from Word Pro.

SUMMARY

In this chapter, you learned how to use Text, Merge to create form letters. You also learned how to sort records within a merge data file, and how to use Create Envelope to create and print a single envelope.

Figure 11.11 **The printed envelope**

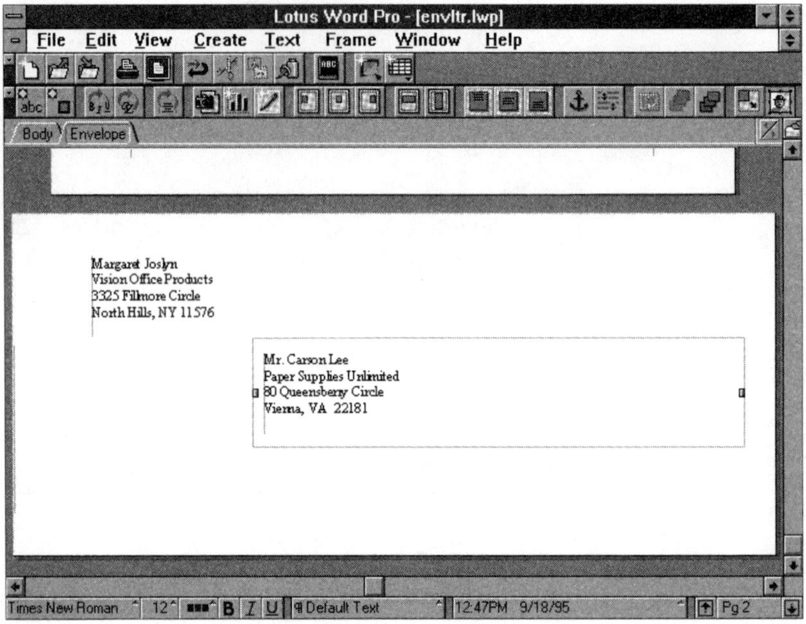

Here is a quick reference guide to the Word Pro features introduced in this chapter:

Desired Result	**How to Do It**
Create merge data file	Choose **Text, Merge**; click on **New Data File** and type field names, clicking on **Add** after each name; click on **OK**; fill in records on Edit Data File dialog box index cards, clicking on **Add Record** and then **New Record** after each record; click on **Close File**; click on **Yes**; type name for merge data file; click on **OK**.
Translate delimited data to electronic index cards	Choose **Text, Merge**; select **Step 1: Data File** (if necessary); click on **Browse**; select merge data file name; click on **OK**; click on **Edit Data File**.

Desired Result	How to Do It
Move to another index card	Click on index card's **tab divider**. Or click on **Go To**; specify record; then click on **OK**. Or click on a **navigation button**.
Edit record on index card	Move to card; edit fields; click on **Update Record**.
Create brand-new index card and record	Click on **New Record**.
Delete index card and record	Display card; click on **Delete Record**.
Manually open Insert Merge Field dialog box	Choose **Text, Insert Other, Merge Field**.
Insert merge field	Open merge document; open Insert Merge Field dialog box; place insertion point at desired location; select field name; click on **Insert**.
Insert standardized text	Type text in merge document.
Merge from merge document	Open merge document; choose **Text, Merge**; open View And Print tab; select **View On-Screen Before Printing**, or **Send Directly To Printer**; click on **Done**.
Sort delimited merge data file records	Translate file to index cards; click on **Sort**; select sort field, sort type, and sort order; click on **OK**.
Create envelope	Open document containing envelope address; choose **Create Envelope**; select envelope size; then click on **Print** or **Done**.

Congratulations! You have now learned how to use many of Word Pro's features. You are now prepared to take all that you've learned and apply it to your own documents. Remember, to master the skills that you've acquired, you must supply the most important ingredient—practice. Only through practice will you be able to get beyond the techniques themselves. Good luck!

APPENDIX A: INSTALLATION

Preparing Your Computer for Word Pro Installation

Installing Word Pro 4.0 on Your Computer

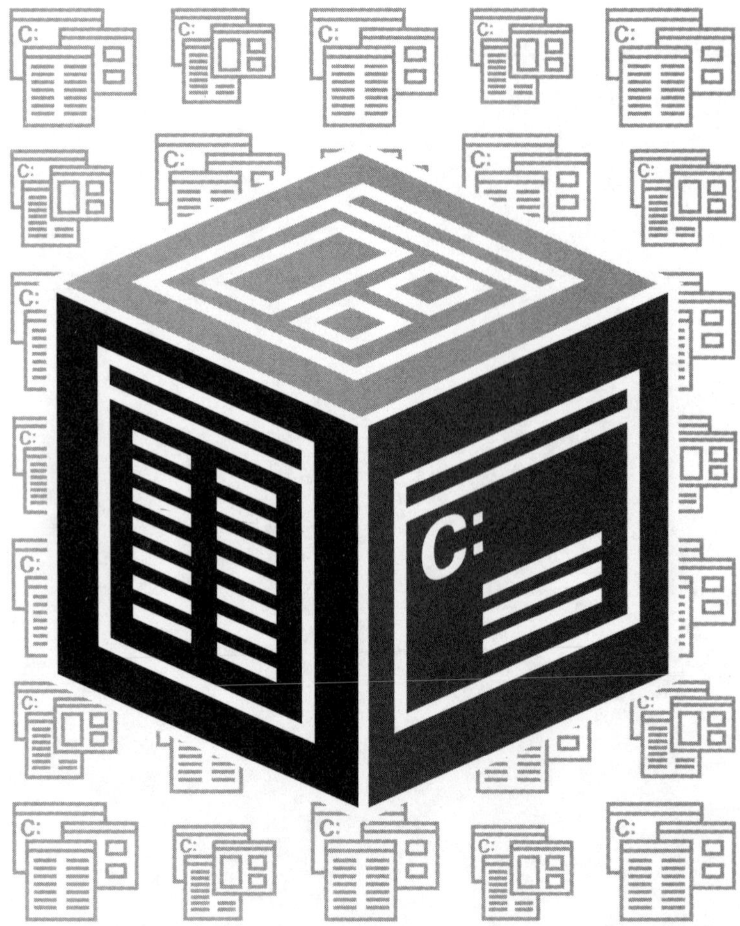

This appendix provides instructions for installing or reinstalling Word Pro 96 on your computer.

To be certain that Word Pro will run as described in this book, you should use the *All Features Install* option when installing Word Pro (we will describe the procedure for doing so later in this appendix). If you already have installed Word Pro, you may want to *reinstall* it to make certain that Word Pro is completely installed. Otherwise, some Word Pro features described in this book may not be available to you.

Note: To get you up and running in Word Pro as quickly as possible, we have used terms in this appendix that you may not understand. Please bear with us. Most of the terms introduced here are explained early in the book.

PREPARING YOUR COMPUTER FOR WORD PRO INSTALLATION

There are three requirements that you must meet before you begin to install Word Pro 96:

- DOS version 3.1 or higher must be installed on your computer. If it is not, install it now. (For help, see your DOS documentation.)
- Windows version 3.1 or higher must be installed on your computer. If it is not, install it now. (For help, see your Windows documentation.)
- There must be enough free space (45 megabytes) on your hard drive to store all of Word Pro's program files and the temporary files that Word Pro creates while running.

Note: If you are *reinstalling* Word Pro, you may need less than 45 megabytes of free space. This is because Word Pro's installation program will replace program files already stored on your hard drive, thereby reducing the overall amount of *new* space needed.

Perform the following steps to meet the third requirement just listed:

1. You need to have your computer on and running in DOS. If Windows is running, you need to exit to DOS. To do this, click on **File** in the Program Manager window, click on **Exit Windows...** in the File menu, and then click on **OK**.
2. At the DOS prompt, type **c:** (or, if you intend to install Word Pro on a hard drive other than C, type the letter of that drive, followed by a colon). Then press **Enter**.
3. Type **dir**, and then press **Enter**. DOS lists the files contained in the current directory and, at the very end of this list, reports the number of free bytes.
4. Observe the number of free bytes. You need at least 45 megabytes (just over 45,000,000 bytes) of free hard-drive space to install and run Word Pro.

5. If the number of free bytes is over 45,000,000, skip the rest of this activity. If the number is very close to or under 45,000,000, delete enough files from your hard drive to free the space required for the installation. *Be sure to back up any files that you want to save before deleting them!*
6. Type **dir** and then press **Enter** again. DOS should now report over 45,000,000 free bytes. (If it does not, return to step 5.)

INSTALLING WORD PRO 96 ON YOUR COMPUTER

Now that you've met the three requirements mentioned earlier, you can begin the actual Word Pro 4.0 installation or reinstallation.

1. From DOS, type **win** and press **Enter** to start Windows.
2. Insert the disk labeled *Install Disk 1* in the appropriate floppy disk drive.
3. If necessary, activate the **Program Manager window**. (If Program Manager is running as an icon, double-click on the icon to open and activate Program Manager in a window. If Program Manager is running in a window, click on the title bar of the window to activate it.)
4. In the Program Manager window, click on **File** and then on **Run...** to open the Run dialog box.
5. Type **a:install** if the Install disk is in drive A, or **b:install** if the disk is in drive B. Then click on **OK** to begin the Word Pro installation program.
6. After a moment, the Lotus installation program opens a window entitled *Welcome To The Lotus Word Pro Install Program*.
7. Type your name in the Name text box and your company name in the Company Name text box, if necessary.
8. Click on **Next**.
9. Click on **Yes** to confirm the names you typed are correct.
10. The installation program next opens the Install Options & Word Pro Directory dialog box, providing three install options: *All Features*, *Minimum Features*, and *Customize Features*. Verify that *All Features* is selected and click on **Next**.

11. Click on **Next** to select *Lotus Applications* as the Program Group for Word Pro application icons.
12. Click on **Yes** to begin copying files to your hard disk.
13. The installation program next opens a Transferring Files dialog box to show you the per-disk and overall installation progress. As it installs, the installation program also provides some general information about Word Pro's features.
14. Follow the on-screen directions to remove the current installation disk and insert subsequent disks. Click on **OK** after inserting each disk.
15. The installation program next opens the Install Complete dialog box to inform you that the installation is complete. Click on **Done** to close this dialog box.
16. The Lotus Word Pro Install Program window closes, returning you to the Program Manager window. There you will find a window entitled *Lotus Applications* that contains the Word Pro icons.
17. Remove the last installation disk and put all your installation disks in a safe place.

APPENDIX B: KEYBOARD SHORTCUT REFERENCE

Movement

Text Selection

Menu Commands

This appendix lists a number of keyboard shortcuts available in Word Pro. In some cases, you may find these shortcuts easier to use than their mouse-based counterparts.

MOVEMENT

To Move	Use This Keyboard Shortcut
One character to left	Left Arrow
One character to right	Right Arrow
One line up	Up Arrow
One line down	Down Arrow
One word to left	Ctrl+Left Arrow
One word to right	Ctrl+Right Arrow
To end of line	End
To beginning of line	Home
To beginning of current or previous sentence	Ctrl+, (comma)
To beginning of next sentence	Ctrl+. (period)
Down one screen	PgDn
Up one screen	PgUp
Down one page	Ctrl+PgDn
Up one page	Ctrl+PgUp
To beginning of document	Ctrl+Home
To end of document	Ctrl+End

TEXT SELECTION

To select text with the keyboard, place the insertion point at one end of the text, press and hold Shift, use any of the movement shortcuts listed in the preceding section, and then release Shift.

MENU COMMANDS

To Issue This Command	Use This Keyboard Shortcut
File, Open	Ctrl+O
File, Save	Ctrl+S
File, Print	Ctrl+P
Edit, Undo	Ctrl+Z
Edit, Cut	Ctrl+X
Edit, Copy	Ctrl+C
Edit, Paste	Ctrl+V
Edit, Find & Replace	Ctrl+F
Edit, Check Spelling	Ctrl+F2
Edit, Go To (opens Go To dialog box)	Ctrl+G
View, Show SmartIcons or View, Hide SmartIcons	Ctrl+Q
Text, Alignment, Left	Ctrl+L
Text, Alignment, Center	Ctrl+E
Text, Alignment, Right	Ctrl+R
Text, Alignment, Full Justify	Ctrl+J
Text, Normal	Ctrl+N
Text, Bold	Ctrl+B
Text, Italic	Ctrl+I
Text, Underline	Ctrl+U
Text, Word Underline	Ctrl+W

To Issue This Command	Use This Keyboard Shortcut
Text, Text Properties	Alt+Enter
Text, Alignment, Indent	F7
Text, Alignment, Outdent	Shift+F7
Text, Fast Format	Ctrl+T

Note: To help you remember these keyboard shortcuts, Word Pro lists them on the menus, to the right of each corresponding menu item.

APPENDIX C: EXCHANGING DOCUMENTS WITH OTHER PROGRAMS

Opening Non-Word Pro 96 Files

Saving Word Pro 96 Documents in Other File Formats

Importing and Exporting for Unsupported Programs

Loss of Formatting When Importing and Exporting

Word Pro 96 has a number of *import file filters* that enable it to open document files created in many other word processing programs, as well as files created by many spreadsheet and database programs. Word Pro also has *export file filters* that enable Word Pro to save documents in a file format that other programs can use. Because of these import and export abilities, you can exchange information electronically with many other computer users, regardless of what programs they use. For example, you can open a coworker's Word for Windows document in Word Pro, edit the document, save the document in Word for Windows format, and then hand the edited document back to your coworker.

This appendix lists the various programs supported by Word Pro's file filters, and shows you how to open and save files in non–Word Pro 96 formats.

OPENING NON–WORD PRO 96 FILES

To open a non–Word Pro 96 file:

- Open the Open dialog box (choose *File, Open*, or click on the *Open An Existing File SmartIcon*, or press *Ctrl+O*).
- In the List Files Of Type drop-down list box, select the appropriate file format. Word Pro will then list in the Files list box any files that have the corresponding file name extension. For example, if you choose to open a Word for Windows document, which uses the .DOC file name extension, Word Pro will list only those files that end with *.DOC*, rather than those that end with *.LWP*.
- If necessary, select the drive and directory where the file is stored.
- Select the desired file in the Files list box; or type the file name (with its extension) in the File Name text box.
- Click on *OK*.
- For certain file formats, Word Pro will next open an Import or Import Options dialog box to enable you to specify exactly how Word Pro should import the selected file. If one of these dialog boxes opens, consult your Word Pro documentation for information on the import options available for that specific file format. Then specify the desired option or options and click on OK.

Word Pro opens the file as an untitled document. You can edit, print, and save this document as you would any standard Word Pro document. When you name and save the document, Word Pro by default will save it in Word Pro 96 format. To save the file in its original or some other non–Word Pro 96 format, refer to the procedure in the next section, "Saving Word Pro 96 Documents in Other File Formats."

Here is a list of non–Word Pro 96 file types that Word Pro can open:

dBase	DCA/RFT
DCA/FFT	DIF

- DisplayWrite
- Enable 4.x
- Excel
- Executive MemoMaker
- FrameMaker (MIF)
- HPTag
- HTML
- Interleaf Publisher 1, 5
- Legacy 1, 2
- Lotus 1-2-3
- Lotus 1-2-3 for OS/2
- Lotus 1-2-3 R3
- Lotus 1-2-3 R4, 5
- Lotus Ami Pro
- Lotus Ami Pro 3.x Macro
- Lotus Ami Pro 3.x Styles
- Lotus Manuscript 2.x
- Lotus Organizer 1.x
- MS Excel 4, 5, 6
- MS Windows Write 3.x
- MS Word for DOS
- MS Word for OS/2
- MS Word for Windows 1, 2, 6
- MS WordPad
- MultiMate 3, 4
- MultiMate Advantage
- ODBC Data
- OfficeWriter 4, 5, 6
- PeachText 5000
- Professional Write 1, 2
- Q&A Write 1, 3, 4
- Rich Text Format (RTF)
- Samna Word
- SGML-ASCII
- Text-ANSI (Windows)
- Text-ASCII (DOS)
- Text-EMail
- WordPerfect 5.0, 5.1, 6.x
- WordStar 2000 R3
- WordStar 3, 4, 5, 6, 7
- WordStar for Windows
- XY Write DOS/Windows

SAVING WORD PRO 96 DOCUMENTS IN OTHER FILE FORMATS

Follow these steps when you want to save an Word Pro 96 document in a non–Word Pro 96 file format:

- Open the Save As dialog box (choose File, Save As).
- In the List Files Of Type drop-down list box, select the desired file format.

- If necessary, select the drive and directory where you want to save the file.
- In the File Name text box, type a name for your file. (Remember, file names must be one to eight characters, and cannot include spaces or some special characters.)
- Click on *OK*.
- For certain file formats, Word Pro will open an Export or an Export Options dialog box to enable you to specify exactly how Word Pro should export your document. If one of these dialog boxes opens, consult your Word Pro documentation for information on the export options available for that specific file format. Then specify the desired option or options and click on OK.

Word Pro saves the current document in the format you specified, leaving a copy of the original document in the active document window. If you want to save the document in Word Pro 96 format, as well, save the document. Otherwise, just close the document window without saving changes.

Once you've saved a document in a non–Word Pro 96 file format, you can open it in the program that uses this file format (for example, WordPerfect). Then you can edit, print, save, or close the file exactly as you would any standard file in that program.

Here is a list of non–Word Pro 96 file types to which Word Pro can export:

DCA/FFT	MS Word for DOS
DCA/RFT	MS Word for OS/2
DisplayWrite	MS Word for Windows
Enable	MS WordPad
FrameMaker	MultiMate
Interleaf Publisher	Office Writer
Legacy	PeachText
Lotus Ami Pro	Professional Write
MS Windows Write	Q&A Write

Rich Text Format
Samna Word
SGML ASCII
Text-ANSI (Windows)
Text-ASCII (DOS)
Text-EMail
WordPerfect
WordStar
XY Write DOS/Windows

IMPORTING AND EXPORTING FOR UNSUPPORTED PROGRAMS

Although you can see from the long lists in this appendix that Word Pro's import and export filters support a wide variety of file formats from other programs, one of the applications you use may not be listed or may be supported for import only and not for export. If this is the case, you may be able to use one of the following three options to transfer your information:

- Create and use an *interim file format* that both programs support. For example, if another program can export to Rich Text Format, save the file in that format and then import the interim file into Word Pro. Conversely, if your other program can read Rich Text Format files, you can export to that format from Word Pro.
- Among Windows applications, use the Windows Clipboard to copy and paste information. If you have an 80386-based (or higher) computer, you can even copy and paste between Windows and non–Windows applications. For more information on using the Windows Clipboard to transfer information between applications, see your Windows documentation.
- Call Word Pro's support line to see if they have filters for your application that did not ship with your original Word Pro package.

LOSS OF FORMATTING WHEN IMPORTING AND EXPORTING

Word Pro's import and export filters are a good way to transfer information between one application and another. However, no import or export filter is perfect. Because each program supports a specific set of features, some formatting information may be lost when you import and export files. For instance, if you export a

Word Pro document that contains a table to another word processing program format that does not support tables, your table-formatting information will be lost.

For details on which formatting information will be retained and which will be lost during importing and exporting, see your Word Pro documentation.

APPENDIX D: TEAM COMPUTING

TeamReview

TeamMail

TeamConsolidate

One of the most innovative new features of Word Pro is its *Team Computing* capability. Word Pro allows you to use tools such as *TeamMail, TeamConsolidate,* and *TeamReview* to work as a group, incorporating everyone's ideas into one document. Team Computing tools make it easier for groups of people to create, review, and edit documents.

TEAMREVIEW

TeamReview allows you to choose whom to share your document with, what rights each reviewer has, and how to distribute the document. To prepare a document for TeamReview:

- Choose *File, TeamReview*. The TeamReview Assistant dialog box opens to the Step 1: Who tab (see Figure D.1).

Figure D.1 **The Step 1: Who tab of the TeamReview Assistant dialog box**

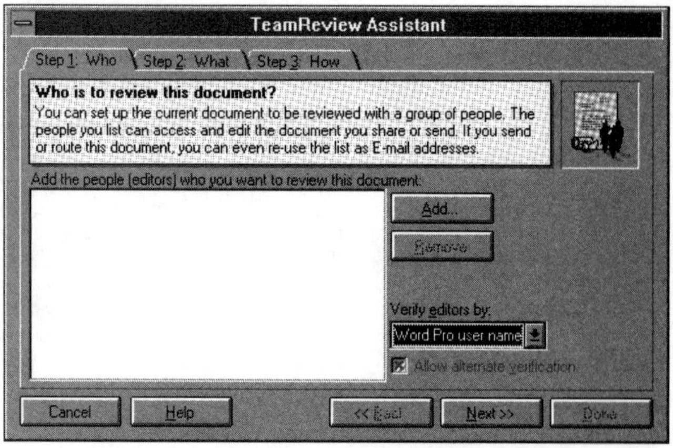

- In the Verify Editors By drop-down list, select the method by which you want Word Pro to verify the people who will review your document. You can choose their Word Pro user name or their e-mail login.
- To add an editor to the document:
  - Click on *Add* to open the New Editor dialog box (see Figure D.2).
  - Type the name of the editor you want to add to the document.
  - Click on *OK*.

Figure D.2 **The New Editor dialog box**

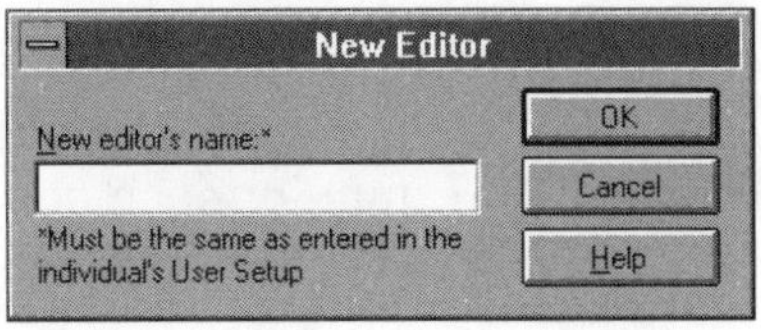

- To delete an editor from the document:
  - Select the editor's name in the Add The People (Editors) Who You Want To Review This Document list box.
  - Click on *Remove*.
  - Click on *Next* to display the Step 2: What tab (see Figure D.3).

Figure D.3 **The Step 2: What tab**

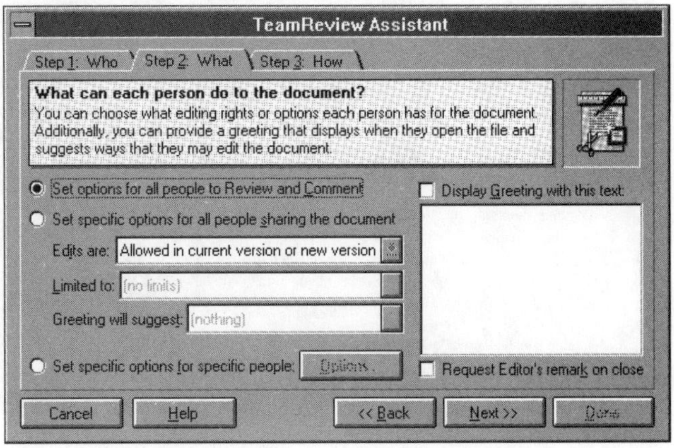

- Select the option for the editing rights you want to give reviewers. There are three editing rights options:
  - *Set Options For All People To Review And Comment* allows all editors to have all editing rights, opens the Review & Comment Tools SmartIcons bar, activates marked edits and allows the user to edit a new version only.

- *Set Specific Options For All People Sharing The Document* allows you to define specific editing rights for all editors.
- *Set Specific Options For Specific People* allows you to define specific editing rights for each editor assigned to the document.

- Check the *Display Greeting With This Text* check box if you want to display a greeting whenever an editor opens the document; then type the greeting in its text box.
- Check the *Request Editor's Remark On Close* check box if you want the editor to comment on the document before he or she closes it.
- Click on *Next* to display the Step 3: How tab (see Figure D.4).

Figure D.4 **The Step 3: How tab**

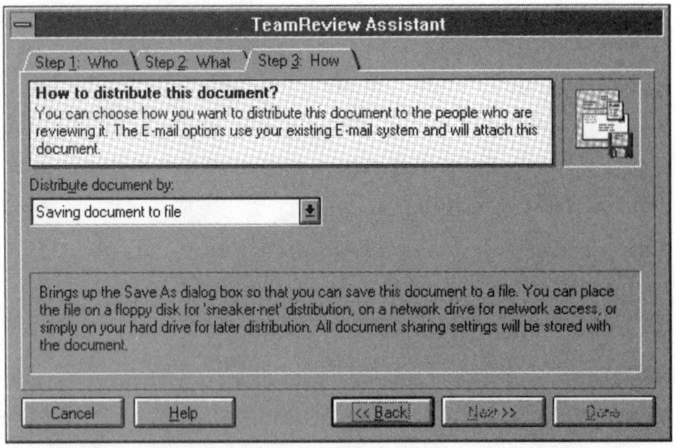

- Select the distribution option you want:
  - *Saving Document To File* saves the document as a file so you can distribute it to the editors.
  - *Saving Document To File On Internet* saves the document to a file server on the Internet.
  - *Saving Document And Sending Via E-Mail* saves the document and opens the Send Mail dialog box so you can

send the document as an attachment in an e-mail to each editor.

- *Saving Document And Routing Via E-Mail* saves the document and opens the Send Mail dialog box so you can route the document from one editor to the next.

- Click on *Done*.

Once you've set up a document for TeamReview, it's time for your editors to mark up the document. For information about using Comment tools to mark up a document, see your Word Pro documentation.

TEAMMAIL

TeamMail allows you to use your electronic mail system to send or receive mail messages. You can send a document to other people (for example, your editor) or to a list of people in the order in which you specify. Obviously, this is a big advantage if you are working closely with a group of people who don't work in the same physical location. You can exchange documents without wasting a lot of time waiting at the post office.

To use TeamMail:

- Choose *File, TeamMail* to open the TeamMail dialog box (see Figure D.5).

Figure D.5 **The TeamMail dialog box**

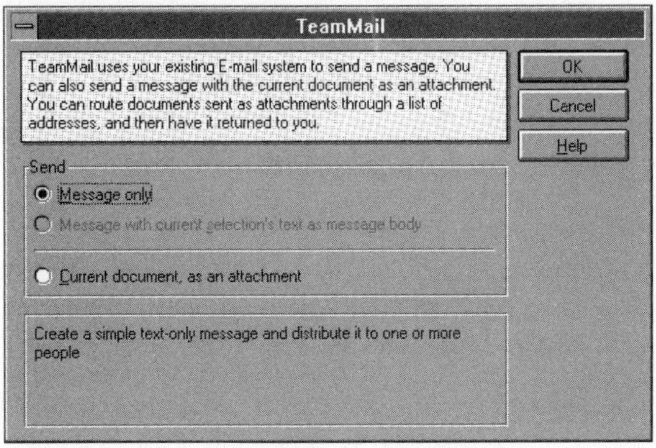

- Select the Send option you want:
  - *Message Only* allows you to send an e-mail message.
  - *Message With Current Selection's Text As Message Body* allows you to send part of the document with the message.
  - *Current Document, As An Attachment* attaches the current document to a message.
- Click on *OK* and type your password and any other information that your e-mail system requires.
- Click on *OK*.
- In the Recipient text box, type the name of the person to whom you wish to send the message.
- In the Delivery Priority list box, select the mail priority level.
- Type a subject in the Subject text box.
- Click the *Tracking tab* and select *Send Return Mail Receipt When Mail Message Is Opened* if you want to track the message.
- Click on *Send*.

TEAMCONSOLIDATE

Once all the editors have reviewed your document, you can use TeamConsolidate to consolidate their edits into one document for you to review. **Note**: Make sure each of your editors saved his/her version of the document as a separate file. Team Consolidate can only compare like documents, it can't compare versions of a document. For more information about versions, see your Word Pro documentation.

To use TeamConsolidate:

- Open the file to which you want to compare the other files (this is probably your original file).
- Choose *File, TeamConsolidate* to open the TeamConsolidate dialog box (see Figure D.6).
- Click on *Add Files* to open the Browse dialog box.

Figure D.6 **The TeamConsolidate dialog box**

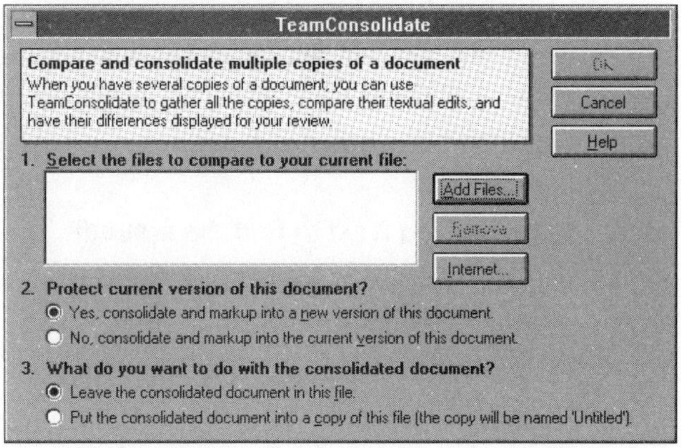

- Select the file(s) you want to compare to the current document. (**Note:** If the files are in the same directory, you can choose more than one file by pressing *Ctrl* and then selecting the second file, third file, and so on.)
- Click on *OK* to return to the TeamConsolidate dialog box and add the file(s) to the "1. Select The Files To Compare To Your Current File" text box.
- Select the appropriate option under "2. Protect Current Version Of This Document?" If you select *Yes*, Word Pro creates a new version of the document with all the markups incorporated. If you select *No*, Word Pro adds the markups to the current version of the document.
- Select the appropriate option under "3. What Do You Want To Do With The Consolidated Document?" If you select *Leave The Consolidated Document In This File*, Word Pro uses the current document. If you select *Put The Consolidated Document Into A Copy Of This File*, Word Pro creates a copy of the consolidated document in a new untitled document.
- Click on *OK*. Word Pro displays the consolidated document and the Review Marked Edits bar so you can compare and consolidate all the versions of the document.

  Note: When you consolidate more than two copies of a document, Word Pro copies the paragraphs that contain edits and displays them below the original paragraph in the order in which you listed the files they come from in the TeamConsolidate dialog box. To lessen the confusion this might cause, Word Pro uses *paragraph tags* to identify each paragraph. For more information about paragraph tags, see your Word Pro documentation.

- Place the insertion point where you want to start reviewing the edits.
- Click on *Find Next* to find the first edit.
- Use the Review Marked Edits bar buttons to accept or reject each edit.
- Click on *Done* to close the Review Marked Edits bar.
- Save the document. (You can either save the document as a new file or overwrite the current file.)

For more information about TeamConsolidate, see your Word Pro documentation.

INDEX

Symbols

< > (angle brackets) around merge fields, 282–283

... (ellipsis), 15

¶ (return symbol), 21

-> (tab symbol), 21

-> (tab symbol), 120

~ (tilde) field delimiter, 275

| (vertical bar) record delimiter, 275

A

Add Entry button (SmartCorrect feature), 182

Add To User Dictionary Spell Check option, 179

aligning paragraphs, 138–142, 152

angle brackets (<>) around merge fields, 282–283

application window, 10, *11–12*

- controlling size of, *12*
- resizing, *13*

arrow keys on numeric keypad, 244

ascending order, sorting fields in, 289

automatic page breaks, 166, 169

B

B (bold text) button, 97–98, 110

Backspace key, deleting text with, 18–19, 29

blank fields, merging records with, 286–288

blank lines, creating, 16

bold text, selecting in Text infobox, 95

borders, adding and changing in tables, 255–258, 266

bubble Help, 65

Bullet 1 style, 210

bullets, adding to and removing from documents, 198–200, 204

buttons on status bar, 102

C

Calendar SmartMaster, 230–*231*

Cancel button, 14–15

cell address, 239–240

cell marker, *237*

cells, 236–*237*

- moving between, *243*
- selecting in tables, *244*, 265

center alignment, *139*

centered tab, *118*, 124

centering paragraphs, 140–141

character movement shortcuts, 304

characters

- deleting with Delete key, 89
- typing, 16

Clipboard, 79, 193, 313

closing documents, 26–27, 30

color, 94

Color button, 102
column guides, 236–*237*
column and row headings, 239-240, *242,* 264
columns, 236–*237*
  changing widths of in tables, 253–254, 266
  deleting from tables, 252, 266
  inserting in tables, 249, 251, 266
  referencing, 239
  selecting in tables, *245,* 265
commands
  accessing, *12*
  issuing through menu bar, 14–15, 29
conditional merges, 285
context-sensitive help, 54–56, 60. *See also* Help table of contents
context-sensitive SmartIcons bars, 240
Control menu box, *8,* 11
copying
  styles, 226–228
  text, 80–82, 89, 192–195, 203
  text between documents, 195–198, 204
Copy Styles From dialog box, *227*
correcting operations, 82–83, 89
correcting text formatting mistakes, 200–204
Create Table dialog box, *237*
Create A Table Grid SmartIcon, 238
creating documents, 27–28, 30
custom tabs
  moving and setting, 125, 151
  setting in ruler, 118–123

D

dates, adding to headers and footers, 158–161, 174
.DBF file name extension, 22
defaults, definition of, 10
definition window, 53–*54,* 60
Delete Entry button (SmartCorrect feature), 182
Delete key versus Del key, 66
deleting text, 18–19, 67–69
delimited data, 275, *280*
descending order, sorting fields in, 289
deselecting text, 72, 89
dialog boxes, closing, 14–15
dir command, 3
directories
  changing, 34
  displaying from DOS prompt, 3
  saving documents to, 22, 30
disk drives, changing, 34
displaying
  documents at different magnifications, 50–51
  nonprinting symbols, 20–21, 30
.DOC file name extension, 310
document descriptions, 36
document magnification, 50–51, 60
document path, 37–39, 59
documents
  closing, 26–27, 30
  closing without making changes to, 144, 152
  creating, 27–28, 30
  displaying names of, 25

moving to beginning and end of, *42*–43, 60, 304
naming, 23–25
opening, 34–37
opening with SmartIcons, 64–66
printing, 25–26, 30
revising, 34
saving, 21–*25*, 30, 34, 56
saving in other file formats, 311–313
selecting, 72, 75
sharing, 318–321
shortcuts for opening, 35–36, 59
viewing preferences for, 20
document statistics, determining after grammar check, 187–188
document windows, 10, *11–13*
opening more than one, 204
switching between, 204
DOS prompt, 3
double-clicking, definition of, 3, 6
down scroll arrow, *40*
Drag & Drop feature, 192-193, 203
copying text with, *195*
moving text with, *194*
dragging the mouse, 14, *71*–73
drives
changing, 3
saving documents to, 22, 30
selecting when naming files, 24

E

editing rights for shared documents, 318–321
Edit menu
commands, 305
opening, 15
edits, consolidating Team features into one document, 322–324
electronic index cards for merging data files, *277*, 292–293
electronic mail system, 321–322
ellipsis (...), 15
Enter key, 16–17
envelopes, creating, 290–*291*, 293
Exact Case option for searching text, 49–50
.EXE file name extension, 22
exiting Word Pro, 28, 30
export formats, 312–313
exporting unsupported programs, 313

F

Fast Format feature, 104–110
field names
adding to data files, *276*
appearance of in data file, 282
marking, 275
fields
field names in merge data files, 270
separating with punctuation, 283
File menu
opening, 3, 14
commands, 305
file names
extensions, 22
guidelines for, 23
files
opening, 34–37
opening from other programs, 310–311

shortcuts for opening of, 35–36, 59
File, Save command, 22–23
File, Save As command, 21–22, 30
Find & Replace bar, 46–*47*
Find & Replace Options dialog box, *48*
fixed headers and footers, 156, 173
floating headers and footers, 156
Font Name button, 102–*103*
fonts, 94, 100–104, 110
footers, creating, 158
Format Check feature, 200–204
formatting, loss of when importing and exporting, 313–314
form letters, merging, 285–286
free bytes, determining, 298–299
free bytes on hard disk, determining, 3
full justify alignment, 141, *139*
Full Page view, displaying page layouts in, *52,* 168–169, 174

G

Go To dialog box, *44*
Grammar Check feature, 186–188
graphical user interface, definition of, 4–5
grid lines, showing and hiding, 257, 264

H

hanging indents, 133–*135,* 137–138
hard disk, determining free bytes on, 3
hard page breaks, 167
headers, creating, 157–158
headers and footers, deleting and editing, 164, 173–174
Header SmartIcons bar, *157*
Heading 2 style, 210
Help hand, 53. *See also* context-sensitive help
Help icon, *55,* 60
Help table of contents, 52–*53,* 60. *See also* context-sensitive help
highlighting menu items, 14
horizontal scroll bar, *11–12*
horizontal scroll box, *40*
horizontal and vertical scrolling options, *41*
hourglass, appearance of, 6

I

I (italicize text) button, 97–98, 110
I-beam, *17*
icon, definition of, 6
importing unsupported programs, 313
Include Properties option (Options button for searching text), 47
Include User Dictionary Alternatives Spell Check option, 179
indent markers on ruler, *115, 127–128*
indents
versus margins, 126–*127*
setting with ruler, 128–130, 151
setting with Text infobox, 130–*132,* 152
index cards for merging data files, *277,* 292–293
Insert Date/Time dialog box, *161*
insertion point, 16–*17*
centering in footers, 160
Insert Merge Field bar, 282, 293
Insert Page Number dialog box, *162*

installation requirements, 298–299
Install Disk 1, 299
installing work directory, 3
interim file format, 313
italic text
  selecting in Text infobox, 96
  and underlined text, *97*

K

kerning, 209
keyboard, moving through documents with, *42*–43, 304-306

L

leading, 142–144, 152
left-aligned tab, setting, *122, 139*
left scroll arrow, *40*
left tab, *118*
line break, inserting, 136–138
lines
  creating, 135–138, 152
  ending, 16, 29
  moving between, 304
line spacing, 142–*144,* 152
  versus paragraph spacing, 215
lines of text, moving along and between, *42*–43, 59
Locations tab in Word Pro Preferences dialog box, 37–38
Lotus Applications Program Group, 300
Lotus installation program, 299
Lotus Word Pro icon, searching for, 9–10
.LWP file name extension, 22, 310

M

macros, 229
magnification, 50–51, 60
mailing labels, creating, 288–290
Manage Styles dialog box, *227*
manual page breaks, 167
  inserting, 169–170, 174
  removing, 171
margin marker on ruler, *115*
margins, *11–12,* 164–166
  versus indents, 126–*127*
Match Case option (Options button for searching text), 47
Maximize/Restore button, *8,* 29
memo, sample of, *19*
menu bar, *8,* 14–15, 29
menu commands, 305–306
Merge Assistant dialog box, *276*
Merge bar, opening, 285
merge data file, creating, 274–281, 292
merge documents, 272–273, 282-285
merge fields, inserting, *284*
Minimize button, *8,* 29
misspelled words, automatic correction of, 183
modeless bars, 46
monitor, definition of, 9
mouse pointer, 3, 6, 16, 105
moving text, 79–*80,* 89, 192–195, 203
moving through documents with keyboard, *42*
multitasking, 5

N

navigating through documents with keyboard, *42*, 304

nonprinting symbols, displaying, 20–21

Number List style, 210, 212

numeric tab, creating, 124, *118*

Num Lock key, 66

O

on-line help, 51–53

Open dialog box, *35*

Open A Document SmartIcon, 65–66, 86

opening documents, 64–66

operating environment, 2

P

page breaks, inserting, 169–170, 174

Page Layout infobox, setting margins with, 165, 174

page layouts, viewing, 168–169

Page Number Options dialog box, *163*

page numbers, adding to headers and footers, 161–163, 174

Page Number text box, *44*

pages, moving through, *42*–45, *60*

Page Status and Page Arrow buttons, *45*

paginating documents, 166–167

paragraphs

- aligning, 138–142, 152
- assigning styles to, 209, 231
- ending, 16, 29
- selecting, 71–73, 89, 116, 151

paragraph spacing versus line spacing, 215

pointing, definition of, 3

point size, 100, 110

Point Size button, 102

Print dialog box, *26*

printing

- document pages, 172–*173,* 175
- documents, 25–26, 30
- merged documents, 285–287

program group and icon, *8*

Program Manager, 2–3, 6-8, 299

properties, inheriting using Style Hierarchy Definition dialog box, 221–226, 232

Q

quick center tab, *118*

quick right tab, *118*

R

readability statistics, 187–188

records

- adding to data files, 277–278, 293
- editing on index cards, 293
- in merge data files, 270
- merging blank fields in, 286–288
- moving between, 279
- sorting in merge data file, 288–290, 293

Redefine Style dialog box, *214*

reinstallation requirements, 298

Replace All Spell Check Option, 179

Replacement Text For box (SmartCorrect feature), 182
replacing found text, 70, 76–78, 89
Restore button, *11*–13
return symbol (¶), 21
reversing operations, 82–83, 89
right alignment, *139,* 142
right margin, calculating on ruler, 116
right scroll arrow, *40*
right tab, *118,* 123
row and column headings, displaying, 239-240, *242,* 264
rows, 236–*237*
  deleting from tables, 252, 266
  inserting in tables, 249–250, 265
  moving between, *243*
  referencing, 239
  selecting in tables, *245,* 265
ruler
  hiding and displaying, 114–116, 151
  indent markers on, *128*
  setting hanging indents with, 133–134, 152

S

Save As command (File menu), 21–22, 30
Save command (File menu), 22–23, 30
saving documents, 21-25, 30, 56
screens
  appearance of, 7
  moving up and down, *42*–43, 59, 304
scripts, 229
scrolling, *12,* 38–41, 59
searching for text, 45–50, 60
search and replacement text, specifying, *77*
search results message box, *49*
selected text, *69*
selecting text, 68, 71–76, 89
send options for TeamMail feature, 322
sentences
  moving between, 304
  selecting, *71–74,* 89
Shift+Enter (new line), 135–138
shortcut menus, 118, 151
  for ruler, *119,* 121
Show/Hide ruler SmartIcon, *115*
Show tab in View Preferences dialog box, *21*
Skip and Skip All Spell Check options, 179
SmartCorrect feature, 182–183
SmartIcons, *11–12*
  displaying names of, *65,* 86
  moving bars, 240–243, 264
SmartMaster style sheets, 228–231, 233
sorting records in merge data files, 288–*290,* 293
source document, 196
Spacebar and text alignment, 18
spacing, 209
  redefining between styled paragraphs, 215–217
Spell Check, 178–181,188
status bar, *11–12*
  applying and removing text attributes with, 97–99
  bar, changing fonts with, 102–104

- Page Status and Page Arrow buttons, 44–45
- Style Hierarchy Definition dialog box, *222*
- Style list, *211*
- styles
  - assigning, 209–212, 231
  - copying, 226–228
  - creating for selected text, 219–221, 232
  - deleting, 222
  - inheriting properties of, 221–226, 232–233
  - overriding, 217–219, 232
  - redefining, 213–215, 232
- style sheets, 228–231
- Style Status button, assigning styles with, 210–212
- subdirectories, saving documents to, 22
- symbol for manual page break, displaying and removing, *170,* 174–175
- symbols, displaying, 20–21, 30
- synonyms, looking up with Thesaurus feature, 184–185, 188

T

- tabbed table, adding line to, *121*
- tabbed text, converting to table, 258–260, 266
- tab character, inserting, 18, 29
- tab dividers in merge data files, 272, 279
- table guides, 236–237, 257, 264
- tables
  - aligning, 255, 266
  - changing width of columns in, 253–254, 266
  - creating, 236–239, 264
  - deleting, 252, 266
  - deselecting, 245
  - entering text in, 248
  - indenting text in, 236
  - moving in, *243*–244, 264–265
  - selecting, *245,* 265
  - selecting components in, *244–245*
- table size, specifying in Create A Table Grid SmartIcon grid, *239*
- Table Style drop-down list box, *237*–238
- tabs, 117–126
  - aligning text with, 17–18
- tabs, clearing, 119, 125–126, 151
- tab symbol (->), 21, 120
- tab types, *117*
- target document, 196
- TeamConsolidate feature, 322–324
- TeamMail feature, 321–322
- TeamReview feature, 318–321
- text
  - aligning, 17–18
  - copying, 80–82, 89
  - correcting input of, 182–183
  - deleting, 18–19, 66-69
  - deselecting, 72, 89
  - entering, 15–21
  - entering in tables, 248
  - extending selection of, *72,* 74–*75,* 89
  - formatting in tables, 255
  - moving, 79–*80,* 89
  - positioning of, 41

replacing, 70, 76–78, 89
searching for, 45–50, 60
selecting, 71–76, 89
selecting by dragging, 68, 89
Text, Alignment submenu, *140*
text attributes, 94–99, 110
Text Bullets tab (Text infobox), *199*
text formatting, copying, 104–110
Text infobox, *101*
applying and removing attributes with, 95–97, 110
changing fonts with, 100–101, 110
setting hanging indents with, 134
Text menu alignment options, 139
Text menu commands, 305–306
text selection shortcuts for keyboard, 304
text selection techniques, *71–72*
Thesaurus feature, 184–185, 188
tilde (~) field delimiter, 275
time, adding to headers and footers, 159–161
title bar, *8, 11*
Title style, 211
typeface, 94, 103
typing area, *11–12,* 16

U

U (underline text) button, 98, 110
underlined text, selecting in Text infobox, 96
undoing operations, 82–83, 89
Undo menu, dimmed appearance of, 15
Universal SmartIcons bar, *241*
up scroll arrow, *40*

V

vertical bar (|) record delimiter, 275
vertical and horizontal scrolling, *40–41*
vertical scroll bar, *11–12*
View menu commands, 305
View Preferences dialog box, 20

W

Whole Words Only option (Find Options drop-down list), 46, 49
window, definition of, 3, 5
window elements, *8*
Window menu listing two open documents, *198*
Windows, starting, 6, 29, 299
.WK3 file name extension, 22
Word Pro 96
exiting, 28, 30
installing, 299–300
saving documents in other file formats, 311–313
starting, 9–10, 29
window elements, *11–12*
words
moving between, 304
selecting, *71*–73, 89
Words Containing option (Find Options drop-down list), 47
Words Ending With option (Find Options drop-down list), 46
Words Starting With option (Find Options drop-down list), 46
word wrap, 16–17, 19

work directory, creating, 2–4
writing style, enhancing, 186–187
WYSIWYG, 15

Z

Zoom options for displaying
documents on screen, 50–51

Ziff-Davis Press Survey of Readers

Please help us in our effort to produce the best books on personal computing.
For your assistance, we would be pleased to send you a FREE catalog
featuring the complete line of Ziff-Davis Press books.

1. How did you first learn about this book?

Recommended by a friend	☐	-1 (5)
Recommended by store personnel	☐	-2
Saw in Ziff-Davis Press catalog	☐	-3
Received advertisement in the mail	☐	-4
Saw the book on bookshelf at store	☐	-5
Read book review in: ______________	☐	-6
Saw an advertisement in: ______________	☐	-7
Other (Please specify): ______________	☐	-8

2. Which THREE of the following factors most influenced your decision to purchase this book? (Please check up to THREE.)

Front or back cover information on book	☐	-1 (6)
Logo of magazine affiliated with book	☐	-2
Special approach to the content	☐	-3
Completeness of content	☐	-4
Author's reputation	☐	-5
Publisher's reputation	☐	-6
Book cover design or layout	☐	-7
Index or table of contents of book	☐	-8
Price of book	☐	-9
Special effects, graphics, illustrations	☐	-0
Other (Please specify): ______________	☐	-x

3. How many computer books have you purchased in the last six months? _____ (7-10)

4. On a scale of 1 to 5, where 5 is excellent, 4 is above average, 3 is average, 2 is below average, and 1 is poor, please rate each of the following aspects of this book below. (Please circle your answer.)

Depth/completeness of coverage	5	4	3	2	1	(11)
Organization of material	5	4	3	2	1	(12)
Ease of finding topic	5	4	3	2	1	(13)
Special features/time saving tips	5	4	3	2	1	(14)
Appropriate level of writing	5	4	3	2	1	(15)
Usefulness of table of contents	5	4	3	2	1	(16)
Usefulness of index	5	4	3	2	1	(17)
Usefulness of accompanying disk	5	4	3	2	1	(18)
Usefulness of illustrations/graphics	5	4	3	2	1	(19)
Cover design and attractiveness	5	4	3	2	1	(20)
Overall design and layout of book	5	4	3	2	1	(21)
Overall satisfaction with book	5	4	3	2	1	(22)

5. Which of the following computer publications do you read regularly; that is, 3 out of 4 issues?

Byte	☐	-1 (23)
Computer Shopper	☐	-2
Home Office Computing	☐	-3
Dr. Dobb's Journal	☐	-4
LAN Magazine	☐	-5
MacWEEK	☐	-6
MacUser	☐	-7
PC Computing	☐	-8
PC Magazine	☐	-9
PC WEEK	☐	-0
Windows Sources	☐	-x
Other (Please specify): ______________	☐	-y

Please turn page.

6. What is your level of experience with personal computers? With the subject of this book?

	With PCs		With subject of book	
Beginner.	☐	-1 (24)	☐	-1 (25)
Intermediate.	☐	-2	☐	-2
Advanced.	☐	-3	☐	-3

7. Which of the following best describes your job title?

Officer (CEO/President/VP/owner).	☐	-1 (26)
Director/head.	☐	-2
Manager/supervisor.	☐	-3
Administration/staff.	☐	-4
Teacher/educator/trainer.	☐	-5
Lawyer/doctor/medical professional.	☐	-6
Engineer/technician.	☐	-7
Consultant.	☐	-8
Not employed/student/retired.	☐	-9
Other (Please specify): ________________	☐	-0

8. What is your age?

Under 20.	☐	-1 (27)
21-29.	☐	-2
30-39.	☐	-3
40-49.	☐	-4
50-59.	☐	-5
60 or over.	☐	-6

9. Are you:

Male.	☐	-1 (28)
Female.	☐	-2

Thank you for your assistance with this important information! Please write your address below to receive our free catalog.

Name: ______________________________

Address: ____________________________

City/State/Zip: _______________________

Fold here to mail.

2249-01-01

____

____

____

NO POSTAGE NECESSARY IF MAILED IN THE UNITED STATES

BUSINESS REPLY MAIL

FIRST CLASS MAIL PERMIT NO. 1612 OAKLAND, CA

POSTAGE WILL BE PAID BY ADDRESSEE

Ziff-Davis Press
5903 Christie Avenue
Emeryville, CA 94608-1925
Attn: Marketing

■ TO RECEIVE 5 1/4-INCH DISK(S)

The Ziff-Davis Press software contained on the 3 1/2-inch disk included with this book is also available in 5 1/4-inch format. If you would like to receive the software in the 5 1/4-inch format, please return the 3 1/2-inch disk with your name and address to:

Disk Exchange
Ziff-Davis Press
5903 Christie Avenue
Emeryville, CA 94608

■ END-USER LICENSE AGREEMENT

READ THIS AGREEMENT CAREFULLY BEFORE BUYING THIS BOOK. BY BUYING THE BOOK AND USING THE PROGRAM LISTINGS, DISKS, AND PROGRAMS REFERRED TO BELOW, YOU ACCEPT THE TERMS OF THIS AGREEMENT.

The program listings included in this book and the programs included on the diskette(s) contained in the package on the opposite page ("Disks") are proprietary products of Ziff-Davis Press and/or third party suppliers ("Suppliers"). The program listings and programs are hereinafter collectively referred to as the "Programs." Ziff-Davis Press and the Suppliers retain ownership of the Disks and copyright to the Programs, as their respective interests may appear. The Programs and the copy of the Disks provided are licensed (not sold) to you under the conditions set forth herein.

License. You may use the Disks on any compatible computer, provided that the Disks are used on only one computer and by one user at a time.

Restrictions. You may not commercially distribute the Disks or the Programs or otherwise reproduce, publish, or distribute or otherwise use the Disks or the Programs in any manner that may infringe any copyright or other proprietary right of Ziff-Davis Press, the Suppliers, or any other party or assign, sublicense, or otherwise transfer the Disks or this agreement to any other party unless such party agrees to accept the terms and conditions of this agreement. This license and your right to use the Disks and the Programs automatically terminates if you fail to comply with any provision of this agreement.

U.S. GOVERNMENT RESTRICTED RIGHTS. The disks and the programs are provided with **RESTRICTED RIGHTS**. Use, duplication, or disclosure by the Government is subject to restrictions as set forth in subparagraph (c)(1)(ii) of the Rights in Technical Data and Computer Software Clause at DFARS (48 CFR 252.277-7013). The Proprietor of the compilation of the Programs and the Disks is Ziff-Davis Press, 5903 Christie Avenue, Emeryville, CA 94608.

Limited Warranty. Ziff-Davis Press warrants the physical Disks to be free of defects in materials and workmanship under normal use for a period of 30 days from the purchase date. If Ziff-Davis Press receives written notification within the warranty period of defects in materials or workmanship in the physical Disks, and such notification is determined by Ziff-Davis Press to be correct, Ziff-Davis Press will, at its option, replace the defective Disks or refund a prorata portion of the purchase price of the book. **THESE ARE YOUR SOLE REMEDIES FOR ANY BREACH OF WARRANTY.**

EXCEPT AS SPECIFICALLY PROVIDED ABOVE, THE DISKS AND THE PROGRAMS ARE PROVIDED "AS IS" WITHOUT ANY WARRANTY OF ANY KIND. NEITHER ZIFF-DAVIS PRESS NOR THE SUPPLIERS MAKE ANY WARRANTY OF ANY KIND AS TO THE ACCURACY OR COMPLETENESS OF THE DISKS OR THE PROGRAMS OR THE RESULTS TO BE OBTAINED FROM USING THE DISKS OR THE PROGRAMS AND NEITHER ZIFF-DAVIS PRESS NOR THE SUPPLIERS SHALL BE RESPONSIBLE FOR ANY CLAIMS ATTRIBUTABLE TO ERRORS, OMISSIONS, OR OTHER INACCURACIES IN THE DISKS OR THE PROGRAMS. THE ENTIRE RISK AS TO THE RESULTS AND PERFORMANCE OF THE DISKS AND THE PROGRAMS IS ASSUMED BY THE USER. FURTHER, NEITHER ZIFF-DAVIS PRESS NOR THE SUPPLIERS MAKE ANY REPRESENTATIONS OR WARRANTIES, EITHER EXPRESS OR IMPLIED, WITH RESPECT TO THE DISKS OR THE PROGRAMS, INCLUDING BUT NOT LIMITED TO, THE QUALITY, PERFORMANCE, MERCHANTABILITY, OR FITNESS FOR A PARTICULAR PURPOSE OF THE DISKS OR THE PROGRAMS. IN NO EVENT SHALL ZIFF-DAVIS PRESS OR THE SUPPLIERS BE LIABLE FOR DIRECT, INDIRECT, SPECIAL, INCIDENTAL, OR CONSEQUENTIAL DAMAGES ARISING OUT THE USE OF OR INABILITY TO USE THE DISKS OR THE PROGRAMS OR FOR ANY LOSS OR DAMAGE OF ANY NATURE CAUSED TO ANY PERSON OR PROPERTY AS A RESULT OF THE USE OF THE DISKS OR THE PROGRAMS, EVEN IF ZIFF-DAVIS PRESS OR THE SUPPLIERS HAVE BEEN SPECIFICALLY ADVISED OF THE POSSIBILITY OF SUCH DAMAGES. NEITHER ZIFF-DAVIS PRESS NOR THE SUPPLIERS ARE RESPONSIBLE FOR ANY COSTS INCLUDING, BUT NOT LIMITED TO, THOSE INCURRED AS A RESULT OF LOST PROFITS OR REVENUE, LOSS OF USE OF THE DISKS OR THE PROGRAMS, LOSS OF DATA, THE COSTS OF RECOVERING SOFTWARE OR DATA, OR THIRD-PARTY CLAIMS. IN NO EVENT WILL ZIFF-DAVIS PRESS' OR THE SUPPLIERS' LIABILITY FOR ANY DAMAGES TO YOU OR ANY OTHER PARTY EVER EXCEED THE PRICE OF THIS BOOK. NO SALES PERSON OR OTHER REPRESENTATIVE OF ANY PARTY INVOLVED IN THE DISTRIBUTION OF THE DISKS IS AUTHORIZED TO MAKE ANY MODIFICATIONS OR ADDITIONS TO THIS LIMITED WARRANTY.

Some states do not allow the exclusion or limitation of implied warranties or limitation of liability for incidental or consequential damages, so the above limitation or exclusion may not apply to you.

General. Ziff-Davis Press and the Suppliers retain all rights not expressly granted. Nothing in this license constitutes a waiver of the rights of Ziff-Davis Press or the Suppliers under the U.S. Copyright Act or any other Federal or State Law, international treaty, or foreign law.